THE SECRET OF SUCCESS IS NOT A SECRET

Dedication

Dedicated to anyone who has ever failed but refused to quit,
including all the individuals featured in this book.
Thank you for being an inspiration. — D. A.

Published by Sellers Publishing, Inc.

ISBN 13: 978-1-56906-997-4
Library of Congress Control Number: 2007935165

Sellers Publishing, Inc.
161 John Roberts Road, South Portland, Maine 04106
For ordering information: (800) 625-3386 toll-free
Visit our Web site: www.rsvp.com • E-mail: rsp@rsvp.com

Cover Design by: The Design Works, Sisters, Oregon

10 9 8 7 6 5 4 3 2 1

Printed in the United States of America.

Credits: *cover image/ladder ; Reiulf Grønnevik/Shutterstock*

THE SECRET OF SUCCESS IS NOT A SECRET

Stories of Famous People Who Persevered

DARCY ANDRIES

Contents

Against All Odds

Something from Nothing

Chart Your Own Course

Inspiration from Within

Turn Lemons into Lemonade

Everyone's a Critic

Introduction

Colin Powell once said, "There are no secrets to success. It is the result of preparation, hard work, and learning from failure." You can learn a lot from failure, but that requires you to continue moving forward despite having failed.

That is exactly what this book is about — learning that the failures are only potholes on the road to success and not stop signs.

Rarely will anyone tell you that the best way to succeed is to fail first. Yet, as this book will illustrate, not everyone succeeds the first time he or she tries — or even the second. Since no one likes to dwell on failures, these events are often overlooked once the person achieves his or her goals.

Sometimes, it is not actual failure that a person must face but rather the prediction of failure. Few have reached the top rung on the ladder of success without meeting at least one person who predicted that the journey was impossible.

This book began as a way to inspire my special education students. I wanted to prove to them that, despite their disabilities, they could do anything. To achieve this goal, I collected stories about the early setbacks experienced by famous figures. Eventually, I had hundreds of stories about people who overcame major obstacles, battled critics, turned setbacks into opportunities, and refused to quit.

When I left teaching to pursue my own dream of becoming a writer, I decided to take that list of names and compile them into a book — written proof that people are not "failures" as long as they do not quit.

"And when it rains on your parade, look up rather than down. Without the rain, there would be no rainbow." — G. K. Chesterton

If at First You Don't Succeed . . .

"Diamonds are nothing more than chunks of coal that stuck to their jobs."

— Malcolm S. Forbes

Eddie Arcaro

250 Losses Later

Jockey Eddie Arcaro (1916–1997) won more American Classic horse races than any other jockey in history and is the only one to have won the U.S. Triple Crown twice.

MOST ASPIRING JOCKEYS GO TO Kentucky, and that is exactly where fifteen-year-old Eddie Arcaro went. He earned $15 a week galloping horses, but it cost him his pride. His boss, Tom McCaffery, told Arcaro he was not good enough to become a jockey. Arcaro hid his tears and kept riding.

With a stubbornness that belied his young age, he packed up his meager belongings, dusted the Kentucky dirt off his boots, and headed west to California, where he found a job with horse trainer Clarence Davison. Davison let Arcaro ride in his first race on May 18, 1931. Arcaro lost. In the next race, he also lost. Arcaro had too much grit to give up after a couple of losses. During the next eight months, he continued to race. Davison did not lose faith either. He saw potential in the rider, and after each loss he and Arcaro sat down and went over every mistake.

With amazing persistence, Arcaro kept riding and losing. Two hundred and fifty losses later, he finally quit — not racing; he simply quit losing. On January 14, 1932, a month before his sixteenth birthday, Arcaro won his first race. He steadily improved under Davison's tutelage, but in 1934 Arcaro cracked his skull, fractured two ribs, and punctured his lung after tumbling off a horse in Chicago. With Arcaro sidelined for at least two months, Davidson sold the rider's contract to Calumet Farms.

Arcaro recovered quickly and resumed racing. Four years later, in 1938, he captured his first Kentucky Derby win. In 1941, ten years after he had been told he would never be good enough to be a jockey, Arcaro became only the fifth jockey to capture the U.S. Triple Crown, riding Whirlaway in the Kentucky Derby, the Preakness Stakes, and the Belmont Stakes. History repeated itself in 1948, when Arcaro won the U.S. Triple Crown astride Citation. Arcaro is the only jockey to win the U.S. Triple Crown more than once. During his thirty-one year racing career, he rode in 24,092 races, won 4,779 victories, placed in the top three 11,888 times, and posted a record 554 stakes victories. Arcaro's skill earned him the nickname "The Master." He was inducted into the Official National Thoroughbred Racing Hall of Fame in 1958, three years before he retired from the sport.

> *"You have to remember that about 70 percent of the horses running don't want to win. Horses are like people. Everybody doesn't have the aggressiveness or ambition to knock himself out to become a success."* — E. A.

Richard Bach

Reluctantly Published

American author Richard Bach (1936–)
wrote *Jonathan Livingston Seagull*, a novel that hit
number one on both the fiction and nonfiction charts, breaking
all hardcover sales records since *Gone with the Wind*.

Twenty-six publishers failed to recognize the best-selling potential of Richard Bach's *Jonathan Livingston Seagull.* The book, less than 10,000 words long, had as its hero a seagull that enjoyed flying. Only Macmillan's editor Eleanor Freide saw the book's value and persuaded her company to publish the novel. The firm printed a mere 7,500 copies and allotted a limited advertising budget to publicize the book. Another publisher predicted that the book would "never make it as a paperback." Still, Avon Books purchased the paperback rights. Before the paperback version could be released, fans had spread the word about *Jonathan Livingston Seagull.*

Although it took two years, *Jonathan Livingston Seagull* reached the top of the *New York Times* best-seller list, where it remained for thirty-eight weeks. Featured on the cover of the November 13, 1972 issue of *Time* magazine, the novel sold more than one million copies in 1972 alone. Within five years, the book had sold more than seven million copies in the United States and thirty million copies worldwide. Bach was inundated with film offers and requests to appear on television talk shows. As of 2007, Bach has written an additional thirteen books, although none have been as successful as *Jonathan Livingston Seagull.*

> *"There are no mistakes. The events we bring upon ourselves, no matter how unpleasant, are necessary in order to learn what we need to learn; whatever steps we take, they're necessary to reach the places we've chosen to go."* — R. B.

Bachman-Turner Overdrive

Twenty-Six Rejections

Bachman-Turner Overdrive, also known as BTO, is a Canadian rock band that produced a string of hits in the 1970s including "Takin' Care of Business" and "You Ain't Seen Nothing Yet."

In 1970, The Guess Who was rapidly rising to the top of the American and Canadian music charts with the hit *American Woman* and was invited to play at the White House by President Richard Nixon. So it seemed odd that band member Randy Bachman chose that time to leave. After releasing a solo album, Bachman teamed up with his brother, Robbie, and another former Guess Who band mate, Chad Allen, to create the band Brave Belt.

After two albums that were only moderately successful, Allen left the group. Fred Turner and another Bachman brother, Tim, soon filled the vacancy. With new members, the band changed its name — and its luck. Now called Bachman-Turner Overdrive, the band quickly compiled a demo tape and sent it out to twenty-six record labels. One by one, their demo tapes came back with firm rejection letters attached until all twenty-six of them had been returned. Out of options, the men contacted the record companies again with the goal of changing at least one mind. Finally, after listening to their demo tape again, Mercury Records offered the band a contract. Bachman-Turner Overdrive went on to sell more than twenty million records with hits such as "Takin' Care of Business" and "You Ain't Seen Nothing Yet."

"Highly successful leaders ignore conventional wisdom and take chances. Their stories inevitably include a defining moment or key decision when they took a significant risk and thereby experienced a breakthrough."
— Larry Osborne

Pat Benatar

Too Feminine

Pat Benatar (1953–) is an American rock star who performed such hits as "Heartbreaker," "Love is a Battlefield," "We Belong," and "Hit Me with Your Best Shot."

Daughter of an opera singer, Pat Benatar originally studied opera at Juilliard before dropping out to marry her high school sweetheart. Together they moved to New York, but the two soon separated and later divorced. With the vision of living happily ever after in ruins, she dusted off her earlier dream of becoming a professional singer and started pursuing it. At night, Benatar worked as a singing waitress and lounge singer. During the day, she pounded the pavement — and the doors of record companies — with her demo tape.

For three years, she endured countless rejections from record labels. Record company executives did not object to her voice; they disliked her style. They said that she was too feminine for the style of music she performed. Then, on Halloween night 1977, Benatar performed her act in a costume — as a modern, urban vampire. The audience went wild. The reaction convinced Benatar to adopt part of the costume — the black tights, short black top, and heavy eyeliner — to transform her look.

The new style gave her performances more edge and landed her a contract with Chrysalis Records. Her first single, "Heartbreaker," headed the Top 40 charts, as did several of her other songs. Benatar won four consecutive Grammy Awards for Best Rock Vocal Performance, from 1980 to 1983, as well as numerous Grammy nominations.

"A woman doesn't have to be hard-ass all the time, she can be soft and tender as well, and she can be a good businesswoman as well as a nice person. She can be pretty and smart at the same time." — P. B.

Larry Bird

From College Dropout to NBA Legend

Larry Bird (1956–), a basketball player for the Boston Celtics from 1979–1992, and is often considered one of the greatest players of all time.

THE PHRASE "BREAK A LEG" might be good luck in the theater, but it can prove problematic on the basketball court — especially when the phrase becomes a reality. Larry Bird learned that lesson when he broke his ankle his sophomore year of high school. Although it cut his basketball season short, the break did not stop him from practicing his shooting, something he did continually until his leg was healed. By the end of the season, Bird was begging his coach for the opportunity to play.

By the time he was a senior, Bird had mastered the sport and was averaging more than thirty points and twenty rebounds each game. Colleges all over the country tried to recruit him. Bird chose Indiana University because it was close to home. However, having spent his childhood in a small town, he was overwhelmed by the large university. Less than a month into his freshman year, he dropped out. Still dreaming of a college education, he enrolled at Northwood Institute. He lasted slightly longer — two months — before dropping out again. Finally, Bird returned home and took a job driving a garbage truck and doing maintenance work. In his off time, he played basketball in an amateur league.

That could have been the end of the story had not Bob King and Bill Hodges made an effort to recruit the young man for Indiana State University. The two had heard about Bird's skill in the amateur league. Not wanting to be known the rest of his life as a quitter, Bird accepted their offer of a scholarship. This time, the school was a better fit — both on and off the courts — and Bird was much happier, even if he was forced to sit out his first season. He was soon averaging thirty points a game and helped the team advance to the quarterfinals his junior year.

The Boston Celtics offered him the opportunity to play professionally for the team after Bird's junior year. Instead, he chose to stay in school and earn his degree. In Bird's senior year, the Indiana State Sycamores advanced to the NCAA championships to play against Michigan State, which was led by Earvin "Magic" Johnson.

It was the first time, but not the last, that Bird would face Magic Johnson. Johnson and Bird developed an intense rivalry during their careers on the court and a deep friendship when they were off the court. Johnson's team walked away with the championship title during their first encounter, but Bird won player of the year trophies from the Associated Press, United Press International, and the National Association of Coaches, as well as a contract to play with the Boston Celtics. With

Bird on the team, the Celtics became regular championship contenders with wins in 1981, 1984, and 1986. After thirteen years, he retired as a player and eventually took up coaching. Bird earned the NBA Coach of the Year his first year. In 1996, Bird was listed as one of the fifty greatest players in NBA history and was inducted into the NBA Hall of Fame in 1998.

> *"A winner is someone who recognizes his God-given talents, works his tail off to develop them into skills, and uses these skills to accomplish his goals." — L. B.*

Jack Canfield and Mark Victor Hansen

Too Positive

Jack Canfield (1944–) and Mark Victor Hansen (1948–) are the coauthors of *Chicken Soup for the Soul* and co-creators of the "Chicken Soup for the Soul" series.

FOR THREE YEARS, JACK CANFIELD and Mark Hansen collected and edited stories for their book. By the time it was finished, they were almost $140,000 in debt. When they managed to land a literary agent — a task almost as difficult as attracting a publisher — it appeared they were on their way. The agent immediately began pitching the manuscript, *Happy Little Stories*, to thirty-three of the biggest names in publishing. One by one, the publishers rejected it saying that there was no market for the book because it was "too positive" and "not topical enough." Executives at one company told the writers, "We just don't get it." Canfield and Hansen were hit by another blow when, after only a month, their agent said he no longer wanted to represent them. "No one buys short stories," he told them, especially ones that lacked sex and violence.

Instead of getting a new agent, they changed tactics and pitched their book at the American Booksellers' Association Convention. Armed with almost two hundred copies of their manuscript crammed into their backpacks, they ruthlessly hunted down every publisher they could find. They handed out dozens of copies, but no one seemed interested. On the second day, they continued their attack. Luck was on their side, because a copy landed in the hands of a publisher at a little-known publishing company that was about to go bankrupt, Health Communications. The publisher read the manuscript that night and called Canfield and Hansen the next morning with good news: he wanted to publish the book.

After a name change, *Chicken Soup for the Soul* hit the *New York Times* best-seller list fourteen months later, where it remained for almost two years. The book also launched a series of more than sixty-five other *Chicken Soup* books directed at specific audiences, many as successful as the original. Titles from the series consistently appear on the *New York Times* best-seller list and in the top fifty on *USA Today*'s list of best-sellers.

"Some people fold after making one timid request. They quit too soon. Keep asking until you find the answers. In sales, there are usually four or five 'no's' before you get a 'yes.'" — Jack Canfield

Paul Cézanne

Dogged by Disappointments

Paul Cézanne (1839–1906) was a French Post-Impressionist painter whose innovative work laid the foundation for cubism and modern abstract art.

In 1861, after many arguments, Paul Cézanne's father agreed to let him drop out of school with the goal of becoming an artist. Cézanne quit studying law, moved to Paris, and immediately applied to the influential art school, École des Beaux-Arts. They rejected him. Discouraged, Cézanne applied and was accepted at a less prestigious institute, the Academie Suisse, but he left after a few months and returned home to work in his father's bank. A year later, after encouragement from writer Émile Zola, Cézanne returned to Paris and tried again to gain admittance to École des Beaux-Arts. As before, he was rejected. Further disappointments dogged him when his submissions were rejected by the Paris Salon, the official art exhibition of the French society Académie des Beaux-Arts. For the next six years, Cézanne continued to submit his art to the Paris Salon, and the exhibition continued to reject his work.

It was not until 1895, after the urgings of fellow artists Camille Pissarro, Claude Monet, and Auguste Renoir, that Cézanne allowed a dealer to show a large number of his paintings. The event increased public interest in his work. Today, Cézanne is considered a dominant figure in the development of modern painting. Many in the art world — including Pablo Picasso — believe that his innovations sparked the movements that followed in cubism and abstractionism.

> *"Right now a moment is fleeting by! Capture its reality in paint! To do that we must put all else out of our minds. We must become that moment." — P.C.*

Winston Churchill

A History of Failure and Rejection

Winston Churchill (1874–1965) was prime minister of the United Kingdom from 1940 to 1945 and again from 1951 to 1955.

Winston Churchill stuttered as a child. His father, who had wanted his son to become a barrister, thought Churchill was retarded because he did poorly in school, usually finishing near the bottom of his class. Churchill failed the sixth grade, took three full terms to get to the next class in mathematics, and was rejected by both Oxford and Cambridge. Churchill's father advised him to pursue a career in the Army. Following his father's advice, Churchill applied to Royal Military College at Sandhurst, the British equivalent to West Point in the United States, but he failed the entrance examination — twice. After intense tutoring and a lot of cramming, Churchill squeaked by the third time around.

After graduation, Churchill entered the British Army, a career that seemed to suit him. By 1911, he had become First Lord of the Admiralty, a position he filled for the next four years. In 1915, during World War I, Churchill helped engineer an unsuccessful battle, referred to as the Gallipoli disaster. Although some argued that the fault for the failure lay with the tactical commanders, Churchill took most of the blame and received a demotion. Churchill later remarked to the publisher of the *News of the World*, "I am finished."

That comment proved to be far from the truth. Churchill held a variety of positions during the 1920s, and he demonstrated his real value as a commander. When World War II broke out, Churchill was reappointed First Lord of the Admiralty and became a member of the War Cabinet. Early in the war, Neville Chamberlain, the British prime minister, resigned. Churchill was the overwhelming choice to replace Chamberlain. He accepted the position and helped lead England to victory. Despite Churchill's success, he was heavily defeated in his bid for prime minister in 1945. Many historians speculate that his success as a wartime leader led people to believe he could not perform as well during a time of peace. However, six years later, Churchill again became prime minister, a position that he held until he resigned in 1955. When not serving in the government, Churchill spent his time writing books on English and world history, for which he won the 1953 Nobel Prize in Literature.

"The pessimist sees the difficulty in the opportunity; the optimist sees the opportunity in each difficulty." — W. C.

Gary Cooper

Fired Seven Times

During his forty-year career, actor Gary Cooper (1901–1961) starred in more than a hundred films.

DETERMINED TO BECOME AN ILLUSTRATOR or a political cartoonist, Frank Cooper knocked on the doors of several newspapers, but the editors he met were unimpressed with his work. Broke, he heard from his friends that money could be made working in the movies. Years earlier, he had been injured in a car accident and had learned to ride horses as part of his physical therapy. Hollywood was looking for a good stunt rider — or rather a good rider who was capable of falling off horses.

A local casting agent thought Cooper could be more than just a stuntman and suggested that he become an actor. There was one problem: two actors already claimed the name Frank Cooper. So Frank became Gary. After he landed a small part in *The Winning of Barbara Worth*, the actor playing the second lead backed out, and the director gave the role to Cooper.

After that, Cooper won a part in a new movie, *Children of Divorce*, but was soon fired because his early shots were terrible. He was eventually rehired, and the scenes were shot again, a trend that would follow Cooper throughout his early career. Overall, movie studios fired and then rehired Cooper seven times. During the 1940s and 1950s, Cooper starred in some of the most prominent Westerns of the time. He received five Oscar nominations for Best Actor, winning for his performances in *Sergeant York* and *High Noon*. He also received an honorary award from the Academy in 1961. In 1999, Cooper ranked eleventh on the Academy's list of the greatest male stars of all time.

"The only achievement I am really proud of is the friends I have made in this community." — G. C.

Bill Cosby

Intermixing Failures with Successes

William Cosby Jr. (1937–), better known as "Bill" Cosby, is an American actor and comedian and the star of the long-running hit television series *The Cosby Show*.

BILL COSBY DID NOT ENJOY school. His report cards often described him as a "disruptive force" or as not being focused on school. He repeated the tenth grade, then dropped out and finished through a correspondence course while in the U.S. Army. Cosby enrolled at Temple University after leaving the Army, but he dropped out to pursue comedy. At one of his first "stage" performances — for which he earned five dollars a night — he had to climb over the bar and perform his act sitting on a chair perched on a table. The bar could not afford a regular stage and used a table instead. Because Cosby was too tall to stand on top of the table, as other comedians did, he had to sit in the chair to perform.

Eventually, Cosby got bigger and better gigs, including several performances on *The Tonight Show starring Johnny Carson*. Following one of his appearances on *The Tonight Show*, television producer Sheldon Leonard contacted Cosby about playing one of the lead roles in a new series he was producing on NBC, *I Spy*. As costar in the show, Cosby became the first African-American actor in a lead role on an American television drama.

After the show left the air, Cosby put together his own show, *The Bill Cosby Show*. Although somewhat successful — at one point it was eleventh in the ratings — the show was canceled after two seasons. Cosby then moved to motion pictures, but his first film, *Hickey and Boggs*, was poorly received. In 1972, Cosby moved back to television with a comedy/variety show. Unfortunately, *The New Bill Cosby Show* was pulled from the lineup after only one episode. This left Cosby open to work on an animated television series, *Fat Albert and the Cosby Kids*, which soon became a fixture on Saturday morning television. *Cos*, Cosby's next television series, a variety show for kids, attracted little attention and was canceled after only two months on the air.

For the next few years, Cosby stayed away from television, except for serving as a guest host on *The Tonight Show*, appearing on several segments of the *Electric Company*, and hosting *Fat Albert and the Cosby Kids* and the "Picture Pages" segment of the *Captain Kangaroo* show. During this time, Cosby earned a master's degree from the University of Massachusetts at Amherst, and in 1977 obtained his doctorate degree in education.

In 1984, Cosby returned to television, starring in a sitcom based on his hit comedy monologues. NBC executives, wary of Cosby's mixed television success, almost did not put it on the air. The show's producers tried ABC, who turned them down. At the last minute, NBC decided to go with the show, but only for a pilot and five episodes. The network extended Cosby's contract when, during its first season, *The Cosby Show* rose to third place in the ratings. For the next four seasons, it remained number one. After reaching the top twenty, the sitcom remained among the top shows until it went off the air in 1992. Although none of his movies has ever done well at the box office, Cosby earns an estimated $60 million a year from his television shows and commercials, making him one of the most highly paid television personalities in America.

"In order to succeed, your desire for success should be greater than your fear of failure." — B. C.

Bob Cousy

One Break Leads to Another

Better known as the "Houdini of the Hardwood" or "The Cooz," basketball star Bob Cousy (1928–) won six championships and played on thirteen All-Star teams during his thirteen-year career with the Boston Celtics from 1951 to 1963.

Bob Cousy never picked up a basketball until he was twelve years old. He got cut from the school team — not once, but twice. Nevertheless, he kept practicing, hoping to improve enough to make the team. Then fate stepped in. While climbing a tree, he slipped and fell and broke his right arm.

Since he could no longer shoot with his right arm, he started practicing with his left. By the time the doctor removed the cast, the teen had become ambidextrous on the court. This unique ability soon caught the eye of the coach, who promptly invited the boy back on the team. Cousy became the team's star player, and during his senior year he won New York City's scoring title.

After high school, Cousy went on to college, where he earned All-American status three times and helped his team win twenty-six straight games. He graduated with a degree in business and considered opening his own driving school. In the end, he decided to try his luck with the draft. Picked by the Chicago Stags, Cousy transferred to the Boston Celtics after the Stags folded before the season even began. He spent the next twelve years with the Celtics, leading the team to six national championships. He also led the NBA in assists for eight consecutive years from 1953 to 1960. Cousy is often referred to as "Mr. Basketball" and "the Houdini of the Hardwood" for his exceptional skills as a point guard. He was voted MVP in 1957, was a ten-time All-NBA First Team, and was on thirteen All-Star teams. Cousy was inducted into the Hall of Fame in 1970.

"Do your best when no one is looking. If you do that, then you can be successful in anything that you put your mind to." — B. C.

Billy Crystal

Cut on Opening Night

Billy Crystal (1948–) is a comedian, actor, writer, producer, and film director who has starred in hit television shows such as *Soap* and *Saturday Night Live* along with successful movies like *When Harry Met Sally* and *City Slickers.*

In 1976, as a new late-night show called *Saturday Night Live* prepared to air, producers reassured Billy Crystal that he would appear on the first show. Crystal had not been hired as one of the main cast, a first-rate ensemble of talented comedians, but he had been told he would eventually become a major character on the show. Crystal turned down a chance to appear on a Bill Cosby television special to prepare for the new series because producers refused to allow him to do both shows. Then, in the final hours before the show aired, the producers informed him that his skit had been cut. He quickly sought the advice of his managers, who encouraged him to leave the show. He reluctantly agreed. It would be some months before Crystal landed another substantial role. Being out of work and hungry led him to take the risky step of accepting the role of Jodie Dallas on a new series, *Soap*, one of the first gay characters depicted on television. The show premiered in 19 million homes — almost 40 percent of the national audience — and stayed on the air for the next four seasons.

In 1984, Crystal hosted *Saturday Night Live* and joined the cast a couple months later. He left the show a year later. Since then, he has hosted *Comic Relief*, an annual program designed to raise money for homeless people in the United States. Crystal has also hosted the annual Academy Awards show eight times and has appeared in several hit movies, including *The Princess Bride*, *When Harry Met Sally*, *City Slickers*, and *Analyze This*. Most recently, he wrote and starred in his own solo show, *700 Sundays*, which won a Tony for Best Special Theatrical Event in 2005. Following that success, Crystal compiled the show's contents into a book of the same title.

"Change is such hard work." — B. C.

Bette Davis

The Little Brown Wren

Bette Davis (1908–1989) is a two-time Academy Award-winning actor who starred in numerous films, including *Dangerous*, *Jezebel*, and *All About Eve*.

Bette Davis's audition for Eva Le Gallienne's acting school was described as "insincere" and "frivolous," and La Galliene advised her not to pursue acting as a career. She was received better at the John Murray Anderson School for the Performing Arts, but she did not impress film producer Samuel Goldwyn at her first screen test. Goldwyn reportedly asked, "Who did this to me?" He informed Davis that she had no audience appeal and sent her on her way.

Down the road at Universal Studios, studio head Carl Laemmle thought that Davis had very little sex appeal and that no one would "want to get her at the end of the movie." His objections were overruled, and Universal signed her anyway. Because Davis was living in New York at the time, she traveled to Hollywood by train. When she arrived, she was surprised to find that no one from the studio was waiting for her. An hour later when she called the studio, she was told that a staff member had been sent to pick her up but had left because he had not seen anyone who looked like an actress. Her nonglamorous appearance earned her the nickname "little brown wren" at the studio.

Nevertheless, by 1934, only four years after Davis had arrived in Hollywood, audiences were so upset that Davis's performance in *Human Bondage* had not earned her an Academy Award nomination that they mounted a campaign on her behalf. Although she did not win an award that year, the Academy allowed her name to be included as a write-in vote. She was officially nominated, and won, the following year for her performance in *Dangerous*. She won her second Academy Award for Best Actress in 1938 for *Jezebel* and eventually became the first woman to receive ten Oscar nominations for Best Actress. Her last nomination came for her work in the movie *Whatever Happened to Baby Jane?* Davis won the role after advertising for work in the *Hollywood Reporter*. She was paid only $25,000 for the role, because she was willing to accept a percentage of the proceeds, which earned her more than $1 million.

"Attempt the impossible in order to improve your work." — B. D.

Morton Downey Jr.

Socked by Rejections

Morton Downey Jr. (1932–2001) was an American talk-show host and is considered a pioneer of the "trash-talk-show" format.

At his sixteenth birthday party, Morton Downey Jr. showed up wearing red socks and brown shoes. Joe Kennedy, father of President John F. Kennedy and Senators Robert and Ted Kennedy, told Downey that he had never met "anyone wearing red socks and brown shoes who ever succeeded." Everyone laughed. The young man's color-blindness led to his choice, but the next day Downey purposefully put on red socks and brown shoes again. Downey continued to wear the distinctive shoe-and-sock combination most of his life, even after he was fired because of it.

When he attempted to get work as a singer, Downey had many doors shut in his face — not because of his clothing but because of his father, who used his influence to keep his son out of show business. Morton Downey Sr. had been a popular singer in the 1930s and 1940s. For a while, his father's efforts succeeded.

Downey was working as a lobbyist in Florida when his wife spotted a newspaper advertisement for a radio talk-show host and urged him to apply. The station hired him. Within a year, he moved from the late, late-night slot to a more popular afternoon spot. In 1986, after Morton Downey Jr. moved his show from radio to TV, the *Morton Downey Jr. Show* quickly rose to fame. It is credited with pioneering the "trash-talk-show" format.

"As long as a person doesn't admit he is defeated, he is not defeated — he's just a little behind and isn't through fighting." — Darrell Royal

Bob Dylan

Booed Off Stage

Bob Dylan (1941–) is a singer-songwriter, author, musician, and poet. His most recent album, *Modern Times*, entered the U.S. charts at number one in 2006, making him the oldest living person to top the charts.

Growing up in northern Minnesota, Robert Zimmerman dreamed of a warmer climate as well as a warmer reception to his music. In high school, Zimmerman took a risk and sang an original song in his high school talent show at one of his first performances. Most of his classmates — not yet attuned to the rock-and-roll music that had barely begun to hit the airwaves in the 1950s — were speechless. The ones who were not booed, and the principal dropped the curtain midway through Zimmerman's song. Zimmerman — who had taught himself to play the piano, harmonica, and guitar — left his hometown in search of a more appreciative audience. He started out playing small clubs in the Midwest, but eventually he headed to New York City. There he found a more receptive audience and a record contract.

In 1962, he released his first album under his new name: Bob Dylan. By 2006, Dylan had produced twenty-nine gold albums and thirteen platinum albums. He has also received the Polar Music Prize, the Grammy Lifetime Achievement Award, and Kennedy Center Honors. He has been inducted into three halls of fame: Rock and Roll Hall of Fame, Nashville Songwriters Hall of Fame, and Songwriters Hall of Fame. He was also listed on *Time* magazine's list of one hundred most influential people of the twentieth century, ranked second on *Rolling Stone* magazine's "100 Greatest Artists of All Time," and had three of his albums included on *Rolling Stone* magazine's "500 Greatest Albums of All Time." He is one of the few songwriters to have been nominated several times for the Nobel Prize in Literature.

"A man is a success if he gets up in the morning and gets to bed at night, and in between he does what he wants to do." — B. D.

Thomas Alva Edison

Unworthy of Attention

Thomas Alva Edison (1847–1931) is considered to be one of America's most prolific and successful inventors. He is credited as the inventor of the phonograph, the incandescent light bulb, and the automatic telegraph.

As a child, Thomas Edison tormented his teachers. He rarely sat still, constantly badgered his teachers with questions, could not focus, and seemed to be ignoring their instructions. He was hearing-impaired, but his teachers believed he was also slow, probably retarded. Before Edison had turned six, he had burned down his family's barn, a fact some used as proof of his mental impairment. His mother tried several different schools, but the results were always the same. Finally, his mother took him out of school and educated him at home.

When Edison was older, he got a position working for the railroad. Not one to let work interfere with his quest for knowledge, he obtained permission to set up a chemistry lab in a baggage car. His boss soon regretted the favor after Edison destroyed a telegraph station while experimenting with a battery. The inventor became so focused on his experiments that he often neglected to do his job. He was fired the following year after he failed to set a danger signal and caused a train to derail.

A few years later, out of money and work, he went to New York City to find a job. After several unsuccessful interviews, he was waiting for yet another interview when he learned that the company's telegraphic gold-price indicator had broken down. He fixed it and landed a job at the firm. Because of this new job, he later invented the Edison Universal Stock Printer, which earned him enough money to set up his own laboratory.

He went on to perfect the electric light bulb, invent the phonograph, and introduce a motion picture machine. Someone once asked him how it felt to have failed so many times before succeeding: "I never failed once," Edison replied. "It happens to be a 2,000-step process."

During his career, he faced many critics. After electric lights had been installed along the Avenue de l'Opéra and the Place de l'Opéra for the Paris Exposition of 1878, Erasmus Wilson, an Oxford professor, predicted that no one would ever hear about the electric light again. A committee set up by the British Parliament to investigate Edison's works reported that they were "unworthy of the attention of practical or scientific men." Henry Morton, president of the Stevens Institute of Technology, wondered how Edison could claim success "when everyone acquainted with the subject will recognize it as a conspicuous failure."

In 1878, Thomas Edison demonstrated his phonograph in front of the French Academy of Sciences. One member, Jean Bouillaud, predicted that it would not work and said, "It is quite impossible that the noble organs of human speech could be replaced by ignoble, senseless metal." After the device worked, Bouillaud attributed the demonstration to simple "ventriloquism."

Over his lifetime, Edison was granted 1,093 patents for his inventions; among them are the incandescent light bulb, an automatic telegraphy machine, the phonograph, and the motion picture machine. After one unsuccessful attempt to create a storage battery, he said, "Well, at least we know 8,000 things that don't work!" Edison became the first person inducted into the National Inventors Hall of Fame.

> *"Many of life's failures are men who did not realize how close they were to success when they gave up." — T. A. E.*

Albert Einstein

A Scientist without a Logical Mind

Albert Einstein (1879–1955) was a physicist who is best known for his theory of relativity and the mass-energy equation $E = mc^2$. His name has become synonymous with the concept of intellectual genius.

ALBERT EINSTEIN WAS THREE YEARS old before he started speaking, and it took him several more years before he could talk fluently. He did not read until he was seven, and his poor performance in elementary school caused many people to suspect he was mentally retarded. When teachers called on him, the boy took forever to answer, often silently mouthing the words to himself before slowly uttering them aloud. Most people believed Einstein would never succeed at anything.

When he applied to the Swiss Federal Institute of Technology, he failed the entrance exam and was required to take it again. The university rejected his doctoral dissertation, which was described as "irrelevant and fanciful." After graduation, Einstein landed a position as a clerk in a patent office. He liked the job because it allowed him free time to research his scientific theories. Known for being incredibly absent-minded, Einstein often forgot basic things, such as putting on his socks, and he once misplaced a $1,500 check after he used it as a bookmark.

It was not until after the first of Einstein's theories, the *Special Theory of Relativity*, was published that the scientific community truly recognized his talent. However, many scientists attacked his theories, calling them "worthless and misleading" and asserted that Einstein "has not a logical mind." Still, he became professor extraordinary at Zurich and later, a professor of theoretical physics at Prague. The highlight of his scientific career came in 1921, when Einstein won the Nobel Prize in Physics.

"Anyone who has never made a mistake has never tried anything new." — A. E.

Michael J. Fox

Not Right for the Part

Michael J. Fox (1961–) is an a Canadian-American actor who starred in the hit television series *Family Ties* and *Spin City* as well as the *Back to the Future* motion picture trilogy.

WITH A SUCCESSFUL CANADIAN TELEVISION series and a movie on his resume, eighteen-year-old Michael J. Fox moved to Hollywood. Instead of finding stardom, he struggled to survive on macaroni and cheese and was reduced to selling his furniture to make his rent payments. A casting director considered him for a role on a new television series, *Family Ties*, but Fox blew his audition. The producers did not think Fox was right for the role, but the casting director convinced them to give Fox another shot. This time, he got the part. It was a fortunate turn of events for Fox since he was so broke that he could not afford a telephone; his agent had to wait for him to call from a pay phone.

Fox's role on *Family Ties* was the start of a brilliant career, which was helped by his performance in *Back to the Future*. Ironically, he almost lost that role because it would not fit into his *Family Ties* schedule. Another actor filled the role when filming for the movie began. When it became apparent that the other actor was not going to work out, the director negotiated with the producers of *Family Ties* to allow Fox to fulfill commitments to both productions. The movie not only launched Fox as an actor, but it also helped boost *Family Ties* into the Nielson's top ten ratings.

"The only thing worse than an opportunity you don't deserve is blowing an opportunity." — M. J. F.

Clark Gable

Performed Poorly in Screen Tests

Nicknamed the "King of Hollywood," Clark Gable (1901–1960) starred in approximately eighty movies from 1924 to 1961, including *Gone with the Wind*, *Mutiny on the Bounty*, and *It Happened One Night*.

Clark Gable spent almost ten years trying to get an acting job, but studio executives did not like his screen tests. He had worked his way from Ohio to Oregon as an actor in a second-class theater company, but he had to sell ties to pay his bills. However, acting was in his blood, and Gable soon found another job in the theater. He eventually met Josephine Dillon, who became both his acting coach and his wife. After getting his teeth fixed, he headed to Hollywood.

Gable landed a screen test for MGM studios, but when production executive Irving Thalberg saw it, he said, "It's awful; take it away." Gable found work as an extra in several silent movies but had no luck in finding a substantial role. Eventually, he quit trying and went back to the stage.

Within four years, Gable was back at the auditions. He tried out for the lead in *Little Caesar* at Warner Brothers, but executives refused to cast him because of his appearance. Jack Warner's response was to ask, "What can you do with a guy with ears like that?" Another executive, Darryl F. Zanuck, is rumored to have compared the actor to an ape.

After Warner Brothers' rejection, Gable tried MGM studios again. This time, he landed a substantial role in the 1931 low-budget Western *The Painted Desert.* Audiences loved him, and the flood of fan mail the actor received forced the studios to take notice and offer him a contract. His popularity skyrocketed. Gable quickly adopted a cocky demeanor and became difficult to work with. According to legend, MGM studio heads lent him out to a smaller studio to teach him a lesson.

Their plan backfired when Gable won the 1934 Academy Award for Best Actor for his performance in *It Happened One Night.* Gable spent the next twenty-five years acting in lead roles, which earned him the title of "King of Hollywood." His most famous role was his portrayal of Rhett Butler in *Gone with the Wind.*

> *"The things a man has to have are hope and confidence in himself against odds."* — C. G.

Nikolai Gogol

Worse than Ignored

Nikolai Gogol (1809–1852) wrote novels, plays, and poetry, including *Dead Souls, Revizor,* and the short story "The Overcoat."

Nikolai Gogol's first poem, "Italy," received little attention when it was published on March 23, 1829, but it gave the young poet confidence to publish, at his own expense, his narrative poem *Gants Kiukhelgarten* (also known as *Hans Kuechelgarten* and *Hanz Küchelgarten*) later that year. This poem was not ignored; it was attacked. The nineteen-year-old writer promptly bought all the copies he could find and burned them. Gogol vowed he would never write poetry again — at least not publicly.

After making an unsuccessful attempt at a career on stage, Gogol returned to writing and bravely published a collection of short stories under the title *Evenings on a Farm Near Dikanka.* The book was an immediate success. Although Gogol turned his attention to fiction, he often referred to his writing as both a "novel in verse" and an "epic poem in prose." He had a huge influence on Russian literature as well as on many modern writers. Two of his best-known works are *The Inspector General* and *Dead Souls,* which is considered by many to be the first modern Russian novel. Many of his works have been adapted into motion pictures, operas, and other formats.

> *"And for a long time yet, led by some wondrous power, I am fated to journey hand in hand with my strange heroes and to survey the surging immensity of life, to survey it through the laughter that all can see and through the tears unseen and unknown by anyone."* — N. G.

Ulysses S. Grant

From Retired Captain to Brigadier General

Ulysses S. Grant (1822–1885) was an important general during the American Civil War and the eighteenth president of the United States.

DESPITE BEING CONSIDERED THE BEST rider at West Point, Ulysses S. Grant was denied a position with the cavalry and assigned to the Fourth Infantry after graduating at the bottom of his West Point class. He spent the next eleven years in the Army, achieving the mere rank of captain before retiring. During the next six years, Grant tried his hand at a variety of careers, including farmer and real estate agent, but he never found any real success.

When the Civil War began, he tried to obtain a suitable position in the Union Army. For six weeks, he was transferred to a variety of positions, including drillmaster, clerk, and mustering officer. Grant finally requested that he be given command of a regiment. After being ignored by the adjutant general in Washington and other superior officers, Grant was appointed colonel of the Twenty-first Illinois Volunteers by Illinois Governor Richard Yates. Within a month, he had risen to the rank of brigadier general. Although newspapers frequently denounced Grant, President Abraham Lincoln never lost faith in him. Grant eventually defeated

Robert E. Lee, negotiated the surrender that ended the Civil War, and — despite never having held public office — was elected president of the United States in 1869.

"My failures have been errors of judgment, not of intent." — U. S. G.

John Grisham

Fewer than Five Thousand Copies Sold

John Grisham (1955–) is the best-selling author of almost two dozen novels, including *A Time to Kill*, *The Firm*, *The Pelican Brief*, and *The Client*.

John Grisham's three years of hard work appeared futile after numerous agents and more than thirty publishers rejected his first novel, *A Time to Kill*. Finally, one publisher, Wynwood Press, agreed to publish it. However, there was a catch — the company would print only five thousand copies. Grisham bought one thousand copies of the novel himself and tried to sell them, but was eventually forced to give away most of them to family and friends.

By then he had already begun writing his second book, *The Firm*. Amazingly, his agent sold the movie rights to the second book to Paramount Pictures for $600,000 before landing a book deal for the manuscript. The deal with Paramount sparked interest in Grisham and his books. *The Firm* became one of the top-ten best-selling novels of 1991, spending forty-seven weeks on the *New York Times* best-seller list. The movie was also extremely successful and took in $100 million after only twenty-three days at the box office. With *The Firm*'s success, the publisher reprinted *A Time to Kill*. This time it sold more than 8.6

million copies and was on the *New York Times* best-seller list for eight weeks in a row. Since then, *Publishers Weekly* has declared Grisham as "the best-selling novelist of the '90s." More than 225 million copies of his novels are in print worldwide; they have been translated into thirty languages. Grisham writes an average of one novel a year, all international best-sellers. Nine of his novels have been made into movies.

"I have learned not to read reviews. Period. Life is much simpler ignoring reviews and the nasty people who write them." — J. G.

Milton Hershey

The Sweetest Failure

Milton Hershey (1857–1945) founded the Hershey Chocolate Company, America's largest chocolate manufacturer.

MILTON HERSHEY OPENED HIS FIRST candy store in Pennsylvania in 1876 at the age of nineteen. For six years, he worked around the clock, manufacturing the candy at night and selling it during the day. After he collapsed from exhaustion, Hershey closed the business and moved to Denver to work for another candy company. After gaining some experience, he moved to Chicago and tried again to run his own business, but it, too, failed. He opened yet another company in New York City, only to fail again.

Finally, Hershey moved back to Lancaster, Pennsylvania, and scraped together enough money — no one would lend him any after so many failures — to start the Lancaster Caramel Company. Despite his failures, he had managed to perfect a recipe for caramels that used fresh milk, making them much creamier than the standard fare. This new recipe proved to be the key to his success. Sales improved, enabling him to procure a loan and expand the business. In 1900, Hershey sold his caramel company for $1 million and focused entirely on chocolate. In just a few years, his chocolate business was worth more than $20 million. His chocolate was so popular that the town where Hershey began his company — Derry Church, Pennsylvania — changed its name to Hershey and is often called Chocolatetown, USA.

"Because a fellow has failed once or twice, or a dozen times, you don't want to set him down as a failure till he's dead or loses his courage — and that's the same thing." — George Horace Lorimer

Rock Hudson

Thirty-eight Takes to Deliver a Line

Rock Hudson (1925–1985) acted in more than seventy movies during his career, including *Pillow Talk* and *Giant*.

Roy Harold Scherer Jr.'s desire to become an actor began in high school, but he failed to get parts because he could not remember his lines. Scherer turned his attention toward other professions, getting work as a truck driver and as a postal service worker. However, his dreams of acting refused to die, and eventually Scherer moved to Los Angeles. He applied to the University of Southern California dramatics program, but his application was rejected because of his poor grades. He sent out resumes and photographs to every movie studio, agent, and talent scout in town. At one point, Scherer did a screen test for

Twentieth Century-Fox Studios that was so bad that it is still shown to acting classes to illustrate what one should not do in a screen test.

Only one person, a Hollywood talent agent named Henry Wilson, responded to Scherer's mailings. Wilson convinced Scherer to change his name to Rock Hudson and landed him his first role. The newly named Hudson, still had trouble delivering his lines — it is rumored that it took him thirty-eight takes to speak his first line correctly on screen. Wilson encouraged Hudson to take acting lessons, which helped him improve his presentation. During the next six years, Hudson starred in more than twenty-eight pictures. At the time of his death in 1985, he had starred in more than sixty movies, had been nominated for an Oscar in 1957 for Best Actor, and had won four Golden Globe Awards in the category of World Film Favorite: Male Actor.

"The most dangerous thing for an actor is to refuse to listen to anyone else, to feel you know more than anybody." — R. H.

Billy Joel

Sounded Just Like Alvin and the Chipmunks

Billy Joel (1949–), an American singer, pianist, songwriter, composer, and musician, has won numerous Grammy Awards and sold more than 150 million albums worldwide. Some of his most famous songs include "Piano Man," "My Life," "It's Still Rock & Roll to Me," "Uptown Girl," and "We Didn't Start the Fire."

A SHORT-TERM RECORDING CONTRACT with Mercury Records and demo versions of two of his songs failed to launch Billy Joel and the Echoes into stardom. Joel left the band and joined the Hassles, but the band's two albums with

United Artists received little acclaim and did not follow the style Joel favored. He then formed a duo with drummer Jonathan Small. Calling themselves Attila, they released one self-titled album with Epic but disbanded after the record company canceled their contract. Depressed over his failures, Joel attempted suicide and spent a short time at a psychiatric hospital, which helped him put things back into focus.

After leaving the hospital, Joel recorded and released his first solo album, *Cold Spring Harbor*. It was, by all accounts, a catastrophe. The album was mastered poorly and released at the wrong speed. This gave Joel a much higher voice and, as he described it, made him sound "like Alvin and the Chipmunks." Embarrassed by the record and aggravated by a contractual dispute, Joel escaped to California and began working on the piano bar circuit under the pseudonym Bill Martin. A short time later, a Philadelphia radio station began broadcasting a tape of Joel performing his songs in concert. This led executives at Columbia Records to track Joel down and offer him a record contract.

In 1973, Joel released his second solo album. It featured two important songs. The first was "Tomorrow is Today," featuring lyrics written from Joel's suicide note. The second was "Piano Man," written by Joel about his experiences on the piano bar circuit. The latter song became Joel's first top-twenty single, led to his first gold album, and remains one of his most popular songs. Since then, Joel has won six Grammy Awards and sold more than one hundred million records worldwide. He was inducted into the Songwriter's

Hall of Fame in 1992 and the Rock and Roll Hall of Fame in 1999.

"You're only human; you're supposed to be making mistakes." — B. J.

Elton John and Bernie Taupin

Received Last Place in Song Contest

The songwriting team of Elton John (1947–) and Bernie Taupin (1950–) has produced "Rocket Man," "Tiny Dancer," "Candle in the Wind," and "Don't Let the Sun Go Down on Me."

REGINALD KENNETH DWIGHT FIRST JOINED a group called Bluesology that backed other bands and eventually became the supporting band for the blues singer Long John Baldry. However, Dwight did not want to play backup; he wanted to be the lead vocalist. He tried out for that position with King Crimson and Gentle Giant, but both bands rejected him. Looking for work, Dwight answered an advertisement in the *New Musical Express* and met Liberty Records executive Ray Williams. Williams was impressed by Dwight and gave him a stack of lyrics written by Bernie Taupin, who had also answered the advertisement. Six months later, Taupin and Dwight met for the first time when they recorded their first song. Dwight changed his name to Elton John and the two joined DJM Records as songwriters. In 1969, Taupin and John entered one of their songs, *Can't Go On (Living Without You)*, in the Eurovision song contest. The song came in sixth place out of six songs.

A short time later, John collaborated with Taupin on several new songs for his debut album, *Empty Sky*. The album received good reviews, but sales were slow. The following year, John released a second album, *Elton John*. This album included a song he and Taupin had written, "Your Song." Both the song and the album made the top-ten charts in the United States, as did John's next album. Taupin and John have collaborated on more than thirty albums to date. Together the duo has written numerous classics such as "Rocketman," "Tiny Dancer," "Don't Let the Sun Go Down on Me," and "Goodbye Yellow Brick Road." They also collaborated on both the original "Candle in the Wind" and the 1997 update written as a tribute to Diana, Princess of Wales, which became the biggest seller in music history.

"So shine on through these days we have to fill." — E.J.

Bob Keeshan

Fired from the Howdy Doody Show

Bob Keeshan (1927–2004) charmed children as the host and title character of the long-running television show *Captain Kangaroo*.

Bob Keeshan was the first Clarabell on the popular *Howdy Doody Show*, but he was fired after a disagreement with the show's creator. At the time, Keeshan was attending Fordham University with thoughts of becoming an attorney. That career was discarded when Keeshan was offered the role as a Corny the Clown on a noontime cartoon show, *Time for Fun*. The position lasted for two years. By the time the show was cancelled, Keeshan had already begun working on a new program, *Tinker's Workshop*, which he also produced. CBS executives liked the show and offered

Keeshan his own children's show on the network.

Although he was only in his twenties, Keeshan decided he wanted to create an elderly character to host the new show, called *Captain Kangaroo*. He donned a gray wig to bring the character to life. Eventually, the wig was discarded — not because it was unpopular, but because the show lasted so long that Keeshan's hair turned gray and the wig became obsolete. *Captain Kangaroo* was on the air for more than thirty years. During its run, the show and Keeshan won numerous awards, including a Sylvania Award, five Emmy Awards, three Peabody Awards, and a National Education Award. Keeshan has also received recommendations from the National Audience Board and the National Congress of Parents and Teachers.

"Small praise will fire great accomplishment in a young child."

Sandy Koufax

An Unimpressive Beginning

Sandy Koufax (1935–) was a major league baseball player who pitched for the Brooklyn-Los Angeles Dodgers, from 1955 to 1966.

As a child, Sandy Koufax preferred basketball to baseball, which he played only occasionally — usually as the first baseman. It was not until he was seventeen and in high school that he pitched a game. After graduating, he attended the University of Cincinnati on a basketball scholarship. He earned a position on the university's varsity baseball team and was soon being scouted by the major leagues. In 1954, a scout for the Brooklyn Dodgers sent a report about Koufax back to the team's front office, but the report was filed away and no action was taken on the scout's recommendations until 1955.

At that point, Koufax had already tried out for the New York Giants and the Pittsburgh Pirates. Branch Rickey, general manager for the Pirates, thought that Koufax had "the greatest arm [he had] ever seen" and wanted to sign him to the team. When his son, Branch Rickey Jr., an official for the Brooklyn Dodgers, learned of his father's plans, he immediately advised him against signing Koufax. "Don't do it," he said. "I've seen a sandlot team clobber him. All he'll do is take up space for two years and give the papers more ammunition to throw at you." Rickey eventually offered Koufax a contract, but by then the young pitcher had already signed with another team — the Brooklyn Dodgers.

During Koufax's first six seasons in the majors, his record was an unimpressive 36-40. He began to improve after convincing his coach, Buzzie Bavasi, to let him pitch more often. With practice, Koufax learned to control his fastball and perfect his curveball. His skills helped him capture five straight ERA titles, pitch no-hitters in four consecutive seasons, and lead the Dodgers to three championships. In 1971, Koufax became the youngest inductee into the Baseball Hall of Fame at the age of thirty-six.

"I became a good pitcher when I stopped trying to make them miss the ball and started trying to make them hit it." — S. K.

John le Carré

From No Future to Immediate Best-seller

John Le Carré is the pseudonym of David Cornwell (1931–), an English writer of espionage novels, such as *The Spy Who Came in from the Cold* and *Tinker, Tailor, Soldier, Spy*.

DAVID CORNWELL'S PROMISING CAREER WITH British Secret Intelligence Service, better known as MI6, was dashed after his cover was blown by a double agent. He had already begun writing fiction under a pseudonym, John le Carré. However, his first two novels did not do well, and he found it difficult to find a publisher for his third book, *The Spy Who Came in from the Cold*. One editor reportedly said, "You're welcome to le Carré — he hasn't got any future."

Le Carré eventually found a publisher for his book. It received good reviews and became an immediate best-seller. Since then, *The Spy Who Came in from the Cold* has sold more than twenty million copies. The novel also won a Gold Dagger Award for Best Crime Novel from the British Crime Writers Association and the Edgar Award from the Mystery Writers of America for Best Mystery Novel. In 2005, *The Spy Who Came in from the Cold* was awarded the "Dagger of Daggers," a one-time-only award given to the Golden Dagger winner regarded as the standout among all fifty winners. Le Carré has written more than two dozen novels since then.

"Sometimes we do a thing in order to find out the reason for it. Sometimes our actions are questions not answers." — J. l. C.

C. S. Lewis

Received Eight Hundred Rejections

C. S. Lewis (1898–1963) was an Irish author and scholar famous for his series *The Chronicles of Narnia* that includes the novel *The Lion, The Witch, and The Wardrobe.*

Inspired by William Butler Yeats, C. S. Lewis's wrote a collection of verses titled *Spirits in Bondage: a Cycle of Lyrics* under the pseudonym of Clive Hamilton. It was not successful. For the next fourteen years, Lewis's only work to be published was a narrative poem. At the time, Lewis was a member of the English faculty at Oxford University and a close friend of J. R. R. Tolkien, author of *The Lord of the Rings*. His connection to Tolkien, however, did not spark interest from publishers in Lewis's work. Lewis continued to submit his work to publishers during this time and, according to legend, amassed a collection of more than eight hundred rejections.

Lewis's fortune began to change after he converted to Christianity, partially because of Tolkien's influence. He wrote a new piece of fiction titled *The Pilgrim's Regress* about a character's philosophical journey toward Christianity. It was his own version of John Bunyan's *The Pilgrim's Progress* and the work that finally ended his fourteen-year publication dry spell.

Christianity continued to have a major impact on his fictional works with lucrative results. Lewis is best known for his popular series of seven children's books, *The Chronicles of Narnia*, which has sold more than one hundred million copies in more than forty languages. His books have been a source of inspiration for many people; authors such as Daniel Handler, Philip Pullman, J. K. Rowling, and Tim Powers have acknowledged Lewis's influence on their writing.

"Love may forgive all infirmities and love still in spite of them." — C. S. L.

Abraham Lincoln

Failed Over and Over

Abraham Lincoln (1809–1865) was the sixteenth president of the United States.

ABRAHAM LINCOLN EXPERIENCED MANY FAILURES during his lifetime, both before and during his political career. In 1831, he opened his first business, a dry goods store, which later went out of business. In 1832, he entered the Black Hawk War with the rank of captain, but left three months later as a private without ever seeing battle. He also lost an election for the state legislature and was defeated as elector. He purchased another store in a different location, but it, too, closed, leaving Lincoln in considerable debt. His brief stint as postmaster produced the worst efficiency record in the county. In 1834, Lincoln ran for the Illinois House of Representatives and won but later lost his bid to serve as Speaker of the House. In 1835, his girlfriend died. The following year, Lincoln had a nervous breakdown. In 1837, he fell in love again, but the woman turned down his proposal.

In 1843, Lincoln lost an election for the U.S. Congress. Although he won the next time he ran, he later failed to win reelection. In 1854, he was elected to the Illinois legislature, but he declined the seat in order to run for the U.S. Senate, only to lose that election. In 1856, he ran for vice president and lost. Two years later, he ran for the U.S. Senate again, and lost, again. In 1860, he ran for president of the United States and won with 40 percent of the popular vote, although he had 60 percent of the electoral votes. In 1864, the editor of the *New York Tribune* predicted, "Mr. Lincoln is already beaten. He cannot be re-elected." Later that same year, Lincoln won with 55 percent of the popular vote and 91 percent of the electoral votes.

> *"My great concern is not whether you have failed, but whether you are content with your failure."* — A. L.

Joe Louis

Floored Seven Times in Two Rounds

Joe Louis Barrow (1914–1981), better known as Joe Louis, was the world heavyweight champion from 1937 to 1949, the longest reign in boxing history.

In his first amateur boxing match in 1932, Joe Louis Barrow hit the floor seven times in only two rounds. The defeat mortified him, and he decided to give up boxing altogether. Louis had been using the money his mother had given him for violin lessons to join the gym. Afraid that she would find out, he dropped his last name when he first began to box. Eventually, she found out, as mothers always seem to do. Although not pleased about his deception, she recognized that her son was following his dream.

When he told his parents he planned to quit boxing, his stepfather urged him to focus on his job, but his mother encouraged him to get back in the ring because she wanted him to do something he enjoyed. This time, Joe Louis listened to his mother. In 1933, he won fifty out of fifty-four amateur boxing matches — forty-three by knockouts. In 1935, he won all of his professional boxing matches, including matches against two former world heavyweight champions. Two years later, he became the world heavyweight champion. His reign lasted for twelve years, the longest in boxing history. In 2003, *Ring Magazine* placed Louis at the top of its list of one hundred greatest punchers of all time. In 2005, Louis was named the greatest heavyweight of all time by the International Boxing Research Organization.

"Every man's got to figure to get beat sometime." — J. L.

Myrna Loy

Failed Screen Test with Valentino

Actor Myrna Loy (1905–1993) was voted "Queen of Hollywood" in 1938. Her most famous role was as Nora Charles, the wife of Nick Charles in *The Thin Man* series.

By the time Myrna Loy was eleven, she was convinced she was destined to be an actor. She moved to Los Angeles, where she met Natacha Rambova, wife of the legendary silent-film actor Rudolph Valentino. Rambova arranged a screen test for Loy with Valentino. Loy failed the test miserably. Despite this, Rambova saw potential in the young woman and refused to give up on her. She gave Loy a role in the 1925 movie *What Price Beauty?*, which Rambova wrote and starred in. The role landed Loy a variety of bit parts. Gradually, the parts grew larger as her on-screen presence became noted by audiences and critics alike. By the mid-1930s, Loy had worked her way up the ranks to become one of the busiest and highest paid actresses in Hollywood. She was voted the "Queen of Hollywood" to Clark Gable's "King" in a national poll. Amazingly, Loy was never nominated for an Academy Award, although she received the Academy's Honorary Award in 1991 "for her career achievement." She also received a Lifetime Achievement Award from the Kennedy Center in 1988.

"Life is not a having and a getting, but a being and a becoming." — M. L.

Douglas MacArthur

Twice Rejected from West Point

A general in the U.S. Army, Douglas MacArthur (1880–1964) played a prominent role in the Pacific during World War II. He earned a Metal of Honor, three Distinguished Service Crosses, five Army Distinguished Service Medals, seven Silver Stars, a Bronze Star, two Purple Hearts, and numerous other medals during his military career.

Considering that his father had been awarded the Congressional Medal of Honor and was a Civil War hero and a top-ranking officer in the Army, Douglas MacArthur should have had no trouble getting into West Point. Yet, he was turned down twice, most likely because he had been a poor-to-average student in school. MacArthur refused to give up and applied a third time. He was finally accepted. While a student at West Point, MacArthur won all the honors offered at the academy and graduated top in his class with the third-best academic record in the school's history. After graduating, MacArthur became a second lieutenant in the U.S. Army Corps of Engineers. He was assigned to work in Wisconsin as an engineering officer, where he received a poor performance rating. Eventually, he was reassigned to serve as an *aide-de-camp* to his father, who was serving as the appointed governor general of the Philippines. The change helped MacArthur mature into a more distinguished officer, although he was known for stupid mistakes that made him the butt of people's jokes.

MacArthur went on to prove himself in the Pancho Villa Expedition (also called the Punitive Expedition), where he performed several acts of personal bravery. MacArthur participated in three major wars: World War I, World War II, and the Korean War. He is one of a handful of people in U.S. history to have achieved the rank of General of the Army. He also received various decorations from the United States and other allied nations, including a Medal of Honor, a Purple Heart, the French Légion d'Honneur, and the British Knight Grand Cross of the Military Division of the Most Honourable Order of the Bath.

> *"You only grow old by deserting your ideals. Years wrinkle the skin; giving up wrinkles the soul."* — D. M.

Akio Morita and Masaru Ibuka

Creators of the Automatic Rice Burner and the Seventy-five-Pound Recorder

Akio Morita (1921–1999) and Masaru Ibuka (1908–1997) cofounded the Sony Corporation, one of the largest manufacturers of consumer electronics and information technology products.

Akio Morita's love of electronics began when he was just a boy and almost caused him to flunk out of school when he became too engrossed in his pastime. He eventually graduated and attended Osaka Imperial University before entering the Navy, where he met Masaru Ibuka. After their discharge, Morita and Ibuka opened Tokyo Tsushin Kogyo, or Totsuko. They had roughly $500 in capital, twenty employees, a rented office located in a burned-out department store, and the dream of creating electronic products.

One of their first products was an automatic rice cooker. They sold only one hundred of these devices, which were more likely to burn the rice than cook it. Next, they created an inexpensive tape recorder for Japanese schools. It did not sell well because it was hard to carry — it weighed seventy-five pounds. In 1975, the two inventors developed the first full-transistorized radio in history. Unlike their bulky tape recorders, the new device was much smaller and could fit inside a pocket.

The following year, they decided to change the company name and make it less Japanese sounding to help attract more foreign sales. In 1958, Totsuko became Sony Corporation. By continuously investing 6 to 10 percent of their annual sales in research and development, Morita and Ibuka made Sony into a company known for its innovative and revolutionary computer products. As of 2007, Sony was one of the largest media conglomerates with revenues exceeding $68 billion. The company continues to manufacture electronics as well as video, communication, and information technology products for consumers.

"Don't be afraid to make a mistake. But make sure you don't make the same mistake twice." — Akio Morita

'N Sync

Out of Sync with Record Companies

'N Sync is an American pop boy band that has sold more than fifty-six million records worldwide since debuting in 1998.

THE NAME OF THE FIVE-MAN vocal team 'N Sync was inspired by a comment made by one member's mother that they were very "in sync." The official name was created by using the last letter of each member's first name: Justi*n* Timberlake, Chri*s* Kirkpatrick, Joe*y* Fatone, Lanste*n* (Lance) Bass, and J*C* Chasez. Finding a name proved to be much easier than finding a recording company. American record companies repeatedly turned down the group's demo record. 'N Sync was just days away from disbanding when BMG/Ariola, a German label, signed the group. 'N Sync spent the next year touring Europe before returning to the United States.

American response to the band's music was less than promising, but the group got a boost when it was chosen as a last- minute replacement on a Disney Channel concert special after the Backstreet Boys backed out. The concert gave 'N Sync some excellent exposure and immediately boosted sales of the band's album. Since then, four 'N Sync albums have gone multiplatinum. The band's third album, *No Strings Attached*, sold one million records the first day it was released and 2.4 million copies the first week, the highest first-week album sales in music history. It went on to sell fifteen million copies and went platinum eleven times.

The group's next album, *Celebrity*, sold thirteen million copies and went platinum five times. The group took a break in 2004, which allowed Timberlake and Chasez to release solo albums. However, the members are expected to reunite to produce three more records for Jive Records.

"Never consider the possibility of failure; as long as you persist, you will be successful." — Brian Tracy

George Patton

Failed West Point

George Smith Patton Jr. (1885–1945) was a U.S. Army general during World War II.

George S. Patton Jr. was often teased by other students in grade school. He did not learn to read until a late age and was a poor speller. He entered the Virginia Military Institute in 1903, and then transferred to West Point, where he flunked out his second year because of deficiencies in mathematics. Working hard to make up for his academic failings, he repeated his second year and completed his classes with honors. Still at West Point, Patton was appointed corporal adjutant, the second highest position for a cadet. He graduated and became a cavalry officer for the Army. During his thirty-six-year Army career, Patton demonstrated his brilliance on the battlefield. Today, he is considered one of the greatest combat generals who ever lived.

Patton was a senior commander of the new tank corps during World War I and a U.S. Army general in World War II. He earned numerous awards and decorations in the United States and abroad, including a Purple Heart, a Distinguished Service Cross, an Order of the British Empire, and the French Légion d'Honneur. In 1970, an Academy Award-winning film, *Patton*, about the general's life helped secure Patton's legacy as a great military leader. Although some have accused the film of being biased, many of those closest to Patton praised the film for its accuracy.

"Success is how high you bounce when you hit bottom." — G. P.

Luciano Pavarotti

Unable to Read Music

Luciano Pavarotti (1935–2007) was an Italian operatic singer and one of the Three Tenors.

Luciano Pavarotti had very little formal musical training as a child and never learned to read music. He considered a career in professional soccer until his mother convinced him to train as a teacher. For two years, he taught elementary school before his interests turned to music. He quit teaching and worked as an insurance salesman while studying voice. For six years, Pavarotti could not find any work as a singer except a few small, unpaid recitals. He was ready to give up on singing when he entered and won the Achille Peri Competition in 1961. The prize was to perform the role of Rodolfo in a production of Puccini's *La Bohème*. The debut was a success and landed him an agent and a few singing contracts. Within two years, he had gained worldwide fame after filling in for Giuseppe de Stefano in *La Bohème* at the Royal Opera House in Covent Garden.

In 1968, Pavarotti made his New York debut at the Metropolitan Opera, but the show was cut short during his second performance when he became ill. It would be four years before he would make it back to the Met to perform the role of Toni in *La Fille du Regiment*. During the performance, Pavarotti belted out nine high C's in a row, impressing audiences so much that he received numerous curtain calls and landed an appearance on *The Tonight Show starring Johnny Carson*. The television appearance helped make Pavarotti one of the most famous living opera singers. Still, he never learned to read music because, as he observed, "Learning music by reading about it is like making love by mail." Pavarotti sold more than a hundred million records and was the only opera singer to perform on the television show *Saturday Night Live*.

"People have a right to criticize. If they boo me because I sing bad, they will do it." — L. P.

Cole Porter

D Student in Music

Composer and songwriter Cole Porter (1891–1964) wrote many songs, including "Night and Day," "I Get a Kick Out of You," and "I've Got You Under My Skin."

Cole Porter barely managed to graduate from Yale University and received mostly D's in the music courses that he took there. His first song on Broadway, "Esmeralda," appeared in the revue *Hands Up*, and he contributed a song to *Miss Information*. Both shows failed, as did the first musical he wrote, *See America First*, which closed after only two weeks. Porter was so disappointed that he packed up his belongings and moved to France, although not to join the foreign legion as is often rumored. Instead, he enrolled in a French school that specialized in music composition. For more than ten years, he continued to write songs for various revues and even composed a ballet, but none of these efforts met with any success.

He returned to the United States in the late 1920s to write a new Broadway show, *Paris*. The show was a success as was one of the songs he wrote for it, "Let's Do It (Let's Fall in Love)." Porter's career finally took off, beginning with a series of hit Broadway shows and then expanding into the movies. Some of his works include the musical comedies *The Gay Divorcee*, *Anything Goes*, and *Kiss Me, Kate*. He also wrote the songs "Night and Day," "I've Got You Under My Skin," and "In the Still of the Night." In 2004, Porter's life was chronicled in a new movie titled *De-Lovely*, which starred Kevin Kline as Porter.

> *"Don't be afraid to fail. Don't waste energy trying to cover up failure. Learn from your failures and go on to the next challenge. It's okay to fail. If you're not failing, you're not growing."* — H. Stanley Judd

Sally Jessy Raphael

Fired Eighteen Times

Sally Jessy Raphael (1935–) is an American radio and television talk-show host who hosted her own syndicated talk show from 1993 until to 2002 called *Sally Jessy Raphael*.

DURING HER FIRST TEN YEARS in broadcasting, Sally Jessy Raphael was fired from eighteen of the twenty-four jobs she held. Each time, she considered leaving broadcasting and starting on a new career track. She had entered law school twice with the intentions of putting broadcasting behind her for good. Nevertheless, she endured twenty-five years of stress and strife until she finally landed a job that allowed her to support her family. Raphael does not look at the numerous firings as failings. She once told a *Saturday Evening Post* reporter, "If you're dumb enough and stubborn enough to stay with broadcasting . . . you'll have lots of firings."

Eventually, Raphael found her forte as a radio talk-show host. At the height of her popularity on the radio, she was asked to guest host a local television talk show in Cincinnati. The appearance caught the attention of executives at Multimedia Entertainment, the same company that produced Phil Donahue's television show. Soon Raphael was offered her own half-hour TV talk show, which aired out of St. Louis, Missouri. Within six months, her show had become so popular that it was syndicated nationally. Sally Jessy Raphael was a hot commodity on morning television for the next eighteen years before she eventually moved back to radio. In 2002, Raphael was named in *Talkers Magazine* (an industry publication) as one of the twenty-five greatest radio talk-show hosts and one of the twenty-five greatest television talk-show hosts of all time.

"A great deal of success is being prepared. The rest is just outlasting everybody else." — S. J. R.

Bill Russell

Failed to Make the Team

During his thirteen years as a professional basketball player for the Boston Celtics, William "Bill" Russell (1934–) won the NBA Most Valuable Player Award five times and was a twelve-time All-Star.

BILL RUSSELL FAILED TO MAKE the basketball team in junior high and as a freshman in high school. He continued to practice and made the junior varsity squad as a sophomore, but just barely. Russell eventually made the varsity team as a junior, but he was forced to share the team's fifteenth uniform with another player. With practice and hard work, he made the starting line-up as a senior and helped the team win the league championship.

After graduation, he received a basketball scholarship from the University of San Francisco (USF). While he was there, the USF basketball team won two consecutive NCAA championships. He was the first draft choice of the St. Louis Hawks in 1956 but was immediately traded to the Boston Celtics. Instead of playing a full season with the Celtics as a rookie, Russell chose to miss a month to be captain of the U.S. Olympic basketball team, which had been his childhood dream. With Russell as captain, the United States brought home a gold medal. Russell's professional career was just as impressive. During his thirteen years with the Celtics, the team won eleven NBA championships. Russell was a twelve-time All-Star and won the NBA's Most Valuable Player Award five times. He was elected to the Basketball Hall of Fame in 1975. Today, he is considered by many as one of basketball's greatest defensive centers.

"Durability is part of what makes a great athlete." — B. R.

William Saroyan

Received More than a Hundred Rejections

William Saroyan (1908–1981) was an American author who wrote numerous plays and short stories popular during the 1920s.

After dropping out of technical school, William Saroyan decided to become a writer. During the next six years, he submitted nearly one hundred articles and stories to magazines. All of them were rejected. He not only continued to submit his work, but he kept every rejection piled up in a rapidly growing stack. Finally, he managed to get a couple of articles accepted at *The Overland Monthly*. However, it would not be until his story "The Daring Young Man on the Flying Trapeze" was published in *Story* magazine in 1934, that Saroyan began to get noticed as a writer. Six years later, he collected his short stories and published them in a collection titled *My Name is Aram*. The novel became an international best-seller.

In 1940, Saroyan's play *The Time of Your Life* was awarded the Pulitzer Prize for Drama. Saroyan sent a telegram to the Pulitzer judges rejecting the prize, stating, "I do not believe in prizes or awards in the realm of art, and have always been particularly opposed to material or official patronage of the arts by government, organization, or individual, a naive and innocent style of behavior which, nevertheless, I believe, vitiates and embarrasses art at its source." Oddly, he did accept the New York Drama Critics Circle Award a short time later. Saroyan's play was the first drama to win both awards.

"Good people are good because they have come to wisdom through failure." — W. S.

Jon Stewart

Canceled after Coming in Second to Beavis and Butt-head

Jon Stewart (1962–) is an American comedian, actor, writer, and producer who is best known as the host of *The Daily Show.* He also cowrote the best-selling book *America (The Book)* and has hosted the Academy Awards.

ALTHOUGH JON STEWART WAS VOTED as having the best sense of humor in high school, he decided to study chemistry and psychology in college. After he received his degree, he realized that he had no desire to go into either field. Instead, he returned home and took a series of odd jobs, including running a puppet show for disabled children, before moving to New York City, where he drove a van for a caterer.

A year later, Stewart worked up the nerve to perform stand-up comedy, and within three years he was hosting *Short Attention Span Theater.* The series quickly ended, and he went on to work for MTV's *You Wrote It, YOU Watch It,* which lasted less than a year. In 1993, he was considered as a replacement for David Letterman on NBC, but he lost out to Conan O'Brien. He later starred in his own show on MTV, *The Jon Stewart Show.* Although the half-hour show had some of the highest ratings — second only to *Beavis and Butt-head* — it was canceled. Stewart then hosted an hour-long show on another network, but it, too, was soon canceled.

In 1996, Stewart turned down an offer to host a new series titled *The Daily Show* to pursue acting. After two years of bit parts in movies such as *First Wives' Club, Half-Baked,* and *Big Daddy,* he returned to New York and, in January 1999, took on the role of host on *The Daily Show,* a "fake news" program.

Since Stewart took over the show, it has won two Peabody Awards for excellence in radio and television broadcasting. As of 2007, *The Daily Show* had won nine Emmy Awards, several Television Critics Association Awards, and several other prestigious honors. Stewart has also won a Grammy Award for Best Comedy Album in 2005 for *The Daily Show with Jon Stewart Presents . . . America: A Citizen's Guide to Democracy Inaction*. He also received a *Publishers Weekly* Book of the Year Award and a Thurber Prize for American Humor for *America (The Book): A Citizen's Guide to Democracy Inaction*, which he cowrote with other members of the show's writing staff. Stewart has also hosted the Grammy Awards twice as well as the Academy Awards. During his first hosting of the Oscars, Stewart quipped, "Tonight we celebrate excellence in film . . . with me, the fourth male lead from *Death to Smoochy*. Rent it."

"I'm doing everything I can to sabotage my career. It's a little thing called 'fear of success.'" — J. S.

James Thurber

Recovered from the Trash Can

James Thurber (1894–1961) was a U.S. humorist and cartoonist best known for his work with *The New Yorker.*

IN THE EARLY 1920S, JAMES Thurber struggled to make it as a writer. Although he landed a job as a reporter, he wanted to write fiction. He tried writing longer novels but always gave up after the first chapter. He submitted short stories to magazines and newspapers. *The Kansas City Star* accepted one, but most of his work was rejected. He took a job with the *Chicago Tribune* before moving to New York to work as a reporter for the *New York Evening Post.* During this time, he continued to submit fictional pieces to publications, but they were all rejected. Finally, in 1927, after countless submissions and rejections, Thurber discovered the perfect way to get published in *The New Yorker.* He accepted a position there as editor and writer.

He never intended to work as a cartoonist, but he got a push from his friend, E. B. White. White came across Thurber's drawings in the trash and submitted them to *The New Yorker* for publication. They were accepted. Thurber went on to draw six covers and numerous classic illustrations for *The New Yorker.* He also published more than twenty books of collected prose and sketches, including his most famous short story *The Secret Life of Walter Mitty.* Thurber's childhood home, now known as Thurber House, has become a literary center and a museum devoted to Thurber. It gives an annual award to writers of outstanding examples of American humor.

"You might as well fall flat on your face as lean over too far backward." — J. T.

Randy Travis

Rejected for Being Too Country

Born Randy Traywick, Randy Travis (1959–) is an American country singer who has released the hit songs "Forever and Ever, Amen," "Too Gone Too Long," and "Three Wooden Crosses."

After Randy Travis was rejected by every major record label for being "too country," he did the only thing he could think of — he submitted his demo a second time. He did not do any better the second time around. In 1978, he recorded two singles for Paula Records, but both of them were unsuccessful. However, he kept singing. Finally, in 1982, still unable to get a record contract, Travis recorded an independent album, *Randy Ray Live*. The album led to a deal with Warner Brothers Records.

When his first single, "On the Other Hand," was released, it failed to hit the Top 40, peaking at sixty-seven on the country charts. His next single, "1982," hit the Top 10 and prompted Warner to re-release Travis's first song, "On the Other Hand" — a rare event in the record industry. This time, the record climbed to number one. In 1985, the Academy of Country Music named Travis the top male vocalist — the first of many awards he has won in his musical career. Since then, Travis has released twenty country albums and has had more than fifty top-ten country songs.

"It's not what you take when you leave this world behind you. It's what you leave behind you when you go." — R. T.

Liv Ullmann

Judged without Talent

Liv Ullmann (1938–) is a Norwegian actress, author, and film director.

LIV ULLMANN FAILED AN AUDITION for the state theater school in Norway because the judges believed she had no talent. Ullmann did not stop acting. Instead she went to London, where she studied at the Webber-Douglas Academy in London for eight months before starring in her first movie, *Fools in the Mountains*. She appeared in a few Norwegian films until she was discovered by Ingmar Bergman, which led to her breakthrough performance in *Persona*. It was only the first of ten movies she would make with Bergman.

Ullmann went on to be nominated twice for a Best Actress Academy Award as well as a Golden Globe and an LAFCA honor. She has won three Best Actress prizes from the National Society of Film Critics, as well as awards from the National Board of Review and the New York Film Critics Circle. In 1974, after her performance in Ingmar Bergman's *Scenes from a Marriage* was disqualified for an Oscar nomination because it had premiered on Swedish television, a group of actors sent a letter to the *Los Angeles Times* demanding that Ullmann be eligible. Although the Academy did not change its position, Ullmann said the effort was "more gratifying than the award itself."

"Persistent people begin their success where others end in failure."
— Edward Eggleston

Betty White

Emmy-Nominated Cancellation

Often referred to as the "First Lady of Television," five-time Emmy Award-winning actress Betty White (1922–) is best known for her roles in the popular sitcoms *The Mary Tyler Moore Show* and *The Golden Girls*.

When a show has your name in the title, you want it to go well. This was the second time that a show had been named after Betty White, and the first time her show would be nationally broadcast. It started out well, and the show was receiving good ratings. Things were going smoothly, until the network decided to move the program from its noon timeslot to 4:30 PM in an effort to use the show to strengthen the ratings of the afternoon offerings. When the move did not improve the afternoon programming ratings, the network decided to move the program to the 12:30 slot. The moves ultimately backfired, and the show was canceled at the end of the season. After the cancellation, the show was nominated for an Emmy Award — a bitter pill for White.

Initially White was devastated, but eventually she starred in another show with her name in the title. After it, too, was cancelled, she believed her show business career was over. However, it turned out to be only the beginning for the talented actress. White went on to star in several hit shows such as *The Mary Tyler Moore Show* and *The Golden Girls*. She was nominated for an Emmy fifteen times and won five of the awards.

"I was always brought up to be an optimist. ... That doesn't mean failure doesn't hurt. But you do learn that failure in one field might lead to an opportunity in another." — B. W.

Tennessee Williams

Producers Apologized for His Play

Thomas Williams III (1911–1983), better known as Tennessee Williams, was an America playwright. He won the Pulitzer Prize for Drama for *A Streetcar Named Desire* and *Cat on a Hot Tin Roof*. He also wrote *The Glass Menagerie*, *The Night of the Iguana*, and *The Rose Tattoo*.

TENNESSEE WILLIAMS'S FIRST PROFESSIONALLY PRODUCED play, *Battle of Angels*, was so poorly received that, according to legend, the producers went on stage and apologized for it. Williams later said, "I'm glad now that the play was not a success. If it had been, it would have gone to my head and I would have thought I knew all there was to know about playwriting." Seventeen years later, he revised the play and revived it under the title *Orpheus Descending*. It was much more successful the second time around.

After the failure of *Battle of Angels*, Williams's agent, Audrey Wood, landed him a screenwriting assignment at MGM working on *Marriage is a Private Affair*, a movie starring Lana Turner. Instead of taking the job, Williams chose to work on another play, which he titled *The Gentleman Caller*. The studio rejected the screenplay, but Williams got it produced as a play titled *The Glass Menagerie* in Chicago. When the producers, despite positive reviews, planned to close the play early in its run, Wood stepped in and convinced them to give it a little more time. The play ultimately enjoyed a successful run in Chicago, then moved to Broadway, where it earned the New York Drama Critics' Circle Award as the best play of the season as well as many other awards. Williams followed this success with

A Streetcar Named Desire, which earned him the Pulitzer Prize in Drama. He was awarded another Pulitzer Prize in 1955 for *Cat on a Hot Tin Roof* and was inducted into the Theatre Hall of Fame in 1979.

"Success is blocked by concentrating on it and planning for it. . . . Success is shy — it won't come out while you're watching." — T. W.

F. W. Woolworth

Not Enough Sense to Wait on Customers

Franklin Winfield Woolworth (1852–1919) was the founder of the F.W. Woolworth Company, a chain of discount stores.

F. W. Woolworth wanted a job in a dry goods store, so he agreed to a six-month trial period during which he would earn no salary. Although his employer did not think Woolworth had enough sense to wait on customers, the boy eventually earned a salary of $3.50 a week, exactly what he was paying for board and lodging. Later, a man in Port Huron, Michigan, hired Woolworth, but the young worker proved to be such a poor salesman that his salary was soon cut. A few years later, Woolworth convinced W. H. Moore to back him in a five-cent store in Utica, New York, but the store closed after three months. He decided that the variety of goods he had sold had not been large enough; amazingly, he persuaded Moore to back him on a second venture. This time, the store was a success. Over the next forty years, Woolworth opened more than one thousand stores in North America and was worth an estimated $65 million at the time of his death in 1919.

"I am the world's worst salesman: therefore, I must make it easy for people to buy." — F. W. W.

Against All Odds

"Success is to be measured not so much by the position that one has reached in life as by the obstacles which he has overcome."

— Booker T. Washington

Marian Anderson

Faced Racial Ignorance

Marian Anderson (1897–1993), a contralto singer with an extraordinary voice, gained fame in America after performing in front of the Lincoln Memorial on Easter Sunday, 1939.

Growing up in poverty in South Philadelphia, Marian Anderson often ran errands and did odd jobs to earn money for her family. She tried to enroll in a Philadelphia music school, but officials there took one look at Anderson and slammed the door in her face — not because she did not have talent, but because she did not have the right skin color. Hers was too dark. The prejudice turned her stomach, but it did not affect her dreams. Instead, Anderson pinched enough pennies together to pay for singing lessons and sought out an audience anywhere she could. She performed in the church choir and sang in black-only railroad cars. Unable to gain recognition in America, Anderson went to Europe to perform. There she met promoter Sol Hursh, who convinced her to return to the United States with him.

Anderson triumphed despite the racial ignorance and slammed doors she had endured in America. Music business associates told Hursh, "You won't be able to give her away." Others commented, "Wonderful voice, it's too bad she's Negro." Even the Daughters of the American Revolution denied her the right to sing at Constitution Hall in Washington, DC, because she was black. The action so incensed First Lady Eleanor Roosevelt that she invited Anderson to perform at the Lincoln Memorial. More than 75,000 people turned out to hear her sing. In the face of all these setbacks and prejudice, Anderson sang with a voice so powerful that eventually people stopped noticing the color of her skin and listened in awe as she demonstrated her talent. On January 7, 1955, Anderson became the first African-American to perform with the New York Metropolitan Opera. She also worked as a goodwill ambassador for the United Nations. Anderson won numerous awards for her work, including the UN Peace Prize in 1972 and the Grammy Award for Lifetime Achievement in 1991.

> *"As long as you keep a person down, some part of you has to be down there to hold him down, so it means you cannot soar as you otherwise might."* — M. A.

Mary Kay Ash

Accused of Thinking Like a Woman

Mary Kay Ash (1918–2001) founded Mary Kay Cosmetics, an international direct seller of skincare and color cosmetics. In 2006, Mary Kay products exceeded $2.25 billion in wholesale sales.

Being ahead of your one's time is difficult enough, but the experience can be especially frustrating for a woman surrounded by men who are stuck in the past. Still, Mary Kay Ash managed to work her way to the top rung of the career ladder — no small feat for a woman in the 1950s. She even earned a position as the sole woman on the board of directors of World Gift Company. Yet whenever she expressed an opinion, the other board members accused her of "thinking like a woman." Considering the sales force was almost entirely women, Ash thought "thinking like a woman" was an asset, but her suggestions were continually rejected. Finally, out of frustration, she retired.

Ash didn't enjoy retirement, and she decided to open her own cosmetics business. Both her accountant and her attorney told her she would be better off throwing her savings into a trashcan. She went ahead with her plans anyway. With her husband's help and support, she designed the packaging, wrote the training manuals, recruited consultants, and prepared the products. Then, a month before she was to open her new business, tragedy struck: her husband suffered a fatal heart attack.

Rather than postpone things, Ash enlisted the help of her twenty-year-old son and opened on schedule in 1964. As part of the marketing plan, she took her products to a beauty show — but sold only about two dollars worth. Still, she refused to give up. By encouraging her sales force of women and awarding pink Caillacs to top sales directors, Ash and her company soon achieved astounding success. During its first year, Mary Kay Cosmetics earned almost $200,000; at the end of the second year, that figure had grown to $800,000. By the time the company went public in 1968, only four years after it began, sales had reached more than $10 million. Today, annual sales exceed $1.6 billion, and Mary Kay products are available in more than thirty markets worldwide.

"Every failure, obstacle, or hardship is an opportunity in disguise. Success in many cases is failure turned inside out. The greatest pollution problem we face today is negativity. Eliminate the negative attitude and believe you can do anything. Replace 'if I can, I hope, maybe' with 'I can, I will, I must.'" — M. K. A.

Elizabeth Blackwell

Right Qualifications, Wrong Gender

Elizabeth Blackwell (1821–1910) was the first woman doctor in the United States as well as an abolitionist and women's rights activist.

Sitting by her friend's deathbed, Elizabeth Blackwell was stunned when the dying woman told her she would make a good doctor. Until then, Blackwell had never even considered the possibility since the obstacles against her were overwhelming. Blackwell lacked the financial means, the medical experience, and the education required for a medical school to consider admitting her. Even if she acquired these things, one obstacle existed that she could not change. She was a woman, and in the 1840s no woman had ever been admitted to a medical school.

Still, the seed had been planted and soon took root. Blackwell took a job as a teacher and began working with a local physician to gain medical experience. This gave her access to medical texts to further her education. She also sought advice from other physicians, who told her the only way she would ever succeed would be to disguise herself as a man.

Prepared with the right qualifications, Blackwell applied to all the top medical schools in the country. All of them rejected her. Undaunted, she tried the smaller colleges. After receiving so many rejections, she was astonished when she finally unfolded an acceptance letter. The faculty at Geneva Medical College, unwilling to reject a qualified applicant merely because she was a woman, permitted the students to vote whether or not to admit her. The students, thinking it was a joke, voted unanimously to allow her to enroll.

Geneva Medical College might have been willing to accept Blackwell's application, but that did not mean those at the institution would accept her. From the start, Blackwell found herself shunned by everyone around her. Professors, uncomfortable because a woman was present, requested that she skip lectures when certain topics were discussed. Her fellow classmates harassed and ostracized her. Townspeople, thinking Blackwell must be insane or morally corrupt for wanting to become a doctor, stopped and stared at her when she walked by. Despite all of this, Blackwell focused on her studies and refused to let anything deter her from becoming a doctor. As a result, she graduated at the top of her class. At the graduation ceremony, the dean of the college applauded Blackwell for her achievements, although he later said he would probably reject future female applicants because of the "inconveniences" of having a woman attend the school.

The dean's views, however, eventually became irrelevant. A door had opened for women and it would not be closed again. Several medical schools specifically for women students opened, including one founded by Blackwell. She also founded a full-scale hospital with beds for medical and surgical patients, which still exists today as the New York University Downtown Hospital. Blackwell eventually left the hospital and the school in the capable hands of her sister, who was also a doctor, and moved to England. There she established a successful private practice, helped organize the National Health Society, and later became a professor at the London School of Medicine for Women.

"It is not easy to be a pioneer — but oh, it is fascinating! I would not trade one moment, even the worst moment, for all the riches in the world." — E. B.

Christy Brown

One Letter at a Time

Christy Brown (1932–1981) was an Irish writer, painter, and poet whose autobiography *My Left Foot* became an international best-selling book and was made into a 1989 movie starring Daniel Day-Lewis.

CEREBRAL PALSY HAD LEFT CHRISTY Brown severely physically disabled at birth. Doctors said the infant was mentally disabled as well. His mother refused to believe it and, despite having to raise twelve other children, spent time talking and reading to her son. Her efforts paid off when Brown managed to snatch a piece of chalk away from his sister, not with his hand but with the only part of his body he could control — his left foot. It was a turning point for Brown and indicated to his mother that his disability was only physical.

His mother began teaching him the alphabet. Brown also developed a love of painting and won a *Sunday Independent* children's painting competition when he was twelve. When Brown was eighteen, orthopedist Robert Collis suggested he go to a clinic for therapy. Brown was hesitant at first because during the initial phases of the therapy he would not be allowed to use his left foot. Closing off his only means of communication, doctors believed, would motivate him to develop other ways to convey messages. Eventually, Brown agreed to participate in the therapy.

To encourage Brown as he struggled to develop the other muscles in his body and master basic speech patterns, Collis allowed him to use his left foot to perform special tasks such as creative writing. Using only his left foot, Brown wrote the story of his life. He had never been to school, and his first draft was so filled with grammatical errors that it was almost impossible to read. Not ready to give up, he asked Collis, who was an amateur playwright, to help him improve his writing skills. His second draft was better, but it still needed revision. In 1954, Brown finished his autobiography, and *My Left Foot* was published when he was twenty-two. The therapy not only helped Brown improve as a writer, it also enabled him to speak and move more easily. He steadily improved and, by the time he was ready to write his second book, he was able to use his fingers to type it on an electric typewriter.

> *"If I could never really be like other people, then at least I would be like myself and make the best of it." — C. B.*

Loretta Claiborne

Saved by Athletics

Loretta Claiborne (1953–) is a motivational speaker, a gold medal winner in the Special Olympics, and a winner of the Arthur Ashe ESPY Award for Courage.

Born legally blind and mentally retarded, Loretta Claiborne did not walk or talk until she was four. Her mother, who was struggling to raise six other children by herself in the projects of York, Pennsylvania, was advised to place her daughter in an institution, but she refused. After corrective eye surgery, Loretta was allowed to attend school, where students and teachers teased and humiliated her. Claiborne responded by lashing out at the world until a social worker, Janet McFarland, introduced Claiborne to the Special Olympics when Claiborne was twelve.

Amazingly, Claiborne, who had been born with a twisted leg and had to wear a leg brace, discovered she could run. "If it weren't for sports," Claiborne says, "I wouldn't be the person I am today. I was very angry before, and sports was the arena that turned that around for me." Claiborne has participated in six world Special Olympics and earned ten medals in eight different events including gold medals in the mile, half-marathon (twice), bowling, and 3,000-meter run.

In 1981, she was the first Special Olympics athlete to run the Boston Marathon. She finished in three hours and nine minutes. By 2007, she had run in more than twenty-five marathons and had had placed in the top one hundred female finishers in the Boston Marathon twice. She also has a black belt in karate. However, Claiborne is more than an athlete. She speaks four languages and has become a renowned motivational speaker. In 2000, Walt Disney Productions made a movie about her life, *The Loretta Claiborne Story.* Claiborne was inducted into the Special Olympics International Hall of Fame in 1996 and the Women in Sports Hall of Fame in December 2000.

"It's not how much you have; it's what you have and how you use it." — L. C.

Chuck Close

Considered Lazy and Unmotivated

Chuck Close (1940–) is an American photorealist painter and photographer.

Unaware that dyslexia made reading difficult for Chuck Close, his teachers considered the boy lazy and unmotivated. This did not staunch his creative spirit or his artistic ability, which Close's parents encouraged by providing him with art supplies and lessons. From the beginning, Close dealt with his art the same way he dealt with dyslexia: by breaking the whole into workable chunks. It did not take long for him to become renowned in the art world, and his photorealism won him a Fulbright grant in 1964 and a National Endowment for the Arts grant in 1973.

In December 1988, his world crashed down around him. Shortly after giving a speech at an arts award ceremony, he was left paralyzed from the shoulders down when an artery in his spine collapsed. He could not grasp a brush; everyone assumed that his artistic career was over.

Everyone, that is, except Close, who simply refused to accept that he would never be able to paint again. At first, he painted by holding a brush in his mouth. However, after months of painful physical therapy, Close began to paint with his hands again, although the brush needed to be attached to his wrist with Velcro. Within three years, Close had a new art exhibit at the Pace Gallery in New York City. Close's new work exhibited a free-spirited style that earned praise from many of his contemporaries.

His paintings are exhibited in the most prominent art museums in the world.

> *"I tried to, with a series of self-imposed limitations, back myself into my own personal corner where nobody else's answers would fit. I've always thought that problem solving is highly overrated and that problem creation is far more interesting."* — C. C.

Roger Crawford

Ignored a Dead-End Prognosis

Motivational speaker and author Roger Crawford (1960–) became the first athlete with four impaired limbs to compete in an NCAA Division One college sport and to be certified by the U.S. Professional Tennis Association.

When Roger Crawford was born, doctors told his parents that he would never be able to walk, take care of himself, or lead a normal life. Crawford had a condition called ectrodactylism, which causes the fingers and the toes to fuse together. Both his legs and his arms were shorter than usual. He had no palms, only a thumblike projection on his right forearm, and a thumb and a finger growing out of his left forearm. His left leg had only a shrunken foot with three toes, which were amputated when he was five. Roger's parents, determined that their son would lead a normal life, refused to listen to the doctors. His father told him, "You're only as handicapped as you want to be." They sent him to public school and encouraged him to participate in sports, which Roger enjoyed, especially tennis.

In high school, Crawford became a tennis champion, captain of his team, and a four-year varsity athlete. He attended Loyola Marymount University, where he became the first athlete with four impaired limbs to compete in an NCAA Division I college sport and to be certified by the United States Professional Tennis Association. He is the author of two books, *How High Can You Bounce?* and *Playing from the Heart*. His story was featured in the original edition of *Chicken Soup for the Soul* and became part of an NBC Emmy Award-winning documentary *In a New Light*. Now a motivational speaker, Crawford was awarded the CPAE Speaker Hall of Fame designation, a lifetime honor for speaking excellence presented by the National Speakers Association.

"A broken spirit is more disabling than a broken body." — R. C.

Glenn Cunningham

Never Walk Again

Glenn Cunningham (1909–1988) was an American distance runner who set a world record for the mile and indoor world records for the 1,500 meter and the mile.

Glenn Cunningham was only seven years old when a classroom stove exploded, injuring him and killing his brother. His legs were severely burned, and the doctors recommended amputation because they doubted that Cunningham would ever walk again. Cunningham's mother, determined that her son would improve, refused to allow the amputation. Sure enough, with the help of his mother, Cunningham learned to walk again. However, Cunningham was not simply satisfied with walking — he wanted to run.

By the time he was twelve, he was not only running, he was running faster than everyone else at his school. His deeply scarred legs prevented him from running smoothly or efficiently, but he made up for his ungainly stride with endurance and strength. Before competing, Cunningham had to spend a lot of time massaging his legs and doing warm-up exercises.

When he was thirteen years old, Cunningham won his first mile-long race. Although he participated in many other sports, he excelled at running. He set records as a University of Kansas student and competed twice in the 1,500-meter run at the Olympics, where he came in fourth in 1932 and won a silver medal in 1936. Cunningham was elected to the U.S. and the National Track and Field Hall of Fame and named the most outstanding track athlete to compete at Madison Square Garden during its first one hundred years.

> *"A runner's creed: I will win; if I cannot win, I shall be second; if I cannot be second, I shall be third; if I cannot place at all, I shall still do my best."*
> — Ken Doherty

Joe DiMaggio

Considered a Cripple

Three-time Most Valuable Player winner and thirteen-time All-Star Joe DiMaggio (1914–1999) played baseball for the New York Yankees from 1936 through 1951.

Joe DiMaggio played his first full year in professional baseball for the minor league team, the San Francisco Seals. DiMaggio had convinced the manager to let him fill in as shortstop. Although by all accounts he did a poor job as a shortstop, he was an outstanding hitter. Everyone believed that DiMaggio was on his way to the major leagues — until a fluke accident nearly crippled him.

In 1934, DiMaggio tore the ligaments in his left knee while going to his sister's house. The injury scared away most teams. The Chicago Cubs turned him down because they believed he would never fully recover. Only one scout, Bill Essick for the New York Yankees, was willing to give him a shot. When New York's farm-system director George Weiss suggested offering DiMaggio a contract, Yankees' general manager Ed Barrow told him, "This is exactly what you were hired not to do." However, Weiss persisted and, after DiMaggio passed medical inspections, he began his major league baseball career with the New York Yankees. Bill Terry, manager of the New York Giants, ridiculed Weiss for the deal, telling him, "You've bought yourself a cripple."

Joltin' Joe DiMaggio remained with the team for his entire major league career. During that time, he led the Yankees to nine titles in thirteen years, four of which were during his first four years with the team. When DiMaggio retired in 1951, he was ranked fifth for the most career home runs and sixth for the best slugging percentage.

"A person always doing his or her best becomes a natural leader, just by example." — J. D.

Anne Frank

Rambling Teenage Girl

While hiding from the Nazis during World War II, teenager Anne Frank (1929–1945) recorded her experiences in her diary, which was later published as *The Diary of a Young Girl.*

AT ONLY FIFTEEN, ANNE FRANK knew that she wanted to be a writer and dreamed of publishing a novel based on her diaries. Frank had received her first diary as a present for her thirteenth birthday. Her first writings included comments about school and boys and the typical ramblings of a teenage girl interspersed with observations about living as a Jew in German-occupied Amsterdam in 1942.

She did not know that she and her family would be forced to go into hiding twenty-four days after she received the diary. Suddenly, she found herself living in a tiny 500-square-foot space with seven other people. For the next two years, Frank spent her time reading, studying, and continuing to write and edit her diary. She dreamed of what she would do once she could come out of hiding. On one page of her diary she wrote, "If God lets me live . . . I shall not remain insignificant." She wrote her final diary entry on August 1, 1944, about three days before the Gestapo discovered her and her family and sent them to a concentration camp. Of the eight people hiding with her, only her father, Otto Frank, managed to survive.

After the war was over, Miep Gies, one of the Dutch citizens who had hidden Frank's family, gave Anne's father the diaries she had been forced to abandon. Realizing that Anne had wanted to become an author, Otto passed the diary to a historian Anne Romein-Verschoor, who tried unsuccessfully to have it published. One editor responded, "The girl doesn't, it seems to me, have a special perception or feeling which would lift that book above the 'curiosity' level." Romein-Verschoor did not give up, and eventually turned the diaries over to her husband, who wrote an article about them. The article attracted the attention of a publisher, who finally published Frank's writings. *The Diary of Anne Frank* has sold more than twenty-five million copies, has been printed in more than fifty languages, and has been required reading in classrooms for more than fifty years.

> *"It's difficult in times like these: ideals, dreams, and cherished hopes rise within us, only to be crushed by grim reality. It's a wonder I haven't abandoned all my ideals, they seem so absurd and impractical. Yet I cling to them because I still believe, in spite of everything, that people are truly good at heart."* — A. F.

Viktor Frankl

Risked Death for the Meaning in Life

Austrian neurologist and psychologist Viktor Frankl (1905–1997) chronicled his experiences in a German concentration camp in his best-selling book *Man's Search for Meaning.*

As a doctor specializing in neurology and psychiatry, Viktor Frankl decided to focus his attention on depression and suicide. He soon discovered that he had a talent for helping patients who had considered suicide. In 1924, he became president of the Sozialistische Mittelschüler Österreich, the association of socialist pupils of secondary schools in Austria, and created a program to help counsel students.

During his tenure, no students committed suicide. He eventually moved his practice to the General Hospital in Vienna, Austria, and became the head of what was called the "suicide pavilion." In four years, he treated more than 30,000 women with suicidal tendencies.

His work with depression led him to develop a theory that psychological health was connected to finding meaning in one's life. Frankl could not have known that he would soon be facing circumstances that would put his theory to the ultimate test. Frankl was still in Vienna in 1938 when the Nazis overran Austria and annexed it into Germany. Suddenly, Frankl, who was Jewish, was prohibited from treating "Aryan" patients — those who were considered "pure-blooded" German.

Frankl decided to open a private practice and began practicing at the Rothschild Hospital, the only Viennese hospital still allowed to treat Jews. As head of the neurological program there, he had to deal with the Nazi's euthanasia program, better known as Action T4. Under this policy, those diagnosed with "terminal neurological conditions" such as schizophrenia, epilepsy, Huntington's chorea, advanced syphilis, senile dementia, paralysis, or encephalitis were put to death. Frankl often gave false medical diagnoses in order to save his patients' lives. During this time, Frankl began working on his first manuscript, *The Doctor and the Soul,* but it was discovered and immediately destroyed. Soon afterward, the Nazis arrested Frankl and sent him to a concentration camp in Theresienstadt. He was accompanied by his parents, his brother, and his wife.

Despite his medical degree, Frankl was assigned to labor detail. Still, he worked hard to try to help his fellow patients and prevent their suicides — an action that was forbidden and would have led to his own death had he been caught. He managed to keep his family's spirits up, even after his father died of starvation. He was later separated from his wife when he, his mother, and his brother were sent to another camp, Auschwitz. Upon arrival, he and the other prisoners were divided into two lines. Frankl was ordered to move to the left. When he realized that the left line was going toward the gas chambers, Frankl managed to slip over into the right line undetected and save himself.

Frankl was eventually separated from all his family when he was transferred to another concentration camp. During this time, Frankl continued his work and often recorded his observations on scraps of paper. He continued to do this until the end of the war when he was finally liberated. Frankl was horrified to learn that his pregnant wife, his mother, and his brother had not survived. Refusing to let these tragedies overcome him, he decided to turn his experiences into something meaningful. Frankl had previously developed what he called "logotherapy," a belief that "those who have a 'why' to live, can bear with almost any 'how.'"

He combined this theory with his experiences in the concentration camps in a book, which he wrote in eight days. Frankl's masterpiece, *Man's Search for Meaning: An Introduction to Logotherapy*, has been translated into more than twenty-four languages, reprinted more than seventy times, and sold more than 1.5 million copies in the United States alone.

> *"The one thing you can't take away from me is the way I choose to respond to what you do to me. The last of one's freedoms is to choose one's attitude in any given circumstance."* — V. F.

Ruth Bader Ginsburg

Overlooked Because of Gender

Ruth Bader Ginsburg (1933–) is the second woman to have served on the U.S. Supreme Court.

RUTH BADER GINSBURG'S CREDENTIALS ARE outstanding. She was Phi Beta Kappa at Cornell University; attended Harvard Law School, where she served on the *Harvard Law Review;* then transferred to Columbia Law School, where she served on the *Columbia Law Review* and graduated at the top of her class. While at Columbia, she was told by a professor that the nine women in her graduating class of five hundred were taking the place of more qualified men. He was not the only one in the law community at the time to hold that opinion, and as a result Ginsburg was often overlooked because of her gender.

After obtaining her law degree, Ginsberg found it difficult to find a job. Law firms would have been eager to hire a student with her credentials had she been a man. Since she was a woman, however, those same law firms refused to consider her for a position. Eventually, she filled a clerkship for a district judge, then taught at Rutgers University before taking a teaching position at Harvard University.

When Harvard denied her tenure in 1972, Ginsburg

moved to the law school at Columbia University, where she became the first tenured female faculty member in the school's history. While there, she authored the first law book on gender equality law. In 1980, President Jimmy Carter appointed her to a judgeship on the U.S. Court of Appeals for the District of Columbia Circuit. President William Clinton nominated her in 1993 as associate justice of the U.S. Supreme Court. The U.S. Senate confirmed her nomination with an overwhelming ninety-six-vote majority. Only three senators voted against her. Ginsburg became the 107th Supreme Court justice — and only the second woman ever to sit on the Court.

"But the greatest dissents do become court opinions and gradually over time, their views become the dominant view." — R. B. G.

Martha Graham

Showed Little Promise as a Dancer

Dancer and choreographer Martha Graham (1894–1991) is considered one of the pioneers of modern dance.

Dance was an unsuitable pursuit for a lady, according to Martha Graham's father. Nevertheless, he unwittingly encouraged his daughter's love of dance by taking her to a performance by Ruth St. Denis. Attending the performance had been his daughter's graduation present. He allowed her to attend a local junior college, even though he would have preferred she go to the more prestigious Vassar College. The junior college allowed her to take regular lessons in dramatics, dance, and speech, but Vassar did not.

When opportunity knocks, it sometimes comes disguised as tragedy. In 1916, Graham's father died, which allowed the twenty-two-year-old woman to pursue her love of dance professionally. Everything about Graham suggested that she would never make it. First, she was heavier and less attractive than most professional dancers. Second, while most dancers had begun training as a child, Graham was an adult by the time she began pursuing her career. Still, she enrolled in a summer dance course at Denishawn, an institute run by the same dancer whose performance had inspired her three years earlier. Ruth St. Denis saw little promise in the young woman and ignored her most of the time. St. Denis's husband, Ted Shawn, disagreed and began working with the girl.

Eventually, Graham acquired enough skill to become a teacher at Denishawn, a job that took her to New York. After eight years of teaching, she decided to venture out on her own and began dancing in a vaudeville revue, Greenwich Village Follies. She loved performing and worked hard to form her own school and dance company. Both became enormously successful and allowed Martha Graham the freedom to create innovative dances that used mobile scenery, symbolic props, and a racially integrated dance company. She won numerous awards including *Dance* magazine's annual award (1956), the Presidential Medal of Freedom (1976), a Kennedy Center Honor (1979), and the National Medal of Arts (1985).

"Dance is the hidden language of the soul." — M. G.

Temple Grandin

Hopelessly Brain Damaged

Despite having been born with autism, Temple Grandin (1947–) has crusaded for the rights of autistic children and adults and campaigned for the humane treatment of livestock. She has written several books and is currently an associate professor at Colorado State University.

Early on, doctors diagnosed Temple Grandin as "brain damaged" and advised her parents to place her in an institution. Instead, her mother took her to another doctor who prescribed various therapies to help her. Grandin, who could not speak until she was almost four, often became so frustrated that she screamed. Her mother did not give up on her and eventually enrolled her in private schools and tutored her to help improve her communication skills. Eventually, she was diagnosed with autism.

One summer, while still in school, Grandin was visiting her aunt's ranch when she became fascinated by a device used to help restrain cows receiving vaccinations. Grandin convinced her aunt to allow her to try it. Normally Grandin hated to be touched, but she discovered that this device calmed and relaxed her. She decided to construct a similar device for her own use. At one point, school officials took the device away from her because they mistakenly believed it was causing her to regress. Grandin insisted that it was beneficial and set out to prove its effects. She began revising and improving the device. Today, Grandin's perfected model is used to help treat children with autism and other disorders in schools and hospitals all over the world.

Grandin did not focus solely on helping people with autism; she also worked to help improve the lives of animals. After high school, she attended college and studied animal science. She used her understanding of autism to give her a better understanding of animals. According to Grandin, "animals are a lot like autistics because of the similar way in which they communicate, by focusing on the visual." Having autism has helped Grandin become the world's leading authority on livestock management. She has designed livestock handling facilities and is an associate professor of Animal Science at Colorado State University. Grandin has won dozens of awards for her efforts to help people with disabilities and to help improve the treatment of animals.

"If I could snap my fingers and become nonautistic, I would not — because then I wouldn't be me. Autism is part of who I am." — T. G.

Ben Hogan

Grim Predictions for His Golf Game

Ben Hogan (1912–1997) is considered one of the greatest golfers in the history of the game.

Ben Hogan had enough talent at eighteen to become a professional golfer, but almost ten years passed before he won a major tournament. The victory came only after he switched his right-handed swing to a left-handed swing. Once he accomplished his first win, he did not stop. Between 1939 and 1941, he won money in fifty-six consecutive tournaments. Hogan placed in the top ten four times in the Professional Golfers' Association (PGA)

Championship before finally winning it in 1946. He won the U.S. Open in 1948. By 1949, the only championship that he had not won was the Masters, although he had placed in the top ten six times and come in second twice. He was determined that 1949 would be his year to win. Then, on February 2, a Greyhound bus slammed head-on into his car. Hogan broke several ribs, his collarbone, an ankle, a leg, and fractured his pelvis. Doctors tied off veins in his legs after he developed life-threatening blood clots. They told him that he probably would never walk again. The possibility that he would ever be able to play golf again was even more remote.

Hogan refused to listen to the doctors' grim predictions. Within eleven months, his legs still in bandages, he played in the Los Angeles Open. He came in second after a playoff with Sam Snead. Five months later, he entered the U.S. Open. Few believed that he would be much of a contender. Hogan may have walked with a limp, but he could still hit with accuracy. He won the U.S. Open that year. The following year, he not only won the U.S. Open, but he also took home the elusive Masters. By 1959, Hogan had won sixty-four PGA tournaments. To date, only two golfers have managed to top his achievement.

"The more I practice, the luckier I get." — B. H.

Rafer Johnson

Injured, But Not Out

Rafer Johnson (1935–) is an Olympic decathlete with silver and gold medals in track and field.

TEN-YEAR-OLD BOYS ARE notorious for getting into trouble, which sometimes leads to tragic results. When Rafer Johnson was ten, he was playing with his siblings outside a food packing plant when he accidentally caught his left foot on a conveyer belt. The belt severely cut his foot. When the wound became infected, doctors feared they would have to amputate. The wound eventually healed, but the foot remained sensitive, and Johnson could not walk barefoot or even rub the foot without causing pain.

When facing this type of pain, most people would stay off the foot as much as possible. Johnson did the opposite. He earned eleven school letters, captained three high school athletic teams, played on three all-league basketball teams, and was a member of the all-state football team his senior year of high school. His favorite was track and field, even though advisers told him the sport would not provide a professional career for him.

After graduation, Johnson turned down several football scholarships in order to accept an academic scholarship to UCLA because it would allow him to participate in track. Johnson excelled at track and, with the help of his track coach at UCLA, he won a place on the U.S. Olympic track and field team. After winning the decathlon at the Pan Am Games in Mexico City in 1955, Johnson was predicted to win the 1956 Olympic decathlon. Unfortunately, just before the games he aggravated his previously injured knee, causing it to swell. Nevertheless Johnson participated in the decathlon and won a silver medal. Afterward, he had surgery on the knee and spent several months in rehabilitation.

Once again, Johnson rebounded from injury. In 1958, he was named *Sports Illustrated*'s Sportsman of the Year. When he returned to the Olympics in 1960, he won a gold medal.

> *"To my mind, the great champions are the ones who are able to react to defeat in a positive way. I'd much rather climb into the head of someone who's lost and see what made that person come back to be a victor, than climb into the head of a winner. You can learn more from the failures rather than the successes of others. That somebody wins all the time does not necessarily mean they are successful."* — R. J.

Helen Keller

Could Not Be Taught

Helen Keller (1880–1968) was the first deafblind to graduate from college. She also was a social activist, writer, and speaker.

Friends and family doubted that Helen Keller, a temperamental deafblind child, was capable of learning. Even if a teacher could be found to teach the child, who would travel to remote Tuscumbia, Alabama, to conduct the lessons? Kate Keller knew that the chances were slim, but that did not stop her from looking for answers. Luckily, she read a passage from *American Notes* by Charles Dickens, in which the British author had written about Laura Bridgman, another deafblind girl who had been successfully educated. After seeking the advice of Alexander Graham Bell, Mrs. Keller contacted the Perkins Institution for the Blind, where she found not only a teacher qualified to teach Helen but also one who was willing to travel to rural Alabama to do so.

The teacher, Anne Sullivan, had to overcome many obstacles before she could educate the ten-year-old girl, who had been allowed total freedom and had never been disciplined. Sullivan had already overcome many obstacles in her own life. Her mother had died when she was eight, and she and her brother had been taken to a state infirmary by relatives. Her brother eventually died there. She also suffered from vision problems but had regained some use of her sight after several operations.

Sullivan taught the young Helen how to fingerspell, read Braille, and write. Keller quickly became desperate for knowledge. She eventually graduated magna cum laude from Radcliffe College, becoming the first deafblind person to graduate from college. Keller could read English, French, German, Greek, and Latin in Braille. She also learned to speak after being inspired by the story of Ragnhild Kåta, a Norwegian girl who was one of the first deafblind people to accomplish this task. Keller, a lifelong advocate for the disabled, became a world-renowned speaker and author, traveling to more than forty countries. For her service, Keller received the highest civilian honor in the United States: the Presidential Medal of Freedom, just one of many awards she was given during her lifetime for her accomplishments.

> *"Character cannot be developed in ease and quiet. Only through experience of trial and suffering can the soul be strengthened, vision cleared, ambition inspired, and success achieved."* — H. K.

Cyndi Lauper

A Ruined Voice

Cyndi Lauper (1953–), a Grammy Award-winning singer, is also an Emmy Award-winning actor in film, television, and theater.

When Cyndi Lauper started singing with the band Flyer, she tried to lower her pitch to please audiences that had, in the past, reacted negatively to her naturally high-pitched voice. This put a severe strain on her vocal cords. A doctor told her that she had ruined her vocal cords and that she would never be able to sing again. Instead of quitting, Lauper decided to take voice lessons from an opera singer. Within a year, she had regained her voice and was able to sing again. She joined a new group, Blue Angel, but when their first record failed to sell, band members became involved in a lawsuit with the manager, and the group disbanded.

Broke and out of work, Lauper was forced to declare bankruptcy. Eventually, she took a job singing in a Japanese piano bar, where she met a rock music manager, David Wolff. Wolff helped her launch her first solo album, *She's so Unusual.* The lead-off single, "Girls Just Want to Have Fun," quickly rose to the top of the charts, peaking at number two in the United States. The song's video, which was produced for less than $35,000, was named MTV's music video of the year in 1983. The second single released from the album, *Time After Time,* which Lauper helped write, was even more popular. It hit number one on the billboard charts and has been performed, in concert or on recordings, by almost a hundred artists. Lauper won a Grammy

Award for Best New Artist in 1984, became the first female artist to have four consecutive hits from one album reach the top five on the "Billboard Hot 100," and was named *Ms.* magazine's Woman of the Year.

> *"I get the greatest feeling when I'm singing. It's other-worldly. Your feet are anchored into the Earth and into this energy force that comes up through your feet and goes up the top of your head and maybe you're holding hands with the angels or the stars."* — C. L.

Wilma Mankiller

Urged Not to Seek Re-election

Wilma Mankiller (1945–) was the first female chief of the Cherokee Nation.

In 1979, Wilma Mankiller was hit head-on in an accident that crushed her face and broke both her legs. In a bizarre, cruel twist of fate, the driver of the other car, who died in the accident, happened to be her best friend. For the next year, Mankiller was confined to a wheelchair and underwent seventeen operations. As she was finally beginning to recover, she developed myasthenia gravis, a rare, paralyzing neuromuscular disease requiring more surgery.

The ordeal helped Mankiller learn how to overcome great odds. She put the lesson to good use in 1983 when she agreed to run as deputy chief on the ballot with Ross Swimmer, who sought to be chief of the Cherokee Nation. Mankiller's candidacy was met with opposition. No woman had ever served as deputy chief of the Cherokee Nation. Mankiller refused to bow down to pressure. Swimmer and Mankiller won the election, and two years later Mankiller became the first woman chief. She assumed the position after Swimmer resigned to become director of Indian Affairs for the federal government.

Initially, Mankiller had intended only to finish the term. Near the end of her term, however, people began urging her not to run for reelection. Their actions convinced Mankiller that she should run, and she began campaigning in earnest, determined to win acceptance based on her abilities instead of being rejected for her gender. She won the election with 83 percent of the vote and served as chief for the next eight years.

> *"I believe in the old Cherokee injunction to 'be of a good mind.' Today it's called positive thinking."* – W. M.

Thurgood Marshall

Refused Admittance to the University

Thurgood Marshall (1908–1993) was the first African-American to serve on the U.S. Supreme Court.

Thurgood Marshall was refused admittance to the University of Maryland in 1930, not because of his qualifications but because of his skin color. Marshall did not let racism prevent him from achieving his goal, nor would he let it stop others from achieving theirs. He attended Howard University Law School, at the time an all-black university. After graduating in 1935, Marshall used his new law degree to sue the University of Maryland. He won the case, forcing the university to admit eligible black students. Soon Marshall became special council for the National Association for the Advancement of Colored People (NAACP). Throughout his career, Marshall continued to attack segregation and promote civil rights by defending people who were not being treated equally. He defended these cases all the way to the Supreme Court, appearing before the high court thirty-two times. Marshall had an enormous success rate, winning twenty-nine of the cases. His most famous case, *Brown* v. *Board of Education*, ended racial segregation in public schools.

In 1961, Marshall was appointed as a judge on the circuit court. Over the next four years, he made 112 rulings — none of which were reversed during appeal. As U.S. solicitor general, a post he won in 1965, Marshall won fourteen out of the nineteen cases he argued for the government. In 1967, Marshall headed back to the Supreme Court, this time to serve as the ninety-sixth justice and the first black man to sit on the Court. As of 2008, only two black men and no black women have served on the Supreme Court.

"None of us has gotten where we are solely by pulling ourselves up [by] our own bootstraps. We got here because somebody bent down and helped us."– T. M.

Jim Morris

The Oldest Rookie

Jim Morris (1964–) entered the world of professional baseball at the late age of thirty-five. His story was recorded in his autobiography *The Oldest Rookie* and made into the Walt Disney movie *The Rookie*.

Even though Jim Morris never played baseball in high school — it was not offered — he managed to be selected fourth overall in baseball's amateur draft. Still in the minor league after three years and with several arm injuries, Morris seemed to be at the end of his baseball career. He returned home and got a job as a teacher and baseball coach. Ten years went by before Morris, in an attempt to encourage his high school baseball team to do better, made them a bet: if they won the title, he would try out for the major league. Since the team had not been playing well, it seemed like a safe bet. The team went on to become the district champions, however, and Morris was forced to hold up his end of the deal.

At tryouts for the Tampa Bay Devil Rays, the team's talent scout was not interested in Morris but agreed to allow him keep his promise to his ballplayers. The scout was astounded when the thirty-five-year-old Morris threw a 98-mile-an-hour fastball. He earned a spot on the minor league team, and on September 18, 1999, Morris made his major league debut. Over the next year, despite continuous problems with his arm, he appeared in twenty-one major league games. He went on to document his story in his autobiography *The Oldest Rookie*, which was made into a movie in 2002 with Dennis Quaid in the starring role. Since leaving the major leagues, Morris spends most of his time giving motivational speeches and coaching high school baseball.

"I consider myself very lucky. God has a funny way of bringing some things around and knocking you in the head with the ultimate destination. Something I should have achieved quite easily took me a long time to get around to. It came in His time, not mine." — J. M.

Sandra Day O'Connor

Limited Job Options

Sandra Day O'Connor (1930–) was the first woman to be appointed to the U.S. Supreme Court.

After graduating from Stanford University Law School, Sandra Day O'Connor found her job options limited because no law firm would hire a woman. One firm did offer her a secretarial position, however. Instead, she took a position as deputy county attorney before setting up a private practice and then later serving as assistant attorney general of Arizona. She became a state senator in 1969 and was the first woman in the United States to serve as a state Senate majority leader. In 1975, she was elected judge of the Maricopa County Superior Court and was appointed to the Arizona Court of Appeals four years later. President Ronald Reagan nominated O'Connor as an associate justice of the Supreme Court in 1981. After winning confirmation by a unanimous vote of the Senate, she became the first woman to sit on the high court. In 2004, *Forbes* magazine named her the fourth most powerful woman in the United States and the sixth most powerful in the world. She served on the Supreme Court until 2006, when she retired.

"I must admit that I personally measure success in terms of the contributions an individual makes to her or his fellow human beings." — Margaret Mead

Bill Porter

Unemployable

Bill Porter (1932–), a salesperson for the Watkins Company, is a successful author and motivational speaker.

As a child, Bill Porter heard people describe him as "slow" and "retarded" many times. However, these were statements made by people who judged him by his outward appearance and not by his real abilities. Porter was born with cerebral palsy, which made walking and speaking difficult for him, but the condition did not affect his intelligence. After graduating from high school, Porter went to the state vocational rehabilitation agency for help in obtaining a job. Staff members there assessed his abilities and labeled him as "unemployable." They urged him to accept the limitations caused by his disability and apply for Social Security.

Porter refused. He would not accept help when he didn't need it. He chose instead to listen to his mother, who urged him to rise above his limitations. He knew he could do something and started searching the help-wanted ads in the local newspaper. One detailed a position at the Watkins Company selling household products door-to-door. Porter applied, but Watkins was reluctant to hire him. However, Porter convinced the manager to give him the company's worst sales route — the one no other sales representative would accept. Porter's unstoppable determination, unwillingness to take no for an answer, and unquenchable spirit helped him overcome the nearly insurmountable odds. Not only did he earn enough money to support himself by selling door-to-door, he eventually outsold the other sales representatives to win the "Salesman of the Year" award.

"You can accomplish anything you want if you just set your mind to it." — B. P.

Christopher Reeve

Down, but Not Out

Christopher Reeve (1952–2004) was an American actor, director, writer, and producer who starred in four *Superman* movies in the 1970s and 1980s.

WHAT HAPPENS WHEN SUPERMAN FALLS? He gets back up. And that is exactly what Christopher Reeve did when he fell off his horse in the summer of 1995. Although suffering from a spinal cord injury that paralyzed him from the neck down and confined him to a wheelchair, Reeve did not let his condition crush his spirit. He used his voice — one of the few faculties not lost in the accident — to rally the scientific community to find cures for spinal cord injuries. Reeve also helped others who were paralyzed to improve their living conditions; lobbied legislators to increase federal funds for research; and with his wife Dana founded the Christopher & Dana Reeve Paralysis Resource Center and the Christopher Reeve Foundation.

He refused to let his accident keep him from his first love, motion pictures. In 1997, Reeve made his debut as a director with the film *In the Gloaming*. The film won four Cable Ace Awards and was nominated for five Emmy Awards including one for outstanding director of a miniseries or special. In 1998, Reeves returned to acting in a remake of the Alfred Hitchcock classic, *Rear Window.* He won a Screen Actors Guild Award and was nominated for an Emmy for Best Actor for his performance in the film. Reeves continued to direct, act in, and produce several more films as well as write his autobiography, *Still Me*, which was on the *New York Times* best-seller list for eleven weeks. He also won a Grammy Award for best spoken word album.

"I think a hero is an ordinary individual who finds the strength to persevere and endure in spite of overwhelming obstacles." — C. R.

Eleanor Roosevelt

A Funny, Old-Fashioned Child

Anna Eleanor Roosevelt (1884–1962), better known as Eleanor Roosevelt, the wife of President Franklin D. Roosevelt, was a prominent advocate for civil rights.

Eleanor Roosevelt knew she was no great beauty — her mother had told her that countless times. She grew up feeling gawky and ugly, and cringed every time she heard her mother tell visitors that she was "such a funny child, so old-fashioned that we always call her Granny." After her parents died, she was sent to live with her maternal grandmother, where she needed three locks on her door just to protect her from her "spirited" uncles.

Amazingly, she triumphed over her insecurities, her shyness, and the emotional wounds of her childhood, but it did not come easily. When she was first married, she was so insecure that she would often burst into tears for no reason. During the early years of her marriage, she was bullied by her mother-in-law, took only a marginal interest in her husband's political ambitions, and gave birth to six children in only ten years.

Tragedy, in the form of her husband Franklin's paralytic polio, helped her to overcome her insecurities and forged her into the woman she was destined to become. She stood up to her mother-in-law and refused to allow her to turn Franklin into an invalid. She nursed him back to health and encouraged him to continue pursuing his political goals by running for governor of New York. He won the election.

By the time Franklin decided to run for president, Roosevelt had become a much stronger woman. She became one of the most assertive first ladies in history. In 1938, *Life* magazine selected her as the greatest woman alive, although she had yet to achieve her most famous accomplishments. She often lent her voice to right the injustices she encountered. In one such incident in 1939, she resigned from the Daughters of the American Revolution when the organization refused to let singer Marian Anderson perform in its Washington hall. Roosevelt served as a delegate to the United Nation's General Assembly and chair of the United Nation's Human Rights Commission. She helped draft the Universal Declaration of Human Rights, and chaired the Kennedy administration's Commission on the Status of Women.

> *"The only man who makes no mistakes is the man who never does anything."* —E. R.

Franklin D. Roosevelt

Three Times Predicted for Massive Defeat

Franklin Delano Roosevelt (1882–1945) was the thirty-second president of the United States.

At Harvard University, Franklin Delano Roosevelt was a "C" student; he later dropped out of Columbia Law School. In 1920, he ran as vice president on the Democratic ticket along with presidential candidate James M. Cox, but they were heavily defeated by Warren G. Harding and Calvin Coolidge. After this defeat, many doubted Roosevelt would ever run for public office again. When polio left him paralyzed from the waist down and unable to stand without assistance the following year, most believed his political career had ended. Nevertheless, seven years later he became governor of New York.

After Roosevelt announced he would run for president, both the *New York Herald Tribune* and the *New York Times* predicted that he would lose to incumbent Herbert Hoover. Roosevelt beat Hoover by more than seven million votes. When Roosevelt ran for reelection in 1936, people again predicted that he would lose. Mark Sullivan, political commentator for the the *New York Times*, wrote, "FDR will be a one-term president." Newspaper publisher Paul Block stated, "I have never felt more certain of anything in my life than the defeat of President Roosevelt. By mid-October, people will wonder why they ever had any doubt about it." California newspaper magnate William Randolph Hearst added his prediction, saying, "The race will not be close at all. Landon will be overwhelmingly elected and I'll stake my reputation as a prophet on it." Again, Roosevelt beat his opponent, Alf Landon, with an overwhelming majority. The third time around, when Roosevelt again ran for reelection, some pundits still predicted that the president would not win. Again, he proved them wrong. Roosevelt served four terms, the only president elected to more than two terms.

"It is common sense to take a method and try it. If it fails, admit it frankly and try another. But above all, try something." — F. D. R.

Theodore Roosevelt

A Sickly, Delicate Boy

Theodore Roosevelt Jr. (1858–1919), also known as "Teddy" Roosevelt, was the twenty-sixth president of the United States and, at forty-two, the youngest to date.

THEODORE ROOSEVELT ONCE DESCRIBED HIMSELF as a "sickly, delicate boy." He worked hard to overcome the severe asthma that prevented him from doing the activities he wanted to do as a child. Roosevelt also had serious heart problems that interfered with his pursuits. Shortly after graduating from Harvard, he was advised by a doctor to find a desk job and avoid strenuous activity. Roosevelt choose to ignore this advice for most of his life.

In 1886, Roosevelt ran for mayor of New York City and lost. He later served as governor of New York for two years and ran on the Republican ticket for vice president under William McKinley, despite objections from Republican party boss Mark Hanna. McKinley and Roosevelt won the election and assumed office in 1897. After McKinley's assassination in 1901, Roosevelt became the youngest president in American history, an office he held for more than eight years. During his presidency, he negotiated a treaty that allowed the United States to build the Panama Canal in 1904 and, in 1906, became the first American to be awarded a Nobel Peace Prize. Roosevelt designated an unprecedented forty-two million acres of national forests, wildlife refuges, and areas of "special interest" during his presidency, a record that would not be surpassed until President Clinton's presidency more than ninety years later.

"It is hard to fail, but it is worse never to have tried to succeed." — T. R.

Wilma Rudolph

Encouraged to Quit

In 1960, Wilma Rudolph (1940–1994) became the first woman to win three Olympic gold medals in track and field during a single game.

The effects of her premature birth did not slow Wilma Rudolph down. Her childhood was marred by double pneumonia and scarlet fever, and a left leg that was paralyzed. Doctors told her mother that Rudolph would never walk again, but her mother refused to believe them. Instead, she took her daughter to a special hospital fifty miles away twice a week for treatment. By the time she was five, Rudolph had learned to walk with the assistance of a metal brace on her left leg. Five years later, she was able to walk without the brace. By the time she was thirteen, all traces of a limp were gone. Though doctors considered her progress a miracle, Rudolph was not satisfied. That same year, she decided to become a runner.

She ran in a race and came in last. People around her told her to quit, but she did not listen to them any more than her mother had listened to the doctors. Rudolph entered another race, and another, and another until, finally, she won. She kept on winning all the way to the Olympics, where she won three gold medals. Before her triumphant appearance at the Olympics, Rudolph set a world record in the 200-meter dash. In 1961, she received the James E. Sullivan Award as the top amateur athlete in the United States. Shortly afterward, she retired as an athlete and worked as a teacher and coach.

> *"Winning is great, sure, but if you are really going to do something in life, the secret is learning how to lose. Nobody goes undefeated all the time. If you can pick up after a crushing defeat, and go on to win again, you are going to be a champion someday."* — W. R.

Gabriel Ruelas

Twisted Out of Shape

Boxer Gabriel Ruelas (1970–) is the former WBC super featherweight titleholder.

Every boxer eventually suffers a loss, but Gabriel Ruelas's first professional loss hit him harder than most. During his first two years in the ring, he won every one of his twenty-one professional fights. He was on his way to winning his twenty-second fight as well when, during a clinch, his opponent grabbed his hand and twisted. Ruelas's arm snapped. Doctors inserted three screws to repair the arm. Unfortunately, two of the screws broke off, and the doctors were forced to perform a second operation that included a bone graft from Ruelas's hip to repair the damage. Doctors warned him that he would never be able to fight again or even regain full use of his hand. When the cast was removed, Ruelas could not completely straighten his arm, which had become three inches shorter than his other arm.

However, he was a fighter, not because of his moves inside the ring, but because of his actions outside it. He began viewing the break as something that could help his career because it forced him to use his brains and not just his brawn in the ring. Ruelas returned to boxing within a year and remained unbeaten until 1993, when he lost to Azumah Nelson in his first shot at the title. Two years later, however, Ruelas got a second chance at the title against Jesse James Leija. This time he won.

"Even after I lost another fight, it didn't bother me one bit. I was stronger. . . . I had learned that no matter what happened I could always come back."
— G. R.

Daniel "Rudy" Ruettiger

Too Many Obstacles in His Way

Daniel "Rudy" Ruettiger (1948–) is a motivational speaker, but is best known as the real-life inspiration behind the movie *Rudy*.

Daniel Ruettiger had one dream: to play football for Notre Dame. Unfortunately, many obstacles stood in his way. He was not a fast runner, had poor grades, and was small — only five foot six and 190 pounds. In addition, he did not have the money to attend the private college nor the qualifications to win a scholarship. After graduating from high school, he joined the U.S. Navy to earn money. After finishing his tour of duty, he was accepted at Holy Cross Community College.

While there, Ruettiger was diagnosed with dyslexia and, with the help of teachers and tutors, began to improve his grades.

With his improved academic record, he began applying to Notre Dame. He received three rejections before the college finally accepted him. Ruettiger earned a spot on the Notre Dame football team as a scrub player — one who practices with the team but does not play in actual games. Working his way up, he reached the sixth string his senior year. Although he was closer to his dream, he again encountered obstacles. NCAA issued a ruling that only sixty players could dress for a game, Notre Dame had a new football coach, and Ruettiger's time as an eligible player was running out. Finally two players convinced the coach, that Ruettiger should be allowed on the field for a game. On the field for the last two plays, Ruettiger sacked the opposing team's quarterback. His excited teammates carried him off the field in triumph.

"Make the decision to take action and move closer to your dream. Create daily success habits and surround yourself with information that will empower and inspire you." — D. R.

Colonel Sanders

Too Old to Start a Business

Harland David Sanders (1890-1980), better known as Colonel Sanders, founded the chain of Kentucky Fried Chicken restaurants now known as KFC.

ALREADY IN HIS SIXTIES, HARLAND Sanders was deemed "too old" by potential investors to start a business. It did not matter to them that he already owned a successful service station or that he had received the honorary title of "Kentucky Colonel" from Kentucky Governor Ruby Laffoon.

Sanders continued to look for investors, and financiers continued to turn him away. After hundreds of rejections, he finally scraped enough money together to progress to the next step — finding people willing to make and sell his unique chicken recipe. For two years, Sanders traveled across the country and met with thousands of business owners in the hopes of developing a franchise. Only five restaurants signed up. Nevertheless, he kept trying. Over the next four years, he convinced another two hundred restaurateurs to buy franchises — a number that would triple in three years. Eventually, as his secret seasonings and "finger lickin' good" chicken won people over, Sanders became the owner of one of the largest fast-food chains in the United States: Kentucky Fried Chicken. As of 2008, more than nine thousand stores in eighty-six countries served the Colonel's chicken.

"Hard work beats all the tonics and vitamins in the world." — H. D. S.

Ronan Tynan

Faced Ongoing Adversity

A former member of the Irish Tenors, Ronan Tynan (1960–) has sung at numerous public events including September 11th memorial services, several New York Yankees games at Yankee Stadium, and President Ronald Reagan's funeral.

Already in his fifth year of medical school, Ronan Tynan decided it was time to pursue another dream. He took voice lessons and began competing in local singing contests. After graduation, he entered and won the British Broadcasting Corporation's talent show *Go for It*. The other doctors who worked with Tynan were so impressed that they raised money for him to study at the Royal Conservatory of Music. At thirty-three, Tynan was old to embark on a musical career, but he was used to facing adversity. Born with a rare lower limb disability, Tynan, had to wear leg supports as a child. After a motorbike accident, he had to have both legs amputated at the knee. Whenever he was faced with a challenge, Tynan remembered his mother's words, "Put courage in your dreams, and leave the rest to the Man above."

While winning international singing competitions, Tynan suddenly lost his voice. Doctors discovered that a blockage had been damaging his vocal cords for years. They needed to remove it, but were uncertain how the surgery would affect his singing voice. Tynan looked at it as a sign that his singing career was over and resumed his medical career. It was not until his father died in 1998 that he began singing in public again. With his voice back to normal, Tynan teamed up with Anthony Kearns and John McDermott to create the Irish Tenors. Their first concert CD, as well as Tynan's first solo album, went platinum. Today, Tynan splits his time between concert halls and his medical practice.

> *"I want people to realize that, regardless of what infirmity or disability, it should never stop you from doing what you want to do. You can mentally make your mind strong enough to overcome any obstacle that comes your way." — R. T.*

Johnny Unitas

Too Small to Play Football

Nicknamed "The Golden Arm," Johnny Unitas (1933–2002) played professional football during the 1950s, 1960s, and 1970s and was the National Football League's (NFL) most valuable player in 1959, 1964, and 1967.

Johnny Unitas played halfback and quarterback on the St. Justin High School football team. He dreamed of playing college football, but to do so he would have had to overcome a multitude of obstacles. Many colleges, including Notre Dame and Indiana University, passed him over because they considered him too small. The University of Pittsburgh offered him a scholarship, but he failed the entrance exam. Ultimately, he went to the University of Louisville. While there, he grew two inches and gained more than fifty pounds. This led the Pittsburgh Steelers, his hometown team, to pick him in the ninth round of the college draft. However, he was cut before he even had a chance to play for the team.

Unitas did not give up on his dream of playing professional football, but he took a job as a construction worker until he could accomplish that goal. During his time off, he played quarterback for a "semipro" football team, the Bloomfield Rams, earning a whopping six dollars a game. A fan, impressed with Unitas's talent, told the Baltimore Colts about his abilities. The team gave him a tryout and then signed him to a contract as a backup to quarterback George Shaw. Unitas got his big break after the starting quarterback got his — literally. Shaw broke his leg during the fourth game of the 1956–1957 season, giving Unitas the chance to fill his spot. Unitas's first throw was intercepted, but it was the beginning of a spectacular professional career. From December 9, 1956, until December 4, 1960, Unitas completed at least one touchdown pass in every game he played. In 1957, he led the NFL in touchdown passes and passing yardage. He was named as National Football League's most valuable player in 1957, 1959, and 1964.

During his eighteen years with the NFL, Unitas threw 5,186 passes, completing 2,830 of them for 40,239 yards, a NFL record at the time, and 290 touchdowns, with 253 interceptions. He also rushed for 1,777 yards and thirteen touchdowns on the ground. When he retired, Unitas held the NFL records for most seasons passing for more than 3000 yards (3); most games passing for 300 yards or more (27); and most touchdowns thrown (290). He also held two postseason records: highest pass completion percentage, (62.9 percent); and most yards gained passing during championship play, (1,177). He is known for having thrown an amazing seventy-five-yard touchdown pass during Super Bowl V.

"There is a difference between conceit and confidence. Conceit is bragging about yourself. Confidence means you believe you can get the job done." — J. U.

Barbara Walters

Not Right for Television

Barbara Walters (1929–) is an American journalist, writer, and media personality. She regularly appears on *The View* and *20/20*, as well as on her own series of *Barbara Walters Specials*, among the highest-rated programs on television.

In 1957, Don Hewitt, a producer at CBS, advised then-writer Barbara Walters, "You're a marvelous girl, but stay out of television." According to Hewitt, he did not believe her voice was right for television. Others shared his opinion. Walters herself observed, "I was the kind nobody thought could make it. I had a funny Boston accent. I couldn't pronounce my R's. I wasn't a beauty."

Walters might have lacked some attributes, but she had plenty of determination and grit. She eventually left CBS and went to work on the *Today Show*. There, she moved from writing to reporting, eventually becoming the show's cohost. In 1976, Walters made history when she became the first woman to be coanchor of a nightly news show. ABC had hoped her presence would raise ratings, but the show was a disaster. In 1979, Walters moved to a new job as a reporter on a weekly news magazine show, *20/20*, where she remained until 2004. She continues to produce the *Barbara Walters Specials* that have been airing for the past thirty years. She also is cohost of the daytime talk show she created, *The View*. To date, Walters has been nominated more than thirty times for Emmy Awards (she won three) and received an Emmy for Lifetime Achievement in 2000.

"Success can make you go one of two ways. It can make you a prima donna — or it can smooth the edges, take away the insecurities, let the nice things come out." — B. W.

Heather Whitestone

Dreams Out of Reach

In 1995, Heather Whitestone (1973–)
became the first deaf Miss America.

Heather Whitestone lost her hearing before she was two years old. Doctors predicted that she would never read beyond a third grade level or learn to speak. Her parents rejected the doctor's opinion and chose instead to encourage their daughter to pursue her dreams, no matter how out of reach they might appear.

After graduating from high school, Whitestone majored in accounting at Jacksonville State University. While there, she decided to enter the Miss Alabama contest. Several people had told Whitestone she would never be able to perform ballet, but she chose to demonstrate her talent at the contest. Although she could not hear the music, she was able to feel the vibrations with her feet. The first two times she entered the state Miss America contest, she came in second. Encouragement from her friends and family led Whitestone to try a third time, in 1994. Third time was the charm, and Whitestone headed to Atlantic City to participate in the Miss America contest. In 1995, Whitestone became the first person with a disability to be crowned Miss America. Whitestone is currently a spokesperson for the Helen Keller Eye Research Foundation and the Starkey Hearing Aid Foundation and is the author of three books.

"You will face obstacles. You will be blown off the path, but because you have a goal, you stay on your path." — H. W.

Something from Nothing

"The only thing that separates successful people from the ones who aren't is the willingness to work very, very hard."

— Helen Gurley Brown

Irving Berlin

An Illiterate Composer

Irving Berlin (1888–1989) was an American composer and lyricist who wrote classic American favorites such as "White Christmas," "God Bless America" and "There's No Business Like Show Business."

Irving Berlin first learned to love music as a young boy growing up in New York's Lower East Side. Singing for pennies was one of the few ways he could help support his family after his father died. He could not afford musical training and never learned to read or write music. He taught himself how to play the piano, however, and sold his first song, "Marie of Sunny Italy," when he was nineteen.

Without formal piano lessons, Berlin created his own style of playing. He typically played everything in F-sharp, which allowed him to use the black keys almost exclusively. Because the black keys are raised and spaced farther apart, they are easier to play. Berlin eventually realized that he needed to be able to write music in other keys, so he invested in a transposing piano to change the key signature, enabling him to alter the key without changing the way he played. As he became more successful, he took piano lessons but soon decided to hire an assistant with musical knowledge instead.

His first assistant, Cliff Hess, worked with Berlin for five years. He was followed briefly by Arthur Johnston before Helmy Kresa accepted the job, a position Kresa filled for sixty years. At one point, Berlin turned down George Gershwin for the job because he thought Gershwin was too talented to be happy in the position. Unfortunately, since Berlin dictated his music to his assistant, some people accused Berlin of plagiarism — saying that it was really the assistant and not Berlin who had composed the music. Both Berlin and Kresa denied the allegations.

After Berlin retired, he donated his transposing piano to the Smithsonian in 1973. During his career, Berlin composed several thousand songs including American classics "God Bless America," "White Christmas" (America's best-selling single for more than fifty years), "Cheek to Cheek," "Easter Parade," "Let's Face the Music and Dance," "Top Hat, White Tie, and Tails," and "Puttin' on the Ritz." He also wrote the scores for seventeen films including *Easter Parade, Top Hat,* and *Holiday Inn*; and twenty-one Broadway musicals, among them his most successful Broadway musical, *Annie Get Your Gun*. Interestingly, one of the earliest reviews of the show, written by Louis Kronenberger, stated, "Irving Berlin's score is musically not exciting — of the real songs, only one or two are tuneful." *Annie Get Your Gun*, which includes the numbers "There's No Business Like Show Business," "Anything You Can Do, I Can Do Better," and "They Say It's Wonderful," ran for several years with more than eleven hundred performances on Broadway.

"The toughest thing about success is that you've got to keep on being a success." — I. B.

George Burns

The Worst Vaudeville Act in the World

For more than ninety years, George Burns (1896–1996) entertained audiences on stage, radio, screen, and television as an actor and comedian.

Despite his early start in show business — he was dancing around the neighborhood's organ grinder when he was only five — Nathan Birnbaum struggled for years before succeeding on the vaudeville circuit. Birnbaum performed as a trick roller skater, taught ballroom dancing, and did impressions. Each time he changed acts or partners, he changed his name — it was the only way he could get another job since he was usually fired after only one performance. "I'd be lying if I said I was the worst act in the world," he wrote in his autobiography. "I wasn't that good." He was known as Willy Delight, Pedro Lopez, Billy Pierce, Captain Betts, Jed Jackson, Jimmy Malone, and Buddy Lanks before finally settling on the name George Burns.

In 1923, Burns met Gracie Allen, who he thought would make a great straight partner to his funny man act. Allen had been a performer, but he had given it up to train as a stenographer. Burns convinced her that they would make a good team — both professionally and personally. Allen reluctantly agreed, but at their first performance the audience did not laugh at the jokes. Instead, they laughed at Allen's straight lines. Burns realized that he had been wrong, and for the next twenty-seven years Burns played the straight man to Allen's comic genius. They were married in 1926 and enjoyed a happy marriage along with a successful career. "I'm the brains," Burns once told the *Daily Mail*, "and Gracie is everything else, especially to me." Together, Burns and Allen moved from vaudeville to radio and then to television before Allen's failing health forced her to retire.

> *"I honestly think it is better to be a failure at something you love than to be a success at something you hate."* — G. B.

Nolan Bushnell

Rejected by Disney

Nolan Bushnell (1943–) founded both the electronics games company Atari and the Chuck E. Cheese's Pizza-Time chain.

NOLAN BUSHNELL HAD ALWAYS BEEN fascinated by the animatronic figures Disney used in its parks and had tried unsuccessfully to get a job with the company for years. He turned his attention toward inventing video games. His first game, *Computer Space*, considered too complicated and too far ahead of its time, was a commercial failure. His next game, *Pong*, was more successful. A simplified version of tennis, it was distributed by his company, Atari.

The success of *Pong* allowed Bushnell to create his own mini-Disneyland restaurants chain — Chuck E. Cheese — that incorporated animatronics figures and video game technology. After a dispute forced Bushnell out of Atari in November 1978, he focused attention on his restaurants. The venture succeeded until overexpansion forced the company into bankruptcy in 1984. Chuck E. Cheese was then purchased by a competing company, ShoBiz Pizza, which merged the two companies under the Chuck E. Cheese name.

A business deal that fell through and an adverse court ruling left Bushnell with nothing. However, the experience taught him valuable lessons, and he used his newly gained knowledge to start over. During his career, Bushnell has created more than twenty companies. He is recognized by many as the father of the video game industry. Bushnell was named one of *Newsweek*'s "Fifty Men Who Changed America." He has also been inducted into the Video Game Hall of Fame and the Consumer Electronics Association Hall of Fame, and has received the *Nation's Restaurant News* Innovator of the Year award.

> *"If you are unwilling to take a risk on something that you know is better than what's out there, but not as good as you think it could be, then you will fail because you are now paralyzed by your requirements of perfection."* — N. B.

Alfred Mosher Butts

Unemployed and Playing Games

Alfred Mosher Butts (1899–1993) invented the board game Scrabble.

Alfred Butts worked as an architect until the Great Depression hit the United States and he found himself unemployed. For four years, he struggled to find a job. During that period, Butts spent most of his free time expanding a game he had played as a child that combined anagrams and crossword puzzles. He used the expanded version to create a game board game by gluing architectural graph paper onto a chessboard. Desperate to generate income, Butts tried to sell the game. He sold a few sets, but he could not find a manufacturer. After Butts found a new job as an architect, he abandoned the game. Ten years later, James Brunot, Butts's friend, urged him to manufacture and distribute the game. Butts agreed, and the two men redesigned the game slightly and gave it a new name: Scrabble.

In the beginning, Brunot manufactured thousands of games in his house with the help of his wife. Unfortunately, they did not sell enough to make a profit. For the first four years, the company lost money and was on the verge of bankruptcy. Then, in 1952, a Macy's executive discovered the game and agreed to stock it in all the stores in the chain. Sales boomed and, within two years, more than one million games had been sold. Today, more than 100 million Scrabble games have been sold worldwide; it is found in approximately one-third of all American homes.

"Success isn't built on success. It is built on failure and frustration, sometimes catastrophe, and learning to turn it around." — Sumner Redstone

Andrew Carnegie

From $100 to $42,000 a Year

Andrew Carnegie (1835–1919) was an industrialist, businessman, and major philanthropist.

As a teen, Andrew Carnegie held his first job at a textile mill, where he earned less than twenty cents a day. By the time he was twenty, he had become his family's only means of support. Unable to attend school, Carnegie spent most of his free time studying at the public library and attending night school. Carnegie did not wait for opportunity to come knocking; he went and searched for it. While working for the railroad, Carnegie took out a bank loan to invest $217.50 in the Woodruff Sleeping Car Company. Within two years, he was receiving an annual return on his investment of about $5,000, three times more than his salary at the railroad. In ten years, Carnegie's annual salary skyrocketed from less than $100 to $42,000.

Eventually Carnegie would earn close to $400 million during his lifetime. More astonishing than his financial successes, however, is the way Carnegie spent his earnings before he died: he distributed 90 percent of his fortune to universities, libraries, the arts, charities that supported scientific research, and other good works.

"It is the mind that makes the body rich. There is no class so pitiably wretched as that which possesses money and nothing else." — A. C.

Clive Cussler

Relied Upon Fake Recommendations

Clive Cussler (1931–) is the author of the Dirk Pitt Adventure novels, which include *Raise the Titanic!*, *Treasure of Khan*, and *Deep Six*.

Most fiction writers create their own worlds, but Clive Cussler works his fiction into the real world. After months of countless rejections, Cussler gave up on his first novel and tried a different approach for his second one. He created a West Coast literary agent named Charles Winthrop. Cussler then printed letterhead (with his father's address and no phone number) and used it to write recommendations for his work from the "agent" who, for some unknown reason (perhaps because he did not exist), was unable to represent Cussler himself. Cussler sent the bogus recommendations to major New York literary agencies. The ploy worked. Within thirty days, Cussler had a contract with agent Peter Lampack. Several years passed, and Lampack had no more luck selling Cussler's manuscript than the author had. Lampack's superiors at the agency decided to drop the writer, but Lampack changed their minds. Finally, after four years, Lampack negotiated two publishing deals: one in paperback and one in hardcover. Only three thousand copies sold.

More bad news followed when Cussler was fired from his other job. Instead of despairing, the novelist used his time off to write a third book. Nine months later, Lampack sent it to an editor who replied, "The book is too long and the cost of paper has gone up. We just feel it's not a viable work." Lampack sent it to another editor, who wanted to do a massive rewrite. Viking eventually purchased the manuscript, but the editor there did not consider it a sound purchase.

By chance, an editor from England was visiting Viking at the time and read a copy of the manuscript. He offered to publish the book and, after a bidding war, the novel, *Raising the Titanic*, sold for $840,000. Cussler's first review, in the *New York Times*, attacked his novel, but Lampack told him not to worry because good reviews do not sell. He was right. Cussler's novels have sold more than seventy million copies. Cussler eventually confessed his use of the fake literary agent to Lampack. Rather than be upset about it, Lampack laughed. Today, Cussler's books are published in more than forty languages in more than one hundred countries, with a readership of more than 125 million.

> *"Behind every successful man, there's a lot of unsuccessful years."*
> *— Bob Brown*

Chris Gardner

Fired on His First Day

Chris Gardner (1954–) is a self-made millionaire as well as a motivational speaker and philanthropist.

As a young man, Chris Gardner was not sure what he wanted to do, but he knew what he wanted: a red Ferrari. When he saw a man drive up in the sports car, Gardner asked him what he did for a living and how he could get that job. The man was a stockbroker. Gardner learned that in order to become a stockbroker he would have to serve as a trainee at an investment house. For the next ten months, Gardner tried tirelessly to land a spot as a trainee, which was difficult because he did not have a college degree nor any connections.

He did have drive, though, and his relentless pursuit of his goal finally paid off when he won a position at E. F. Hutton. When Gardner showed up for his first day at the firm, he discovered that the man who had hired him had been fired three days earlier. Gardner did not give up and eventually made it through several rounds of interviews at Dean Witter, the largest investment house on the West Coast at the time. With only one interview left, Gardner found himself in jail for having more than $1,000 in outstanding parking tickets. Because he had no money to pay the tickets, he was forced to stay in jail for a few days. When he got out of jail several days later, he discovered his girlfriend had left him and taken their son and all his possessions. Gardner had no choice but to show up at the interview in the old clothes he had worn before going to jail. Instead of lying to the interviewer, Gardner told him the truth and landed the position.

As a trainee, Gardner received a small stipend that was barely enough to cover the rent on a small room at a boardinghouse. When his girlfriend told Gardner he would have to take care of his young son, Gardner was forced to move from the boardinghouse, which did not allow children. He could not afford an apartment, and Gardner found himself homeless. For the next year, he and his son lived on the streets finding shelter wherever they could — at flophouses, parks, and the Bay Area Rapid Transit station — until the Reverend Cecil Williams agreed to let them stay at the Glide Memorial United Methodist Church's shelter, which had been strictly for homeless women.

Despite the odds against him, Gardner succeeded as a stockbroker. A year later, he and his son moved into their own place. No matter how bad things got, Gardner never stopped working. He eventually opened his own brokerage firm in Chicago. Gardner's story, *The Pursuit of Happyness*, was published by HarperCollins in 2006 and was made into a major motion picture by the same name.

> *"One of the things young people always ask me about is what is the secret to success. The secret is there is no secret. It's the basics. Blocking and tackling. And more important than that, find something that you love. Something that gets you so excited, you can't wait to get out of bed in the morning. Forget about money. Be happy. That takes a certain amount of boldness to say, 'This is what I like.'" — C. G.*

Tommy Hilfiger

Bankrupt, Fired, and Failed

Tommy Hilfiger (1951–) is an American fashion designer and creator of the "Tommy Hilfiger" and "Tommy" brand clothing lines.

With no formal training in fashion design, Tommy Hilfiger started at the bottom — literally. His first clothing store was located in a friend's basement. From there, he had nowhere to go but up. Hilfiger eventually expanded his basement store into a series of seven jean boutiques before financial difficulties forced him and his partner to declare bankruptcy under Chapter 11. Hilfiger found the entire experience "embarrassing" and rarely discusses it.

With everything he had created gone, Hilfiger went back to what he knew best. He began sketching new clothing designs and used them to land a job with Jordache Jeans. He was with the company for about a year before his bosses fired him for reasons neither side has ever disclosed. With financial help from friends, Hilfiger opened his own sportswear company, Twentieth Century Survival. The company folded the following year.

After three unsuccessful businesses, Hilfiger decided to stick to freelance work. During this time, he met fashion mogul Mohan Murjani, who offered him a job overseeing a design team for a line of Coca-Cola clothing. He also gave Hilfiger the opportunity to develop his own line of clothing. Both clothing lines became huge successes. In its first year in 1984, the Coca-Cola line of clothes sold more than $100 million. Tommy Hilfiger's own line sold $5 million wholesale its first year in 1985 and increased to $16 million wholesale the following year. The Tommy Hilfiger Corporation went public in 1992. By 2004, it had about 5,400 employees and was earning more than $1.8 billion in revenues. Hilfiger sold the company in 2005 for $1.6 billion to Apax Partners.

> *"It takes hard work, resourcefulness, perseverance, and courage to succeed." — T. H.*

Jay Leno

Admonished for Being a Comedian

Jay Leno (1950–), an American comedian and writer, took over as host of *The Tonight Show* when Johnny Carson retired in 1992.

Growing up with dyslexia, Jay Leno discovered he would have to work twice as hard as the other students to earn the same grades. When he was in the fifth grade, his teacher wrote on his report card that if he "spent as much time studying as he does trying to be a comedian, he'd be a big star." Leno took all this advice to heart, but with a twist to fit his own ambitions. He knew that becoming a comedian would require hard work, especially if he were going to become a big star.

He attended college, and earned a degree in speech therapy. However, he had no desire to work in the field and decided instead to pursue a career as a comedian and an actor. Leno had worked at McDonald's in high school (according to him, because he flunked the test to work at Woolworth's) and had won the McDonald's talent show. Hollywood proved a harsher judge of him. During one television casting meeting, the casting agent said, "We really like Jay, but we feel his face could be frightening to children." The agent suggested he get his jaw fixed, but when Leno discovered that the surgery would leave him unable to talk for at least a year, he decided against it. He won a few bit parts in several unsuccessful movies, all the while continuing to pursue comedy.

In 1977, he appeared on *The Tonight Show starring Johnny Carson*. For the next several years, he appeared frequently on *The Tonight Show* as well as on *Late Night with David Letterman*. In 1987, Leno became the exclusive guest host for Johnny Carson, a job he held until taking over as the show's permanent host in 1992. He has hosted the show for more than fifteen years, earning numerous awards including four Emmy Awards. Leno is scheduled to retire in 2009, when Conan O'Brien will take on the job as permanent host.

"The worst thing you can do in show business is make thirty thousand a year by doing something else to support yourself." — J. L.

Vince Lombardi

Too Old to Become an NFL Coach

Vince Lombardi (1913–1970) is one of the most successful coaches in the history of American football.

Vince Lombardi dropped out of law school to teach high school and become the assistant coach for the football team at St. Cecilia High School in Englewood, New Jersey. Three years later, he became the head coach for the football team and coached the basketball and baseball teams as well. In 1947, after seven years and six state championship wins in football, he left to coach at Fordham University before moving on again just two years later to coach at West Point.

Lombardi really wanted to coach football for the National Football League (NFL). By the time he accepted a position as offensive coach for the New York Giants in 1954, he was forty-one and considered by many as "too old" to be entering the NFL coaching world. In 1959, less than five years later, Lombardi had proven himself as a coach and was offered a head coaching position with the Green Bay Packers. Lombardi agreed to take the position only if he could be the head coach and the general manager. The directors accepted the terms but only if Lombardi could revive the team within five years. Considering the Green Bay Packers had not had a winning season in twelve years and had just finished their worst season ever with only one win, experts predicted that such a turnaround would be impossible. Of course, they did not know Lombardi.

In his first season as coach, Lombardi led the Green Bay Packers to a third-place finish in the western division. The Packers won their division the next three years and the league championship their third and fourth years. Under Lombardi's direction, the team won six division titles, five NFL championships, and the first two Super Bowls, in 1967 and 1968. As of 2007, no coach in NFL history has come close to repeating Lombardi's success.

> *"The greatest accomplishment is not in never failing, but in rising again after you fall." — V. L.*

Jack London

Six Hundred Rejections and No Education

Jack London (1876–1916) was an American writer and author of *The Call of the Wild, White Fang,* and numerous other novels.

Financial difficulties forced Jack London to leave grammar school and find work to support his family. Yet, a lack of schooling did not prevent him from dreaming of being a writer. Although he never graduated from high school, he dreamed of attending the University of California. After cramming and studying, he gained entrance to the college, but financial difficulties once again forced London to drop out of school before graduating. A short time later, the Klondike Gold Rush lured London and his brother-in-law to Alaska. Although he never struck gold, London found it the perfect setting for some of his most successful stories.

Over his lifetime, London held a wide variety of jobs as he struggled to get his works published. Initially, rejections came frequently while payments came infrequently, and London almost abandoned his writing career. London reportedly received more than six hundred rejection letters from publishers. Like the protagonists in his novels, he refused to give up and eventually became one of the highest paid and most popular living writers of his era.

Ironically, he made the most money and earned fame from novels based on the life experiences he garnered before becoming successful. His best known short story, "To Build a Fire," relates the experiences of a new arrival to the Klondike, while the main character in *The Call of the*

Wild, also set in the Klondike, was based on a dog owned by London's landlord. London published more than seventy novels, novellas, and short stories including the American classics *Martin Eden*, *Sea Wolf*, and *White Fang*.

"You can't wait for inspiration. You have to go after it with a club." — J. L.

Sophia Loren

Known as Sophia the Toothpick

Sophia Loren (1934–) is an Italian Academy Award–winning actress who has starred in many films, including *Two Women*, *Grumpier Old Men*, *A Countess From Hong Kong*, *Man Of La Mancha*, *The Voyage*, *Brief Encounter*, and *Cassandra Crossing*.

SOFIA SCICOLONE, LATER KNOWN AS Sophia Loren, had two advantages growing up: "to have been born wise and to have been born in poverty." She recalls her early years in a small Italian village during World War II as a time of cold, hunger, and illness. A fearful, shy, unattractive child, she was so thin that she was nicknamed Sofia Stuzzicadente, or "Sofia the toothpick." Eventually, she transformed into a beautiful young woman. As a teenager, she was a finalist in a local beauty pageant. She obtained work in *fumetti* magazines, comics that use real photographs instead of drawings. She appeared in eight movies using her real name, and then, after a director suggested she change it, she used the name Sofia Lazzaro for her next three films.

She came in second in a Miss Rome competition, where one of the judges happened to be Carlo Ponti, Italy's leading film director. That chance encounter led to a screen test with Ponti. At this time, she changed her last name again as well as the spelling of her first name, and Sofia Scicolone became Sophia Loren. Between 1950 and 2006, Loren appeared in almost ninety movies. In 1960, she won an Academy Award for Best Actress for her performance in Vittorio De Sica's *Two Women* — the first major Academy Award for a performance not in English. She also earned best performance awards at Cannes, Venezia, and Berlin film festivals.

> *"Getting ahead in a difficult profession requires avid faith in yourself. That is why some people with mediocre talent, but with great inner drive, go so much further than people with vastly superior talent."* — *S. L.*

R. H. Macy

Repeated Failures and Bankruptcy

Rowland Hussey Macy (1822–1877) was an American businessman and founder of R. H. Macy and Company, a department store chain whose employees began the annual Macy's Thanksgiving Day Parade in New York City.

Four years on a whaling ship did not prepare R. H. Macy for shop ownership. Still, he took his hard-earned, diligently saved money and opened his own thread and needle store in Boston, Massachusetts. The store failed less than a year later. He tried again, this time opening a store that sold mostly European-made dry goods. Again, the store failed. Out of money, Macy took a job working with his brother-in-law before heading to California with his brother. They hoped to strike it rich in the gold rush. Together the two men opened a store that sold goods to the miners, but when the gold ran out, the miners left, and the store foundered. Macy sold the business to a competitor and moved back East.

This time he opened a store north of Boston, in Haverhill, Massachusetts. This store soon failed, too. After declaring bankruptcy, Macy moved to New York City and opened another store. Again, he met with disaster; his new store was robbed, then it burned down. Macy rebuilt, added new merchandise, and expanded. This time his store succeeded. Although his first day's sales were a meager $11.06, before year's end his store had grossed nearly $90,000. By the 1870s, Macy's stores were averaging more than $1 million in annual sales. One hundred and fifty years later, Macy's continues with more than 850 stores across the United States, Puerto Rico, and Guam.

"I think everyone should experience defeat at least once during their career. You learn a lot from it." — Lou Holtz

Tom Monaghan

Hundreds of Lawsuits and $1.5 Million in Debt

Tom Monaghan (1937–) is the founder of Domino's Pizza, the second largest pizza chain in America when it went public in 2004.

Tom Monaghan's high school grades were so low that he graduated at the bottom of his class. The local university rejected his application, but he managed to enroll at the University of Michigan. A few weeks later, he dropped out because he lacked money for tuition and books. In 1960, Monaghan agreed to buy a pizza store with his brother. When his brother decided he wanted out a year later, Monaghan traded his Volkswagen Beetle for his brother's half of the business.

For the first year, Monaghan worked all the time but barely made any money. He soon found himself deep in debt. He began simplifying the business, selling only three sizes of pizza, instead of five. The change helped Monaghan make a profit, which enabled him to expand his three stores under a new name, Domino's.

Just when life seemed to be improving, Monaghan faced a series of setbacks. In 1967, a fire destroyed his anchor store in Ypsilanti, Michigan, which supplied the other stores with food and served as the company's offices. Most of the damage was not covered by insurance. In an effort to recover his losses, Monaghan continued to expand his franchise, but was unable to keep up with the growth. Without Monaghan's guidance, many of the new stores foundered. By 1970, Monaghan was $1.5 million in debt and facing lawsuits from nearly 150 creditors, including many of his franchise owners. In the ensuing financial settlement, Monaghan lost 51 percent of his company to the bank.

Rather than focus on his losses, Monaghan concentrated on building the 49 percent of the business he still owned. Slowly, he began to work his way out of his financial difficulties. He defended himself in court since he could not afford an attorney. He sold his furniture and his car. When things started to turn around, he ordered checks printed with the name Operation Surprise and sent a payment and a thank you note to every creditor — even those who had already written off the debt. In about a year, he managed to pay off all his debts.

These hard times taught him a valuable lesson in how to run a business. Instead of charging a franchise fee, he required people to work successfully as store managers before they could apply. He also set up a company to help finance franchise buyers. Under these new guidelines, Domino's began to flourish and, by 1978, two hundred Domino's stores had opened. By 1983, the number of stores surpassed a thousand; by 1989, the chain had more than five thousand stores. The company had more than six thousand pizza delivery stores when Monaghan sold it for $1 billion in 1998. He has spent his retirement doing philanthropic work for Catholic charities and conservative political causes.

> *"You always get negative reactions. If you worry about that, you would never do anything." — T. M.*

Paul Orfalea

Unhireable

Paul Orfalea (1947–) is the founder of Kinko's, an international chain of stores that provides printing, copying, and binding services.

Paul Orfalea flunked the second grade, graduated from high school 1,192 out of 1,200, and earned a C average in college. Orfalea, who has dyslexia and attention deficit hyperactivity disorder, knew he would have to make his own way. He had had only two jobs in his life and neither of them had lasted longer than a day. After noticing the long lines at the copy machines in the small college town where he lived, he took out a $5,000 loan and, in 1970, started his own copier business. He opened his first store, which he called Kinko's after a nickname he had been given as a child, in an eight-foot-by-twelve-foot storefront. Orfalea stood out front selling pens and pencils from his backpack. The store was so small that he had to move the copy machine to the sidewalk to use it.

People told him it would never work, but he refused to listen. "I knew what I was going to do," Orfalea said later. His first store did well enough for him to expand. Within ten years, he had eighty Kinko's located around the country. By 1990, the number had grown to 420 stores — and doubled by 1997. In 2004, Orfalea sold Kinko's to FedEx for $2.4 billion.

"My learning disability gave me certain advantages, because I was able to live in the moment and capitalize on the opportunities I spotted." — P. O.

Al Pacino

Screen Test Reject

Actor Al Pacino (1940–) has appeared in numerous films including *The Godfather* trilogy, *Scent of a Woman*, *Serpico*, and *Dog Day Afternoon*.

At seventeen, Al Pacino was forced to drop out of Manhattan's High School for the Performing Arts in order to work full-time. He worked as a delivery boy, usher, and porter, and at several other odd jobs before studying with acting coach Lee Strasberg, who compared him to a young Marlon Brando. Pacino loved acting, but he found it incredibly difficult to make any money at it. He began performing in New York theaters and won both an Obie

Award and a Tony Award for his performances. His first television appearance, in an episode of *N.Y.P.D.* in 1968, was followed in 1969 by his movie debut in *Me, Natalie*.

Hollywood began to take an interest in him, and he landed a role in *The Panic in Needle Park*. The role won him the attention of director Francis Ford Coppola, who selected him to play Michael Corleone in his upcoming movie, *The Godfather*. Paramount executives disagreed and rejected Pacino several times for the role. With actors such as Robert Redford and Warren Beatty vying for the part, it seemed foolish to cast an unknown. Coppola insisted and eventually got his way. Pacino's portrayal won him critical acclaim as well as an Academy Award nomination for Best Supporting Actor. The actor has also starred in the movie's two sequels, as well as *Scarface*, *Serpico*, *Scent of a Woman*, *Dog Day Afternoon*, and *Glengarry Glen Ross*. In 1997, Pacino was ranked fourth in *Empire* magazine's list of the "Top 100 Movie Stars of All Time." He has also been awarded the American Film Institute Life Achievement Award and the Golden Globe Cecil B. de Mille Award.

"It's easy to fool the eye, but it's hard to fool the heart." — A. P.

Van Halen

A Band With No Commercial Potential

Van Halen, an American rock band, has sold more than eighty million albums worldwide and earned a place in the *Guinness Book of World Records* for having the most number one hits on the *Billboard* Mainstream Rock Tracks chart.

In 1974, Eddie and Alex Van Halen started their own band, called Mammoth. Because they could not afford their own sound system, they were forced to rent a system from the member of another band, David Lee Roth. Ironically, the Van Halens had turned Roth down earlier when he had auditioned to become a member of their band. When they realized they could avoid paying Roth rental fees by allowing him into the band, they invited him to join them. Soon afterward, Michael Anthony joined the trio. When the group decided that the new band needed a new name, Roth had to convince the other members that his suggestion of "Van Halen" was the best choice.

By 1976, Van Halen had become a staple in clubs around Los Angeles, where they caught the eye of Gene Simmons, the lead singer of the popular band KISS. Under Simmons's guidance, Van Halen produced the band's first demo tape and landed an audition for a major record producer. The producer was not impressed and said he saw no commercial potential in the band. A short time later, Simmons relinquished rights to the demo, and Van Halen went back to playing in the clubs around Los Angeles.

One rainy Monday night a year later, record producer Ted Templeman and Warner Brothers Record executive Mo Ostin heard the band playing for a nearly empty Starwood Club. They liked the band and quickly signed them to a contract. Van Halen's first album was released the following year. The album, which contains one of Van Halen's best-known songs, "Ain't Talkin' about Love," went gold in less than four months. The song, written by Eddie Van Halen, almost did not make the album, because Eddie believed it was not good enough to show his band mates.

From 1978 to 1998, Van Halen released eleven Top 20

albums. They have sold more than seventy-five million albums worldwide and appear in the *Guinness Book of World Records* for having the most number one hits on the *Billboard* Mainstream Rock Tracks chart. The Recording Industry Association of America ranks Van Halen in the top twenty on its list of the top-selling artists of all time. The band is also one of only five rock groups to have had two albums sell more than ten million copies in the United States. The other four bands are Led Zeppelin, the Beatles, Pink Floyd, and Def Leppard. In 2007, the band was recognized for its many contributions to American music when it was inducted into the Rock and Roll Hall of Fame.

> *"You come to the planet with nothing and you leave with nothing, so you'd better do some good while you are here."* — Alex Van Halen

James McNeill Whistler

Rejected by the Paris Salon and the Royal Academy

James McNeill Whistler (1834–1903) was a painter and etcher. His most famous works include *Arrangement in Grey and Black: Portrait of the Painter's Mother* (better known as *Whistler's Mother*), *Symphony in White, No. 1: The White Girl,* and his famous *Nocturne series.*

James Whistler had originally intended to be a soldier and attended the U.S. Military Academy at West Point. While there, he failed chemistry and constantly broke the rules, earning a record 218 demerits before he was dismissed in 1855. Whistler then decided to be an artist and went to Paris. In 1859, he submitted one of his paintings, *At the Piano*, to the Paris Salon (*Salon de Paris*), the official art exhibition of the Académie des Beaux-Arts, which was considered the greatest art event in the world at the time. The exhibition judges rejected the painting, as did the Royal Academy of Arts in London, England, although the Royal Academy reversed its opinion about the painting in 1860.

Whistler tried again in 1863, this time submitting a painting titled *The White Girl* for the exhibition. Again his painting was rejected by both the Paris Salon and the Royal Academy. It was, however, accepted by the Salon des Refusés, a separate exhibition that featured works rejected by the Paris Salon. Although other artists admired the painting, members of the general public laughed at it.

Whistler persisted, and slowly his paintings grew more and more popular. By the early 1890s, Whistler had achieved worldwide recognition. His influence can be seen in the works of a variety of artists including John Singer Sargent, William Merritt Chase, Oscar Wilde, Walter Sickert, and Arthur Frank Mathews. His work has been featured at numerous museums and art exhibits. His most famous work is *Arrangement in Grey and Black: Portrait of the Painter's Mother,* usually referred to as *Whistler's Mother.*

"If more than five percent of the people like a painting then burn it for it must be bad." — J. M. W.

Oprah Winfrey

Executives Didn't Like her Look

Oprah Winfrey (1954–) has won multiple Emmy Awards as host of *The Oprah Winfrey Show*, the highest-rated talk show in television history.

OPRAH WINFREY BEGAN HER TELEVISION career as a news anchor in Baltimore, but she was fired because executives thought she did not project herself as a hard-nosed reporter. She moved to the morning show, *People Are Talking*, but station executives did not like her appearance. They said her eyes were too far apart, her nose was too wide, her chin was too long, and she had a weight problem. They also did not like her hair, which they tried to change by sending Winfrey to a salon. She ended up nearly bald from a botched permanent.

Apparently, her appearance did not faze the viewers because the morning show steadily increased its ratings, and she was offered another job as host of *AM Chicago*. Winfrey took *AM Chicago* from the bottom of the ratings to the top, successfully toppling the reigning daytime talk show host Phil Donahue. A year later, the show — renamed *The Oprah Winfrey Show* — went into syndication. Winfrey has earned numerous Emmy Awards for her program, today the highest-rated talk show in television history.

"Challenges are gifts that force us to search for a new center of gravity. Don't fight them. Just find a different way to stand." — O. W.

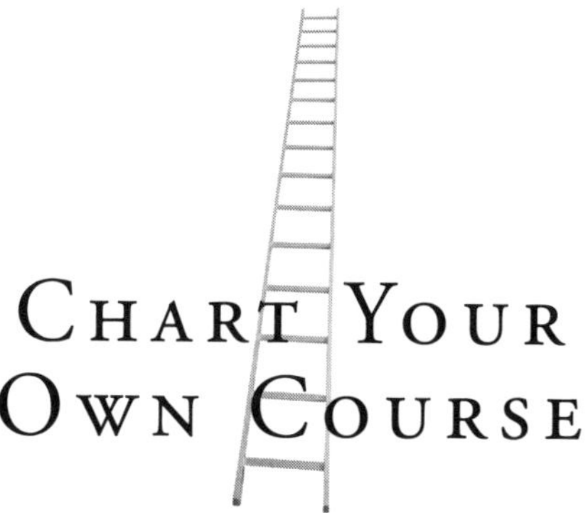

Chart Your Own Course

"I owe my success to having listened respectfully to the very best advice, and then going away and doing the exact opposite."

— G. K. Chesterton

Leon Leonwood Bean

Early High Failure Rate

Leon Leonwood Bean (1873–1967) was the founder of the mail order and retail company L.L. Bean.

Traipsing through the woods in Maine was a soggy, uncomfortable affair. Rubber galoshes kept your feet dry, but did not give enough support. Leather boots offered support, but quickly became soaked. Frustrated by cold, wet feet while trying to enjoy the outdoors, Leon Leonwood Bean set out to find a solution. In 1911, he attached the soles of a pair of rubber galoshes to his beloved leather boots. The idea worked. He was so pleased with his creation that he decided to offer the modified boots for sale in his dry goods store.

The idea proved to be a sound one, even if the construction of the boot was not. The first batch of boots was too flimsy, and most of them quickly fell apart. Bean was not simply an outdoor enthusiast; he was also a good businessman with an exceedingly lenient return policy. He believed that if a customer was not happy, he or she should be able to return the product — even if it meant the store had to take back more than 90 percent of the new boots.

This high failure rate did not discourage Bean. He worked to improve the new boot until he succeeded. Eventually, he developed new ideas and turned his single store in Maine into a leading distributor of outdoor specialty merchandise: L. L. Bean. Almost one hundred years later, the original

Maine store is still open and successful, although today catalog sales account for much of the company's annual $1.5 billion business.

> *"No sale is really complete until the product is worn out and the customer is satisfied." — L. L. B.*

Sarah Bernhardt

Not Very Talented

Sarah Bernhardt (1844–1923) was a famous stage actress of the late 1800s and one of the premier performers in the silent film industry.

Born in 1844, Sarah Bernhardt was the illegitimate daughter of a Dutch courtesan and an unknown Frenchman. She was educated in a French convent. Bernhardt considered becoming a nun, but a friend convinced her to enroll in drama school instead and even agreed to be her sponsor. Bernhardt soon regretted this decision. The school turned out to be a nightmare. Her teachers constantly criticized her and told her that she was not very talented. Bernhardt survived at the school for two years before dropping out.

Despite her lack of training, Bernhardt landed a contract with the Comédie-Française theatre company, which cast her in a production of *Iphigenia*. However, after three lackluster performances and a fight with another performer, she was fired. With the help of friends, she managed to get a job with another theater company, but her performances continued to be ignored and she began to question if she was meant to be an actress. She decided to leave the theater.

Her departure did not last long and actually may have helped her career. Her renewed determination to succeed on the stage gave new life to her performances. After receiving critical and popular attention for her portrayal of Anna Damby in Alexander Dumas's *Kean,* Bernhardt was even invited to perform for Napoleon Bonaparte. As her fame grew, she found herself in demand throughout Europe and the United States. Bernhardt became one of the most popular actors of the nineteenth century. She later became a pioneer in silent movies, making her debut in a French version of *Hamlet* in 1900. She went on to star in eight more motion pictures and two biographical films. Bernhardt refused to slow down, even after her leg was amputated in 1915. Her final film, *La Voyante*, was in the process of being made when she died in 1923, and a body double had to assume her role.

> *"Life engenders life. Energy creates energy. It is by spending oneself that one becomes rich." — S. B.*

Laura Bridgman

From Hopeless to Inspirational

Laura Bridgman (1829–1889) was the first deafblind American child to receive a formal education.

Laura Bridgman was barely two years old when she and her siblings contracted scarlet fever. Laura was the only one of the four children to survive, but the illness left her deaf and blind and severely reduced her sense of smell and taste. Their daughter's disabilities presented the Bridgmans with a dilemma. In the 1830s, schools for the blind and for the deaf existed, but no school accepted students with both disabilities. The family's only options were to keep Laura at home or to commit her to an asylum, which is where most deafblind people were sent at the time. Her parents consulted doctors, but none gave them any hope.

Having already lost three children, the Bridgmans decided to keep their daughter at home and manage the best they could. Laura proved to be a bright girl and learned both sewing and knitting by mimicking her mother, but she had no way to communicate. In 1837, Samuel Howe told the family that he believed that, with the right instruction, Laura and people with similar disabilities could lead productive lives. To prove this theory, he wanted Laura to be his first student.

With the Bridgmans' approval, Howe took seven-year-old Laura to Perkins School for the Blind in Boston, where he was a teacher. Laura made rapid progress. Before long, she was using tactile sign language and, by the end of the year, she could write intelligently. Bridgman's education grew rapidly as did her fame. Howe recorded his student's progress in a series of reports, which were translated into several languages and served as the inspiration for countless others.

British author Charles Dickens learned of Bridgman's progress and met her when he visited the United States. He was so impressed by her accomplishments that he wrote about her in his travelogue, *American Notes*. Bridgman became a teacher at Perkins School and remained there for the rest of her life. Decades later, a young mother read about her in *American Notes* and contacted Perkins School hoping to find a teacher for her own daughter, Helen Keller, who had also contracted scarlet fever as an infant and was now deafblind. Anne Sullivan, a student at the school, became Keller's teacher. Before Sullivan left for the Keller home, Bridgman taught her how to use manual sign language and gave her a gift for Helen: a doll Bridgman had made herself.

"When we do the best that we can, we never know what miracle is wrought in our life or in the life of another." — Helen Keller

Charlotte Brontë

Criticized for Her Writing and Her Gender

Charlotte Brontë (1816–1855) was an English novelist who wrote *Jane Eyre*.

When Charlotte, Emily, and Anne Brontë decided to publish their collection of poems, they were faced with two problems: lack of a publisher and disregard for women authors. They overcame the first problem by publishing the collection themselves. How to convince people to focus on their writing and not their gender proved to be more difficult. As Charlotte wrote later in the preface to the 1910 edition of *Wuthering Heights*:

> *[W]e did not like to declare ourselves women, because — without at that time suspecting that our mode of writing and thinking was not what is called "feminine" — we had a vague impression that authoresses are liable to be looked on with prejudice; we had noticed how critics sometimes use for their chastisement the weapon of personality, and for their reward, a flattery, which is not true praise.*

To resolve this issue, the three women decided to use the pseudonyms Currer, Ellis, and Acton Bell. However, the name change proved irrelevant because only two copies of the book were sold.

Not dissuaded from their chosen path, the sisters began writing their own novels. Charlotte made the first attempts at getting her novel, *The Professor*, published. Again, she faced rejection after rejection. She tried one final publishing house. Like the other publishers, this one was not interested in *The Professor*. However, editors at the publishing house were interested in the narrative she had told them she was writing. Three weeks later, she submitted the new novel. Called *Jane Eyre*, the novel was published in 1847, sold out within three months, and received critical acclaim from reviewers.

It was only after this success that Charlotte decided to drop the pseudonym and reveal her identity. This led to the unveiling of her two sisters' identities. They had also published novels under their pseudonyms. *Wuthering Heights* by Emily Brontë and *Agnes Grey* by Anne Brontë had also been released in 1847. Tragically, Emily died shortly afterward, in 1848, before writing any other novels. Anne wrote and published one additional novel, *The Tenant of Wildfell Hall*, before dying of pulmonary tuberculosis in 1849. Charlotte wrote two more novels, *Shirley*, published in 1849, and *Villette*, published in 1853. *The Professor* was published posthumously in 1857. The works of all three sisters have become enduring classics of English literature and continue to be read today.

"Life appears to me too short to be spent in nursing animosity, or registering wrongs." — C. B.

Richard E. Byrd

More Successful in the Navy after Retirement

Richard Evelyn Byrd (1888–1957) was a pioneer in aviation and polar exploration.

Richard E. Byrd attended the University of Virginia before financial difficulties led him to switch to the U.S. Naval Academy. Byrd graduated in 1912 and enlisted into the Navy. During his tour of duty, Byrd learned to fly and eventually became a Navy flight instructor. Flying soon became his passion, but he was forced to retire from the Navy after a shipboard accident left him with a permanent limp in 1914.

Byrd continued to serve in the Navy as a retired officer on active duty and eventually became the Navy's liaison officer to Congress. One of his assignments was to help create the Bureau of Aeronautics.

He also arranged one of the first transatlantic flights in 1919, but Navy rules prevented him from participating as part of the crew. Byrd then attempted the first flight over the North Pole, but he failed to present navigational data to support his claims. After returning to the United States, he began focusing on making the first solo transatlantic flight. This dream was shattered after his plane crashed during a test flight. Before Byrd could repair his plane, Charles Lindberg accomplished the transatlantic feat.

Twice thwarted, Byrd switched focus to one of the only places left uncharted by flight: the South Pole. In November 1929, he participated in the first flight to the

South Pole. When he returned to the States, the Navy promoted him to the rank of rear admiral.

> *"Few men during their lifetime come anywhere near exhausting the resources dwelling within them. There are deep wells of strength that are never used." — R. E. B.*

Chester Carlson

Inventor of an Unwanted Machine

Chester Carlson (1906–1968) invented the process of instant copying known as xerography, which launched the Xerox company.

For seven years, Chester Carlson tried to sell his invention, which copied images instantaneously using a process he called electrophotography. His still-primitive invention created poor quality images that were either smudged or printed on paper damaged from the heat involved in the process, but it was a work in progress. Carlson approached IBM twice. The company rejected the invention both times. Eastman Kodak and RCA also turned him away. Carlson tried other companies — more than twenty in all — but each one declined to do business with him. One executive asked him, "Who the hell wants to copy a document on plain paper?"

Finally, a little-known company in upstate New York called Haloid became interested in the machine after reading an article about Carlson's work. On October 22, 1948, ten years after Carlson had made his first copier, the Haloid Company made its first public announcement about the process of electrophotography, which Carlson now called xerography. Two years later, the firm sold the first Haloid Xerox copier. By 1958, the company had produced the Xerox 913 photocopier. Within three years, the first Xerox machine had earned nearly $60 million for the company, which renamed itself the Xerox Corporation in tribute to Carlson's invention. By 1965, revenues from the Xerox machine had surpassed $500 million. Today, the Xerox trademark has become so identified with photocopying that the word *xerox* is often used as a generic term for copiers and for photocopying. Carlson earned more than $150 million from his creation, most of which he donated to a variety of charities before he died. He was inducted into the National Inventors Hall of Fame in 1981.

"You may be disappointed if you fail, but you are doomed if you don't try." — Beverly Sills

Christopher Columbus

Proven Incorrect by Court Advisors

Christopher Columbus (1451–1506) was a European explorer and navigator whose quest for a route to the Far East led to America and eventually to the spread of European colonies in the territory.

According to legend, medieval Europeans believed that the world was flat. In reality, however, most educated Europeans understood that the Earth was a sphere. Still, Columbus was one of the few who believed it would be easier and quicker to travel to China by sailing west. Columbus based this belief on mistaken information that underestimated both Asia's size and the Earth's circumference.

In 1484, Columbus pitched this idea to the king of Portugal, John II. The king deferred the matter to his court advisors, who concluded correctly that Columbus had underestimated of the distance between Lisbon, Portugal, and Japan. Columbus believed that he would have to travel about 2,400 nautical miles between the two points, instead of the actual distance of more than 10,000 nautical miles. Columbus tried to raise money in Genoa and Venice, Italy, without luck. He traveled to England, where King Henry VII said he would consider the idea. When his trip to England failed to produce results, Columbus renewed his request to King John, who again rejected his proposal.

Finally, he approached two Spanish monarchs, Ferdinand II of Aragon and Isabella I of Castile. Their advisors agreed with those in Portugal that Columbus's calculations were incorrect. Although they initially turned Columbus down, Ferdinand and Isabella gave the adventurer an annual annuity and provided him with food and lodging. Columbus persisted and, in 1492, Ferdinand agreed to fund the westward journey.

Although many credit Columbus with "discovering" America, it is more accurate to say he sparked European exploration and colonization of North and South America, with positive results for Europeans and negative results for Native Americans.

"The only way to discover the limits of the possible is to go beyond them into the impossible." — Arthur C. Clark

Marie Curie

No Money, No Laboratory, No Help

Marie Curie (1867–1934) was a pioneer scientist in the field of radioactivity. She received two Nobel Prizes for her work.

Although she received high honors in high school, Marie Skłodowska was barred from entering the University of Warsaw because she was a woman. Instead, she worked as a governess while attending an informal "floating university" and later enrolled at the Sorbonne. She graduated first in her class in the spring of 1893 after earning first place in the master's exam in physics. The following year, she earned a master's degree in mathematics after placing second in that subject's master's exam. While at the Sorbonne, Marie met Pierre Curie, a professor at the school.

After their marriage, Pierre gave up his own research on magnetism and joined Marie's work on radioactivity. Together, they worked to isolate an unknown element present in the ore pitchblende. Times were hard, and the Curies had to work out of a shed that was often too hot in summer and too cold in winter. "We had no money, no laboratory, and no help," Marie Curie later wrote. "In the evening, I was broken with fatigue." Money problems persisted, but the Curies refused to profit or patent their research because they wanted to make it available to other scientists.

Marie later said of this time, "I was taught that the way of progress is neither swift nor easy." After years of hard work, they discovered not one, but two new elements. They discovered the first one, polonium, in July 1898. Six months later, they discovered radium. The scientific community met their discoveries with skepticism until four years later when Marie isolated approximately one-tenth of a gram of pure radium.

In 1903, the Royal Swedish Academy of Sciences awarded Pierre Curie and Marie Curie the Nobel Prize in Physics "in recognition of the extraordinary services they have rendered by their joint researches on the radiation phenomena." Marie Curie was the first woman to be awarded the Nobel Prize. In 1911, she became the first person to win a second one when she received the Nobel Prize in Chemistry for "her services to the advancement of chemistry by the discovery of the elements radium and polonium, by the isolation of radium and the study of the nature and compounds of this remarkable element." She is one of only two people to have been awarded a Nobel Prize in two different fields (Linus Pauling is the other) and the only woman to have won two Nobel Prizes.

"Life is not easy for any of us. But what of that? We must have perseverance and, above all, confidence in ourselves. We must believe that we are gifted for something and that this thing must be attained." — M. C.

Walt Disney

No Good Ideas

Walter Disney (1901–1966), better known as Walt Disney, was an American film producer, director, screenwriter, animator, and entrepreneur. He was the cofounder of Walt Disney Productions, known today as the Walt Disney Company.

The film *Snow White and the Seven Dwarfs* was not Walt Disney's first business venture. In fact, at least three of

Disney's previous businesses had failed and, after one such failure, he was forced to file for bankruptcy. Disney had once been fired by a newspaper editor who told him he "had no good ideas." Somehow, Disney knew that the *Snow White* venture would be different and that this idea was a good one. Not everyone agreed with him, and early in production others warned him that he was going too far. The whole concept of creating such an extravagant family film seemed ludicrous to his critics. For four years, Disney ignored the skeptics and critics as he worked. Costs for the film exceeded $1.5 million and pushed his company to the edge of bankruptcy before he was done.

Snow White and the Seven Dwarfs, the first full-length animated feature presentation, became the most successful motion picture of 1938 and earned an honorary Oscar in 1939, in part because it "pioneered a great new entertainment field." Since its release, the film has earned more than $400 million. Disney holds the record for having received the most Academy Awards, twenty-six, including four honorary awards. He was nominated for sixty-four awards during his lifetime.

After the initial popularity of Mickey Mouse, Disney's first successful creation, Walt's brother and business partner, Roy Disney, wanted to phase out the character, which he believed was outdated. Walt disagreed and made Mickey the central character of Disney's enterprises. On November 18, 1978, Mickey Mouse became the first cartoon character to earn a star on the Hollywood Walk of Fame.

"You may not realize it when it happens, but a kick in the teeth may be the best thing in the world for you." — W. D.

Edwin Drake

Crazy Drake

Edwin Drake (1819–1880) was the first man to drill for oil, a concept that revolutionized the oil industry.

THE TOWNSPEOPLE OF TITUSVILLE, PENNSYLVANIA, were kind to Edwin Drake, although they considered him insane and gave him the nickname "Crazy Drake." Drake had the preposterous idea that he could get oil by drilling into the ground. That idea worked for extracting salt, but no one except Drake believed it would work for oil.

For more than a year, Drake struggled in pursuit of his "crazy" idea. He began by purchasing a steam engine and building an engine house. These efforts took longer than a year to accomplish and, by April 1859, Drake had spent all the money Seneca Oil Company had given him with nothing to show for it. Everyone in the company agreed that it was a pointless venture and refused to invest any more money — everyone, that is, except one director, James Townsend.

Townsend could not convince the company to invest more money, but he sent Drake $500 from his own pocket. In Pennsylvania, Drake struggled and finally succeeded in finding a crew to work on the project. Work continued six days a week through the long hot summer. Finally, on August 28, 1859, the crew struck oil. Drake's success launched the first oil rush, and real estate prices in Pennsylvania skyrocketed. Within ten years, petroleum production in the United States went from a mere two thousand barrels in 1859 to more than four million barrels in 1869. Drake never made any money from his discovery, but he is still called the "father of oil drilling."

> *"The thing always happens that you really believe in; and the belief in a thing makes it happen."* — Frank Lloyd Wright

Richard Paul Evans

Rejected from All Angles

Richard Paul Evans (1962–) is the *New York Times* best-selling author of *The Christmas Box.*

Richard Paul Evans was working as an advertising executive in 1993 when he wrote *The Christmas Box* as a gift for his family and friends. Evans printed about twenty copies of the book himself. People loved the book so much they began sharing it with their friends. Before long, readers began asking local bookstores for copies of the book. One bookstore reportedly had orders for ten copies before Evans even thought about publishing the book.

With the demand for his book growing, Evans sent it to several major publishers. They all rejected it with comments that told him the book was "uncategorizable," "too short," or "too long." Evans tried local publishers, who also rejected it. Even so, Evans had a gut feeling that readers would buy the book and decided to publish it himself. He printed three thousand copies and began distributing them. Once those had sold out, he printed a few thousand more, then a few thousand more, and then a few thousand more.

Before long, his book had made history as the only self-published novel to hit the top spot on the *New York Times* best-seller list. Publishers now knocked on his door, with a dozen participating in an auction for the hardcover rights to the book. Evans had sold 700,000 copies by the time Simon & Schuster bought the rights for a $4.2 million advance and a contract for a follow-up book. Since then, he has written ten additional books, all of which have appeared on the *New York Times* best-seller list.

> *"If we believe that we can't do something, we can't. If we think we will fail, most likely we will." — R. P. E.*

Alexander Fleming

Penicillin Not Worth Pursuing

Sir Alexander Fleming (1881–1955) was a biologist and pharmacologist who earned a Nobel Prize for his work on the development of penicillin.

ALEXANDER FLEMING WORKED FOR TWENTY years before he discovered, by accident, a substance that would kill bacteria. Fleming was trying to duplicate the work of another scientist for an article he was writing when he picked up a dish of staphylococcus and noticed it was contaminated with a mold that had killed the bacteria. For the next eight months, he analyzed the contents and then cultivated it. He discovered that the mold, *Penicillium*, was difficult to grow and extracts from it were unstable and tainted with foreign proteins.

Fleming presented a report on his findings at a scientific meeting in May 1929. He hoped that he could pique the interest of the other bacteriologists there, who would then help him find solutions to the problems he encountered with the mold. Unfortunately, the timing of Fleming's presentation coincided with the release of new sulfa drugs, which seemed to be effective at killing infections and which captured the attention of his fellow scientists.

Fleming had no alternative but to move on to other research. Luckily, he did not give up completely on his drug, which he called penicillin, and kept a strain of the mold growing in the corner of his laboratory. Ten years later, it became apparent that sulfa drugs were not as effective as originally believed and that they could have bad side effects. At that point, the scientific community renewed its search for an antibiotic drug.

Scientist Howard W. Florey came across an old report on penicillin and paid a visit to Fleming, who gave him a sample of the *Penicillium* mold in his laboratory. Florey, with the help of another scientist, Ernst Chain, isolated penicillin and concentrated it. By 1945, production of penicillin had become a reality. Fleming, Florey, and Chain were jointly awarded the Nobel Prize for Medicine in 1945 for their work. More than sixty years later, penicillin is still the most widely used antibiotic.

"One sometimes finds what one is not looking for." — A. F.

Betty Friedan

The Neurotic Housewife

Betty Friedan (1921–2006) was an activist and writer whose book, *The Feminine Mystique*, is credited with starting the "second wave" of feminism.

Hoping to combine career and family, Betty Friedan was working for the union newspaper *UE News* when she became pregnant. Although the company granted her maternity leave for the first baby, they denied it when Friedan became pregnant a second time, and she was fired. She filed a complaint, but in 1949, she could not find support for her plight. Friedan had little choice but to embrace her role as a stay-at-home mom. While she loved being a mother, she found she was not content. In her search to find the source of her unhappiness, she started talking to college classmates who were in similar roles and discovered that they felt the same way.

Friedan wrote about her findings in an article, but no magazine — not even women's magazines such as *McCall's*, *Redbook*, and *The Ladies Home Journal* — would publish it. Some editors suggested that she revise the article, but they still rejected it even after she made changes and resubmitted it. Others dismissed Friedan as a "neurotic housewife." Instead of giving up, Friedan used the rejections to expand the article into a book. It became *The Feminine Mystique*, a book that helped launch the modern woman's movement. It also led Friedan to become cofounder of the National Organization for Women (NOW) to help combat discrimination against women.

> *"A girl should not expect special privileges because of her sex, but neither should she adjust to prejudice and discrimination." — B. F.*

Mahatma Gandhi

A Mediocre, Stupid Student

Mahatma Gandhi (1869–1948) was a political activist and spiritual leader of India and the Indian independence movement. His promotion of civil disobedience helped India gain independence and served as an inspiration to millions around the world.

If greatness were measured by report cards or school performance, then Mohandas Karamchand Gandhi would never have been more than "mediocre," the term he used to describe his academic record. When Gandhi misspelled the word "kettle," his teacher called him stupid because he was the only student to miss that word. Throughout his school career, Gandhi never achieved a rating much higher than "mediocre." When it came time to go to college, he barely passed the matriculation exam for Samaldas College at Bhavnagar, Gujarat.

Greatness, however, cannot be measured by something as mundane as a spelling test or a report card. After graduating from law school, Gandhi began fighting for civil rights in South Africa before moving back to his native homeland of India. There, he fought to free India from British control — not with his fists but with civil disobedience.

At first, those in power dismissed Gandhi's efforts. Winston Churchill dismissed him as a "seditious Middle Temple lawyer, now posing as a fakir." Men with guns failed to understand a man who said, "There are many causes that I am prepared to die for but no causes that I am prepared to kill for." His opponents learned, however, that

Gandhi did not need to use violence; he had courage and spirit that could not be crushed. Although he was imprisoned many times during his life, he refused to give up. Gandhi's efforts eventually helped bring independence to India.

This mediocre student rose to be labeled by another term: *mahatma*, which means "great soul." For all of his life, Gandhi used nonviolent means to help those oppressed. His example and teachings have inspired civil rights leaders and freedom movements in the United States, South Africa, and across the world. Although Gandhi was nominated for the Nobel Peace Prize in 1937, 1938, 1939, and 1947, he was never given the award. In 1948, Gandhi was considered for the prize a fifth and final time. However, he was assassinated two days before the nominations closed. The Nobel Committee considered awarding him the prize posthumously that year, but the prize had always been awarded to a living person. Instead, the committee decided to make no award in 1948, because "there was no suitable living candidate."

"Live as if you were to die tomorrow. Learn as if you were to live forever." — M. G.

Thor Heyerdahl

A Crazy Scandinavian

Thor Heyerdahl (1914–2002) was a Norwegian ethnographer and adventurer most famous for his expedition on the *Kon-Tiki*, a raft on which he sailed 4,300 miles.

Thor Heyerdahl had a theory. He spent years searching for evidence to prove his theory, but found that nothing could convince his colleagues. Instead, the scientific community ridiculed his ideas and refused to take him seriously. Heyerdahl believed that some of the earliest inhabitants of the Polynesian islands had come from Peru, not Asia as most experts thought. No one believed that anyone could travel across the Pacific Ocean safely on the balsa wood rafts used in South America at that time. He set out to prove his theory.

Heyerdahl decided that the only way to convince people that he was right was to make his own voyage across the Pacific in the same type of boat the Peruvian Indians had used. In 1947, he set out with five other Scandinavians on a forty-five-foot-long raft. The trip took 101 days and proved that Heyerdahl's theory was technically possible.

When the trip was over, Heyerdahl wrote about his experiences. He soon discovered, however, that publishers were not interested in his journey. Who would want to read about a "bunch of crazy Scandinavians floating around the ocean on a raft?" one publisher asked. William Styron, editor of McGraw-Hill, rejected the book, noting that "a long, solemn, tedious Pacific voyage [was] best suited, I would think, to some kind of drastic abridgment in a journal like the *National Geographic*."

Used to rejection and scorn, Heyerdahl kept trying. Eventually he found a publisher willing to take a chance on the book. *The Kon-Tiki Expedition* stayed on the *New York Times* best-seller list for more than a year. It has been translated into nearly seventy languages and has sold fifty million copies worldwide. Heyerdahl also made a documentary about his voyage, which won an Academy Award in 1951 for Best Documentary. Heyerdahl later said that the film won the Oscar because "it was so badly shot they knew it couldn't have been faked."

"In my experience, it is rarer to find a really happy person in a circle of millionaires than among vagabonds." — T. H.

Janis Joplin

Laughed Out of Class and Out of Town

Janis Joplin (1943–1970) was a singer and songwriter. Her hits include "Piece of My Heart," "Me and Bobby McGee," and "Mercedes Benz."

Janis Joplin left the University of Texas at Austin in 1963 after being voted "the ugliest man on campus." According to her, she had already been "laughed out of class, out of town, and out of the state" by her high school classmates. After traveling around and singing in a few out-of-the-way places, she contemplated leaving it all behind, settling down, and getting married. Then she met Chet Helms, who thought she would make a good lead for a new rock group, Big Brother and the Holding Company. The group signed with Mainstream Records, which released an album after Joplin won over the audience singing the song "Love is Like a Ball and Chain" at the Monterey International Pop Festival.

Joplin's distinct vocal style, flamboyant dress, outspoken nature, and liberated views smashed through the stereotypes for female performers. She helped pioneer a new style for women in the world of rock while at the same time becoming an internationally famous singer. Long after her death, her influence is still felt in the industry. *The Rose*, a movie based loosely on Joplin's life, was released in 1979 and earned Bette Midler (in her screen debut) an Academy Award nomination. In 1988, Joplin's hometown unveiled the Janis Joplin Memorial, an original bronze, multi-image sculpture of Joplin by Douglas Clark. In 1995, Joplin was inducted into the Rock and Roll Hall of Fame. Janis's sister, Laura Joplin, published the best-selling biography *Love, Janis* in 1992. It was later transformed into a musical of the same name in the late 1990s. The musical has packed houses and been held over several times since it opened.

"I think you can destroy your now worrying about tomorrow." — J. J.

Rush Limbaugh

Fired from All but Two Jobs

Rush Limbaugh III (1951–), an American conservative talk show host and political commentator, is the host of *The Rush Limbaugh Show.*

Rush Limbaugh's career in radio began in 1967 when he was a teenager in his hometown of Cape Girardeau, Missouri. After high school, Limbaugh attended Southeast Missouri State University, where he flunked Speech 101 before dropping out to work at a radio station. He did not last long. For the next few years, he bounced from station to station. Tom Leathers, publisher of *The Squires*, knew Limbaugh at the time and recalls, "[Limbaugh] was nothing special. He did not have that dominating personality you hear now. He was painfully shy." Finally, under pressure from his father, who wanted him to quit radio, Limbaugh took a job as a public relations assistant for the Kansas City Royals.

After five years, Limbaugh left the job because he still wanted to work in radio. He soon landed a position at a Kansas City station as a talk show host and commentator. Ten months later, he was fired. In fact, he once admitted that he has been fired from all but two of the jobs he ever held. A year went by before a San Diego radio station agreed to give him a chance, mainly because it was desperate and in dire financial trouble. The job was exactly the chance he needed. Soon Limbaugh's three-hour morning show became the most popular program in the city and spread to radio stations across the United States.

In 2001, Limbaugh faced a new crisis that threatened to take him off the air — deafness. Limbaugh went completely deaf in his left ear and had substantial hearing loss in his right. At first, he attempted to modify the way he did his program to cover up his disability. Eventually, he confessed his problem to listeners and underwent cochlear implant surgery, which restored some hearing in his left ear. As of 2008, Limbaugh's radio show was still being broadcast on almost six hundred AM radio stations in the United States and on audio streams over the Internet. Limbaugh's popularity is often credited with reviving AM radio. His show has also helped numerous Republican political candidates.

> *"Being stuck is a position few of us like. We want something new but cannot let go of the old: old ideas, beliefs, habits, even thoughts. We are out of contact with our own genius. Sometimes we know we are stuck; sometimes we don't. In both cases, we have to do something."* — R. L.

Joseph Lister

Ridiculed for His Theories

Joseph Lister (1827–1912) was an English surgeon who pioneered the concept of sterile surgeries and carbolic acid to sterilize surgical instruments and to clean wounds.

Being a surgeon in the mid-1800s was not a pleasant task. No matter how skilled a doctor might be, only about 20 percent of patients usually survived. Many developed fatal infections shortly after surgery. Joseph Lister was determined to reduce infections in his patients. After studying the ideas of Louis Pasteur and doing his own experiments, Lister developed methods to destroy the microorganisms he believed caused infections. Among the radical ideas he implemented were sterilization of surgical instruments, the use of carbolic acid to kill germs, and washing the hands before surgery.

It did not take long for Lister's ideas to make a difference. Fewer of his patients developed infections. Yet, other doctors were slow to accept his suggestions. Some doctors were unwilling to spend the time and the money required, others did not believe in germs, and some carried out Lister's procedures incorrectly and, as a result, could not duplicate his success. When Lister published his findings in 1867, doctors still ridiculed his ideas. By 1870, his ideas were gradually being accepted in Germany, and his clinics were soon crowded with students eager to learn about his procedures. In his home country of Great Britain and in the United States, however, doctors still had not adopted his life-saving methods. It was not until 1877, after Lister was appointed professor of surgery at King's College Hospital in London, that he was able to convince English doctors to try his procedures. Finally in 1881, Lister was recognized for his achievements at the International Congress held in London, where his work was hailed as "the greatest advance that surgery had ever made." Today, Lister is often considered "the father of modern antisepsis."

"Next to the promulgation of a new truth, the best thing, I conceive, that a man can do, is the recantation of published error." — J. L.

Nelson Mandela

From Prisoner to President

Rolihlahla "Nelson" Mandela (1918–) is the former president of South Africa and the first South African president to be elected in a fully representative democratic election. He was also an anti-apartheid activist and leader of the African National Congress.

As THE SON OF A tribal chief and a descendant of the royal family of the Xhosa people, Rolihlahla Mandela was destined for good things, although his life took some unanticipated twists and turns. But perhaps his first name — which means "making trouble for yourself, bringing things upon yourself or taking things on" in Xhosa — accurately predicted the course his life would follow. True, Mandela did not go by the name Rolihlahla for long, choosing instead to adopt the nickname Nelson, which he had been given by a teacher who had difficulty pronouncing his real name.

Mandela, the first member of his family to go to school, eventually graduated with a law degree. He could have lived a prosperous life, but he chose instead to join the African National Congress (ANC), an organization eventually banned by the government for actively engaging in protests against the ruling National Party's apartheid policies. Arrested in 1962 for incitement and illegally leaving South Africa, he was sentenced to five years hard labor. While in jail, he was brought to trial along with other members of the ANC and charged with treason. On June 12, 1964, at the age of forty-five , Mandela was sentenced to life and sent to Robben Island Prison. Conditions were harsh for all prisoners at Robben Island, but black political prisoners like Mandela endured the worst treatment. They were given the least food and the fewest privileges. Mandela was forced to do hard labor and allowed only one letter — usually made unreadable by the prison censors — and one visitor every six months.

Instead of fading into obscurity in prison, Mandela developed a worldwide reputation. Not only did he serve as a natural leader and teacher to the other prisoners, he also became an international symbol of resistance against apartheid in South Africa. The National Party government tried to negotiate Mandela's release, but Mandela rejected offers for a conditional release. He released a statement through his daughter explaining his position, "What freedom am I being offered while the organization of the people remains banned? Only free men can negotiate. A prisoner cannot enter into contracts."

In 1985, Mandela began secretly meeting with the National Party government. The meetings continued for the next four years with little progress. Finally in 1988, after the ANC conducted a bombing campaign, Mandela again opened discussions with President Pieter Willem Botha from his prison cell in the hopes of averting a civil war. Shortly after negotiations began, Botha suffered a stroke and was replaced by Frederik Willem de Klerk. A year later, de Klerk rescinded the ban against the ANC and all other antiapartheid organizations and ordered Mandela's release. A week later, on February 11, 1990, after twenty-seven years in prison, Mandela was finally freed, but his fight was not over. Mandela worked with de Klerk for four years to establish a representative government in South Africa and to end apartheid. In April 1994, South Africa held its first democratic elections. The ANC won the majority, and Mandela was inaugurated as the nation's first black state president. De Klerk, still a member of the National Party, became Mandela's deputy president.

Through the years, Mandela has received more than one hundred awards for his actions. Among the more notable awards are the Nobel Peace Prize in 1993 (which he shared with de Klerk), the Order of Merit and the Order of St. John from England's Queen Elizabeth II, the U.S. Presidential Medal of Freedom, and Amnesty International's Ambassador of Conscience Award.

"The greatest glory in living lies not in never falling, but in rising every time we fall." — N. M.

Kyle Maynard

Lost His First Thirty Wrestling Matches

Kyle Maynard (1986–) won the 2004 ESPN Espy Award for Best Athlete with a Disability and is the author of *No Excuses: The True Story of a Congenital Amputee Who Became a Champion in Wrestling and in Life.*

Kyle Maynard's family refused to treat him differently even though he had a severe disability, and they would not allow anyone else to treat him differently either. He played football as a nose tackle in elementary school before turning to wrestling as a high school student. His high school coach and his father helped him develop his wrestling technique. He lost his first thirty-five matches — the same number of matches that he would eventually win on the varsity wrestling team his senior year of high school. He was twelfth in his 103-pound class at the National High School Wrestling Championships.

While these feats may seem ordinary for most young boys, for Maynard they were extraordinary. Maynard was born with a rare birth disorder called congenital amputation, leaving him with shortened limbs, deformed feet, and no hands, knees, or elbows. Throughout his life he has had to deal with strange looks from people who assume that his disability limits him more than he will allow it to.

"I really feel like I'm average," Maynard said in a *USA Today* interview, "but people seem to think otherwise." However, Maynard rarely gives a thought to what other people think, instead choosing to behave like everyone else. After high school, Maynard attended college, where he continued to wrestle. He is the author of a memoir, *No Excuses: The True Story of a Congenital Amputee Who Became a Champion in Wrestling and in Life*.

"It's not what I can do: it's what I will do." — K. M.

Gregor Johann Mendel

Unqualified to Teach Physics at the Lower Schools

Gregor Johann Mendel (1822–1884) was a priest and scientist, and is known today as the "father of modern genetics" for his detailed reports on the inheritance traits of pea plants.

Gregor Johann Mendel's plan to become a teacher came to a halt when he failed to pass the tests required to obtain a teaching certificate after several tries. The final report of the Examiners' Board of the University of Vienna noted that Mendel "lacks insight, and his knowledge is without the requisite clarity." The examiners declared him "unqualified to teach physics at the lower schools." Without a certificate, Mendel could teach only as a substitute. Although he eventually entered a monastery and became an ordained priest, Mendel never stopped experimenting in his garden and observing the plants there.

He continued to work as an amateur scientist and pored over most of the scientific literature available at the time. He also became interested in determining how plants in his garden obtained unusual characteristics. In an effort to satisfy his curiosity, he began conducting his own experiments. Between 1856 and 1863, Mendel cultivated and tested nearly thirty thousand pea plants. He publicized the results of his tests in a paper, "Experiments on Plant Hybridization," which the scientific community ignored and criticized during Mendel's lifetime. Mendel's work remained unrecognized until the turn of the twentieth century, when it was rediscovered. It served as the foundation for modern genetics and earned Mendel the honorary title of "father of modern genetics."

> *"Character consists of what you do on the third and fourth tries."*
> — James A. Michener

Carlos Montoya

Shunned by Flamenco Aficionados

Carlos Montoya (1903–1993), a prominent flamenco guitarist, became an international sensation and influenced a number of today's major guitarists.

Carlos Montoya's mother began teaching him guitar when he was only eight. An amateur guitar player herself, she asked her brother, a professional flamenco guitarist, to give him lessons, but he was too busy teaching his own son. Instead, she hired a local barber to teach Carlos and introduced him to other flamenco guitar players. Montoya developed his skill on the guitar by studying other players, and learning chords, keys, and rhythms from them. He created his own style, which other flamenco players — including Montoya's uncle — criticized as being "less brilliant" than their own style. "I play the way I do," Montoya once said, "because to me, that is exactly the way the flamenco guitar should sound. It seems strange to me that the unknowing public should agree, while the real flamenco aficionados clearly do not . . . but that's the case."

By the time he was fourteen, Montoya was playing in concert halls across the world. As *Billboard* magazine reported, "Montoya was a performer whose passionate style and improvisational skills earned him enormous public acclaim and provided a model for other flamenco guitarists." During his career, Montoya recorded more than forty albums. Other legendary guitar players such as Carlos Santana, Eddie Van Halen, Steve Howe, and Robbie Krieger praised him as a source of inspiration. Montoya also composed flamenco music for orchestras, even though he had no formal training and never learned to read music.

"Learning music by reading about it is like making love by mail."
— Luciano Pavarotti

Samuel Morse

A Man with Ridiculous Ideas

Samuel Morse (1791–1872) created the single-wire telegraph system and Morse Code (with Alfred Vail).

Samuel Morse was a struggling portrait artist in 1832 when, by chance, he overheard a conversation about an experiment in electromagnetism. Intrigued by the concept, he adapted it to send messages over a wire using electricity. For the next five years, he worked to perfect his invention until, in 1837, he applied for a patent for his Electromagnetic Telegraph in the United States and England. The patent was rejected in England because a similar device had already been introduced there, but he was awarded a U.S. patent in 1840. Morse also invented a method of conveying messages in which dots and dashes represented letters and numbers, better known as Morse code.

In 1842, Morse demonstrated his device in front of several members of Congress in a failed effort to win funding to build a telegraph line. Oliver Hampton Smith, a U.S. senator from Indiana, later recalled that his fellow legislators were not impressed by Morse's presentation: "I was assured by other Senators after we left the room that they had no confidence in it." After unsuccessfully trying to find other funding, Morse approached Congress again in 1843. Although many still considered his ideas ridiculous, on the last night of the Congressional session he was granted $30,000 to lay a telegraph line from Washington to Baltimore.

On May 24, 1844, he tapped out the first message, "What has God wrought?" Finally able to prove that his invention worked, Morse offered to sell his rights to the telegraph to the U.S. government for $100,000. When his offer was rejected, Morse formed the Magnetic Telegraph Company with several partners. In the first three months, the firm earned less than $200, while expenses exceeded $1,800. Morse refused to quit and eventually began profiting from his invention as others scrambled to create their own telegraph companies. By 1861, a transcontinental telegraph system was established in the United States. Five years later, the first successful transatlantic telegraph cable was developed. The telegraph allowed newspapers to cover significant world events quickly, revolutionized business, and for the first time created a global community.

"The only gleam of hope, and I cannot underrate it, is from confidence in God. When I look upward it calms any apprehension for the future, and I seem to hear a voice saying: 'If I clothe the lilies of the field, shall I not also clothe you?' Here is my strong confidence, and I will wait patiently for the direction of Providence." — S. M.

Isaac Newton

An Unpromising Student

Isaac Newton (1643–1727) was a physicist, mathematician, astronomer, natural philosopher, and alchemist known for his descriptions of gravity and the laws of motion.

Born prematurely, Isaac Newton had not been expected to survive. He did, but he encountered many other obstacles during his life. His father died before he was born. His mother eventually remarried, but Newton and his stepfather developed an instant dislike for each other. Newton was sent to live with his grandmother until he was eleven. He went to school, but officials there reported that he was an "unpromising student." His poor academic performance prompted his mother to bring him home to work on the family farm. Newton proved to be worse as a farmer than he had been as a student.

Thankfully, his uncle recognized potential in Newton and encouraged him to go to college. While there, Newton often pursued his own interests rather than complete his schoolwork. He also failed a scholarship exam because he did not understand geometry.

Although he wanted to earn a master's degree, an outbreak of the bubonic plague forced him to return to the farm. It was here that Newton watched an apple drop and wondered what had caused it to fall. This led him to pursue his groundbreaking work on gravity and motion. He also contributed to the study of light, developed a form of calculus, and built the first reflecting telescope. Newton was a physicist, mathematician, astronomer, alchemist, philosopher, and inventor. Today, he is often listed among the most intelligent people in history.

"An essential aspect of creativity is not being afraid to fail." — I. N.

Anne Nichols

Wrote the Season's Worst Play

Anne Nichols (1891–1966) was an American playwright and director. Her most famous work is *Abie's Irish Rose.*

Anne Nichols had already written several successful plays and a number of vaudeville sketches when *Abie's Irish Rose* opened in San Francisco and Los Angeles. Nichols had written the play in only three hours, but it was enormously popular among audiences. Yet, every producer she approached about bringing the play to the East Coast turned her down. The concept for her play seemed too implausible: a romance between an Irish girl and a Jewish boy. Finally, Nichols decided to stage the play herself (even if she had to mortgage her house to do it) and serve as its director, an unheard-of occupation for a woman in the 1920s.

Abie's Irish Rose opened at the Fulton Theater in the heart of the Broadway theater district in New York. Some of the most powerful Broadway critics tore it to shreds, calling it "corny," "insulting," "a synthetic farce," and even "the season's worst" play. This last comment was said by Robert Benchley, who continued criticizing the play week after week. However, the public was too busy attending *Abie's Irish Rose* to take notice of the bad reviews. The play ran uninterrupted for five years — 2,327 performances — and became the smash hit of Broadway in 1922. It was revived several times, turned into a weekly radio show, and even made into two movies. The play made Nichols a millionaire.

> *"Failure? I never encountered it. All I ever met were temporary setbacks."*
> — Dottie Walters

Louis Pasteur

His Theories Were Considered Ridiculous Fiction

Louis Pasteur (1822–1895) was a chemist regarded as one of the founders of microbiology. Pasteur introduced pasteurization and created the first vaccine for rabies.

Louis Pasteur earned only a "mediocre" rating in his chemistry class at Royal College. After graduation, he worked for a brief time as a professor of physics at Dijon Lycée. His doctoral thesis on crystallography earned him a position as a chemistry professor at the College of Strasbourg.

In his role as a chemistry professor, Pasteur began studying the fermentation process and the growth of microorganisms. At the time, many scientists believed that microorganisms grew in nutrient broths through spontaneous generation. Pasteur examined the "germ theory," an idea that had been suggested by earlier scientists but still remained unproven. Other scientists mocked Pasteur's ideas. Pierre Pachet, a professor of physiology at Toulouse, wrote that Pasteur's "theory of germs is a ridiculous fiction. How do you think that these germs in the air can be numerous enough to develop into all these organic infusions? If that were true, they would be numerous enough to form a thick fog, as dense as iron."

Pasteur ignored his critics and continued his experiments. Through his research, he demonstrated that microorganisms did not grow spontaneously as others had theorized but instead fermented, contaminating the substances around them. He invented a process, now known as pasteurization, to kill most bacteria and molds in milk and other liquids by heating them. His experiments helped another scientist, Joseph Lister, to develop groundbreaking antiseptic methods that revolutionized surgery. Pasteur also developed an effective immunization that helped eradicate typhus and polio, and he created one of the first vaccines for rabies. Today, he is often considered the "father of microbiology."

"In the fields of observation, chance favors the prepared mind." — L. P.

Pablo Picasso

A Madman at Work

Pablo Picasso (1881–1973) was a Spanish painter, sculptor, and one of the co-founders of cubism.

When Pablo Picasso was ten, his father yanked him out of school because he was barely able to read or write. A tutor hired to teach the boy quit soon after because he believed that Picasso refused to learn. Picasso did not want to study academics; he wanted to paint. He eventually went to Madrid to study at the Academia de San Fernando, but he left after less than a year and moved to Paris, where he tried to earn a living as a painter. During this time, he was so poor that he often burned his paintings to stay warm. Ironically, paintings from this period — referred to as Picasso's blue period — are now among his most popular works.

Around 1907, Picasso began developing an innovative new style of painting. Others in the art world were not impressed. Ambroise Vollard, a French art dealer, told him, "It's the work of a madman." Painter and sculptor Georges Braque remarked, "To paint in such a way was as bad as drinking petrol in the hopes of spitting fire."

Picasso, unaffected by these comments, kept on painting. Braque eventually changed his mind about Picasso's work, and together they cofounded cubism, an important and influential art movement. Although Piscasso's work became popular while he was alive, he still had most of his paintings in his possession when he died because he sold paintings only when he needed money. Picasso produced approximately 13,500 paintings. Today, several of his works are among the highest-selling pieces of art: Picasso's painting *Garçon à la pipe* became the sixth most expensive painting in the world when it sold for more than $104 million in 2004. Another seven of Picasso's paintings have also ranked in the top twenty-five most expensive.

"La inspiración existe, pero tiene que encontrarte trabajando."
Translation: *Inspiration exists, but it has to find you working. — P. P.*

Mary Pickford

Predicted to Fade into Obscurity

Mary Pickford (1892–1979) was an Oscar-winning film star and a cofounder of United Artists in 1919.

Director and playwright William C. de Mille tried to dissuade Mary Pickford from leaving Broadway to pursue a career in motion pictures. In 1909, when movies were still relatively new, de Mille believed the young actress would have a more promising future on the well-established Broadway stage than she would in films. When Pickford did not listen, de Mille wrote a friend saying, "I suppose we'll have to say goodbye to little Mary Pickford. She'll never be heard of again and I feel terribly sorry for her."

However, Pickford did not fade into obscurity as de Mille predicted. She became a pioneer in early Hollywood and gained international fame through her acting roles. Between 1909 and 1927, Pickford starred in 142 one-reel and 48 feature-length silent movies. She had an enormous influence in the development of film acting, cofounded United Artists, and became only the second woman to win the Academy Award for Best Actress. In 1999, Pickford was chosen as one of the American Film Institute's "50 Greatest American Screen Legends." Ironically, a few years after advising Pickford not to leave Broadway, de Mille followed her lead and went to Hollywood, where he became a successful screenwriter and director.

"If you have made mistakes, even serious ones, there is always another chance for you. What we call failure is not the falling down but the staying down." — M. P.

Robert Pinsky

A Bum in the Bowery

Robert Pinsky (1940–) is an American poet, essayist, and literary critic. He has published nineteen books and served as Poet Laureate of the United States from 1997–2000.

Cs and Ds were the best grades Robert Pinsky received in high school. It was not that he had a problem reading; he simply had a problem reading the work assigned to him. His high school teachers told him that he was "going to end up a bum in the Bowery." Determined to prove them wrong, he went to college, earned a B.A. at Rutgers University and an M.A. and a Ph.D. from Stanford University. Over the years, Pinsky's works have received numerous rejections from publishers and publications, but he did not quit writing and he did not turn into a bum.

Pinsky has published almost twenty books, most collections of his poetry. One was nominated for the Pulitzer Prize in Poetry and won the Ambassador Book Award in Poetry of the English Speaking Union and the Lenore Marshall Poetry Prize. Pinsky was named Poet Laureate of the United States, a position he filled from 1997 to 2000.

"Failure is instructive. The person who really thinks learns quite as much from his failures as from his successes." — John Dewey

Elvis Presley

Fired After One Performance

Often referred to as the "King of Rock and Roll," Elvis Presley (1935–1977) remains a music icon more than thirty years after his death.

A rusted 1935 Plymouth carried Elvis Presley and his parents out of Mississippi to a better life — which for them meant public housing in Memphis, Tennessee. Life did not improve for thirteen-year-old Elvis, however, who was immediately pegged as being different from the other teens in his neighborhood. Instead of sporting the crew cut favored by other boys, Elvis slicked back his dark blonde hair, which smelled faintly of roses from the rose oil that he used. He wore bright colors instead of the more subdued tones other students preferred. Even the way he spoke set him apart. He talked with a thicker southern accent than his classmates and had a slight stutter. He also suffered from a bad case of acne. Not surprisingly, young Elvis avoided social situations.

One of Elvis's few pleasures was music, an interest that his mother encouraged by buying him a guitar. While he had sung for his Mississippi classmates, most of his Tennessee classmates were unaware of his musical abilities until he performed for the student talent show his senior year. He made his first demo album the summer after graduation, but instead of submitting it to record labels, he gave it to his mother. After Presley performed at an audition, singer Eddie Bond, shook his head and told the eighteen-year-old, "You're never going to make it as a singer."

His confidence shaken, Presley took a job at Crown Electric Company while taking classes at night to become an electrician. A couple of months later, however, he was back in the studio making another demo record. This time, the owner of the studio, Sam Phillips, heard him perform. Six months later Phillips called Presley and asked him to perform the song "Without You." Although Phillips was impressed with Presley, he did not like the way he performed the song. At Phillips's suggestion, Presley recorded two other songs, "That's All Right" and "Blue Moon of Kentucky." These two singles helped him land performances at local clubs. Although he was not earning enough to quit his day job, it was a start. The future looked bright when Presley landed a four-week engagement in Las Vegas, but the tour was cut in half because of poor ticket sales. Frustration turned to hope when Presley landed a potentially career-launching gig on the Grand Ole Opry. He was fired after only one performance, and the manager told him, "You ain't goin' nowhere, son. You ought to go back to drivin' a truck."

Perhaps the disappointment led him to release "Heartbreak Hotel" the following year. The song topped the R&B, pop, and country music charts and launched Presley's career. He has more than one hundred Top 40 hits to his credit and ninety-seven gold albums, fifty-five of which went platinum, and twenty-five multiplatinum. More than twenty-five years after his death, Presley remains the best-selling solo artist in popular music history.

"Truth is like the sun. You can shut it out for a time, but it ain't goin' away." — E. P.

Orville Redenbacher

A Laughing-Stock Salesman

Orville Redenbacher (1907–1995) is an American businessman and the creator and founder of the popcorn brand that bears his name.

Orville Redenbacher graduated from Purdue University in 1928 with a degree in agronomy. Even then he knew exactly what he wanted to do — create the perfect brand of popcorn. For more than forty years, he hand-pollinated thousands of cornstalks a year and created more than thirty thousand hybrids before he finally came up with the perfect popcorn. In 1965, he began selling the popcorn throughout Indiana, operating out of the back of a station wagon. Wherever he went, people made fun of him. They did not believe that anyone would pay three times as much for his "gourmet popcorn."

They changed their minds when they tasted it. 1970, Orville Redenbacher's Gourmet Popping Corn debuted at Marshall Field's department store in Chicago. Sales quickly took off, and soon the popcorn was on grocery store shelves across the country. Redenbacher popcorn soon became the number one selling popcorn in the United States and has remained the most popular brand for almost forty years. Orville Redenbacher appeared in more than one hundred commercials to promote his popcorn, including one created with digital technology in 2007, twelve years after his death.

"Just don't give up trying to do what you really want to do. Where there is love and inspiration, I don't think you can go wrong." — Ella Fitzgerald

Gene Roddenberry

Known as the Guy Who Made an Expensive TV Flop

Eugene "Gene" Roddenberry (1921–1991) is best known as the creator of the *Star Trek* universe.

WHEN GENE RODDENBERRY APPROACHED TELEVISION executives with his concept for a show, they were not impressed. They called his proposed series "a childish concept" about unexciting aliens. They did not even like the name of the show, *Star Trek*. Two pilots later, the executives finally approved Roddenberry's "crazy idea" for television. During its run, *Star Trek* was twice nominated for two Emmy Awards for Best Dramatic Series, but it had terrible ratings. Only its extremely loyal and supportive fans kept it on life-support for three years before it was finally cancelled in 1969. Roddenberry became known as "the guy who made an expensive flop" and found it difficult to get work.

By 1970, Roddenberry was working with MGM Studios on a new movie, *Pretty Maids All in a Row*, a romantic comedy far removed from science fiction. The movie was expected to be one of the biggest blockbusters of 1971, but when it barely broke even, MGM terminated its relationship with Roddenberry. By 1973, Roddenberry had begun working on a new television series, *Genesis II*, for CBS. At the last moment, CBS pulled it from the schedule and replaced it with *Planet of the Apes*. During the next two years, Roddenberry pitched three other sci-fi TV series without success. Roddenberry also served as an executive consultant for an animated version of Star Trek, which was even less successful than its predecessor.

The original show, however, had developed a growing cult following. By 1972, Star Trek fan conventions had begun to spring up, and Roddenberry became a popular lecturer at colleges. A measure of the show's popularity was revealed when, in 1976, the first U.S. space shuttle was named *Enterprise* after the fictional *Star Trek* spaceship. NASA officials invited Roddenberry to attend the space shuttle launch. Around the same time, Paramount executives were lining up new shows for their proposed new network, Paramount Television Service. Executives gave Roddenberry the go-ahead to develop a sequel to Star Trek, based around many of the original cast members. *Star Trek: Phase II* was set to air in 1978; scripts were developed, sets created, and test footage filmed before the network was scrapped. Instead of discarding the series, the pilot script was retooled and used as the basis for a motion picture. Ironically, Roddenberry had proposed a *Star Trek* movie to the network several times, but the idea had been rejected. It was only after the success of *Star Wars* that executives conceded that science fiction could work on the big screen.

Star Trek: The Motion Picture premiered in 1979, grossed more than $80 million, and spawned four sequels. Its success led to five new television series and five additional movies. In addition, fans can choose from myriad *Star Trek* novels, books, comics, video games, trading cards, and other merchandise.

"The way you win in this game is you must be unimaginably stubborn and keep doing it over and over again, hoping that the break comes and the way you get your break is you have to be unimaginably lucky." — G. R.

Margaret Sanger

Repeatedly Arrested for Distributing Obscene Materials

Margaret Sanger (1879–1966) was the founder of the American Birth Control League, which eventually became Planned Parenthood.

SIXTY YEARS BEFORE THE SUPREME Court decided the *Roe* v. *Wade* case that gave women legal access to abortions, fifteen years before Martin Luther King Jr. was born, and six years before women gained the right to vote, Margaret Sanger used civil disobedience in her fight to legalize contraceptives. Growing up in the late 1800s, Sanger watched her own mother's health weakened by eighteen pregnancies, and she resolved to change the laws and guarantee other women did not suffer her mother's fate.

Sanger started by distributing a pamphlet titled *Family Limitation* in the poorest neighborhoods around New York City. The pamphlet provided women with information about contraceptives. Sanger's actions violated the Comstock Law of 1873, which labeled such information as obscene. Sanger was indicted on numerous charges and arrested eight times, but she continued to fight, gradually making birth control available to more people. She also opened the first family planning and birth control clinic in the United States in 1916. Police raided the clinic nine days after it opened, and Sanger was given a thirty-day jail sentence. The outcry over her many arrests helped overturn laws that prevented doctors from discussing and later prescribing birth control. Sanger went on to help found the American Birth Control League, the National Committee on Federal Legislation for Birth Control, and the first World Population Conference in Geneva.

In 1955, the Reverend Martin Luther King Jr. said, "Our sure beginning in the struggle for equality by non-violent direct action may not have been so resolute without the tradition established by Margaret Sanger and people like her."

"Woman must not accept; she must challenge. She must not be awed by that which has been built up around her; she must reverence that woman in her which struggles for expression." — M. S.

Jerry Seinfeld

Too New York, Too Jewish

Jerry Seinfeld (1954–) helped create *Seinfeld*, an Emmy award–winning half-hour comedy show that ran on NBC from 1989 to 1998.

Comedian Jerry Seinfeld's career was doing extremely well in the late 1980s. He performed several times on *The Tonight Show* and *Late Night with David Letterman*, appeared on three episodes of the ABC sitcom *Benson*, and hosted his own HBO special. He was even offered the lead in a sitcom by Rob Reiner's Castle Rock Entertainment production company. He accepted, but ABC vetoed Reiner's casting choices.

Still, the idea of doing a TV show intrigued Seinfeld, and he approached his friend Larry David about developing a show together. David suggested that instead of a tightly structured sitcom, they should do a show based on a more flexible, observational humor — a concept that would later be referred to as "a show about nothing."

Seinfeld agreed and the two developed a script for *The Seinfeld Chronicles*.

The pilot centered on Seinfeld, his neurotic friend George, and his eccentric neighbor Kessler. NBC executives thought the show was funny, but NBC President Brandon Tartikoff said the show was "too New York, too Jewish" to appeal to a mainstream audience. Focus groups hated the characters, thought Seinfeld was a weak leading man, and were confused by the lack of typical sitcom story lines. One viewer commented, "You can't get too excited about two guys going to the laundromat." When NBC aired the pilot as a special in July 1989, ratings were abysmal. The production company offered the show to the Fox network, but it was not interested.

The show might have died there had it not been for NBC executive Rick Ludwin. Ludwin believed in the show and managed to scrape together enough money from his own budget to order four more episodes. The cast now included a regular female character, Elaine, played by Julia Louis-Dreyfus. The new version was called *Seinfeld*, and the name of Seinfeld's neighbor became Kramer. The show premiered in May 1990. This time the ratings improved, though they still were not spectacular. Research showed that the show appealed to young adult males, a favorite target of advertisers. Because of this, NBC decided to stick with the show.

Seinfeld's audience steadily grew during the 1990–1991 season and increased even more after NBC moved the show to the slot directly after the hit series *Cheers*. By 1994, it was the highest rated show in the country.

Seinfeld ran nine seasons before the final episode aired on May 14, 1998. That night, approximately seventy-nine million people — almost half of all television viewers — tuned in to see the show's conclusion. During its run, the show received sixty nominations and more than twenty major awards, including an Emmy, a Golden Globe, and three People's Choice Awards.

> *"The whole object of comedy is to be yourself and the closer you get to that, the funnier you will be."* — *J. S.*

Shel Silverstein

Work Labeled as Too Short and Too Sad

Sheldon "Shel" Silverstein (1930–1999) was an American poet, songwriter, musician, composer, cartoonist, screenwriter, and writer. He is best known for his children's books, which include *The Giving Tree, Where the Sidewalk Ends*, and *A Light in the Attic.*

Shel Silverstein never intended to write children's books. As a young man, he attended the Chicago Academy of Fine Arts before being drafted into the Army. Although he made a terrible soldier, he discovered while in the Army that he was a good cartoonist. After he returned to civilian life in 1956, Silverstein had his Army cartoons published in a book, *Grab Your Socks*. He got work as a cartoonist for *Playboy* magazine, and wrote another two books, both for adults, *Now Here's My Plan*, published in 1960, and *Uncle Shelby's ABZ Book*, published in 1961. That same year, Silverstein published his collection of *Playboy* cartoons in a book titled *Playboy's Teevee Jeebies*.

This was not the resume of a children's book author, yet several of Silverstein's friends urged him to become just that. His first children's book, *Uncle Shelby's Story of Lafcadio, the Lion Who Shot Back*, the story of a lion who learned to handle a gun, was surprisingly well received. Despite this success, he had difficulty finding a publisher for a book he had written four years earlier, *The Giving Tree*, about the friendship that develops between a boy and a tree. Silverstein recalled the response to the book: "Everybody loved it, they were touched by it, they would read it and cry and say it was beautiful, but no one would publish it." William Cole, editor for Simon Schuster, told Silverstein that the book "ain't a kid's book, and it ain't an adult one. I'm sorry but I don't think you're going to find a publisher for it." Other publishers thought it was too short, while still others thought it was too sad. Ursula Nordstrom, an editor at Harper Children's Books, agreed to take a risk on the book and published it. Since then, *The Giving Tree* has become one of Silverstein's best-known titles and has been translated into more than thirty languages. Silverstein also wrote several other children's books, including *The Missing Piece*, *A Light In The Attic*, *Where the Sidewalk Ends*, and *Falling Up.*

> *"I think that if you're a creative person, you should just go about your business, do your work, and not care about how it's received. I never read reviews because if you believe the good ones, you have to believe the bad ones, too. Not that I don't care about success. I do, but only because it lets me do what I want. I was always prepared for success, but that means that I have to be prepared for failure, too." — S. S.*

Robert James Waller

Sequel Rejection

Robert James Waller (1939–) is a writer, photographer, and musician. He has written several best-selling novels including *The Bridges of Madison County* and *Slow Waltz in Cedar Bend.*

Ten years after the release of his first book, *The Bridges of Madison County*, which sold more than 12 million hardcover copies and spent 164 weeks on the *New York Times* best-seller list, Robert James Waller submitted a sequel to it. When his original publisher rejected the new manuscript, Waller took it to a small Texas press, which agreed to print 25,000 copies of the book. The publisher quickly abandoned these plans, however, when news of the upcoming sequel sparked advance orders for more than 400,000 copies. Although the sequel, *Slow Waltz in Cedar Bend,* did not hit the heights of its predecessor, it appeared on the *New York Times* best-seller list and went on to sell almost a million copies in the United States alone.

"Life is never easy for those who dream." — R. J. W.

Sam Walton

Ignored Conventional Wisdom

Sam Walton (1918–1992) founded Wal-Mart and Sam's Club discount stores.

Sam Walton already owned fifteen Ben Franklin hardware stores when he approached the company's executives about starting a new chain of discount stores. The executives rejected the idea. "What I heard more often than anything was: a town of less than 50,000 population cannot support a discount store for very long," Walton wrote in his book, *Sam Walton: Made In America*. He rejected the warning and did what he later advised others to do, "swim upstream" and "ignore the conventional wisdom."

Convinced that his idea would work, he sold his Ben Franklin stores and opened the first Wal-Mart in Rogers, Arkansas, in 1962. It sold a million dollars worth of merchandise in its first year. Within twenty years, Walton had opened more than 750 stores nationwide. Walton, who had to borrow money to open his initial Ben Franklin stores, was listed in 1985 by *Forbes* magazine as the "richest man in America." He received the Presidential Medal of Freedom in 1992 for his "pioneering efforts in retail" and was included in *Time* magazine's list of "100 most influential people of the 20th century" in 1998. As of 2007, there were more than 1,000 Wal-Mart discount stores and 2,300 Wal-Mart Supercenters in the United States. Wal-Mart also owns approximately 2,700 stores in fourteen other countries. The original Ben Franklin stores filed for bankruptcy in 1996, and another company purchased the rights to the name.

> *"If everyone else is doing it one way, there's a good chance you can find your niche by going in exactly the exact opposite direction. But be prepared for a lot of folks to wave you down and tell you you're headed the wrong way."* — *S. W.*

Theodore H. White

Discouraged from Writing Nonfiction

Theodore Harold White (1915–1986) was an American political journalist, historian, and novelist, best known for his accounts of the 1960, 1964, 1968, and 1972 U.S. presidential elections.

In 1956, Theodore H. White, a summa cum laude graduate of Harvard and former correspondent for *Time* magazine, *The Reporter*, and Overseas News Agency, found himself without a job when *Collier's Weekly* closed. Unable to find a journalism job that he liked, he decided to write a novel. His first solo novel, *The Mountain Road*, was accepted by the Book-of-the-Month Club and spawned a movie of the same name. His second novel, *The View From the Fortieth Floor,* was also a best-seller and a Literary Guild selection with the film rights sold to Gary Cooper for $80,000, although no film was ever made.

White based his books on his experiences. He wanted to write a political book on the 1960 presidential election and decided to go on the campaign trail to research it. When he told Bennett Cerf, president of Random House Publishing and his friend, about the plan, Cerf said, "I beg you not to waste a year and a half of your life on this book." White went ahead with his plans anyway. Several publishers rejected the manuscript because they believed readers had no use for a political book only a few months after the election. Undeterred, White kept submitting the work until he found a publisher. Within six weeks of its release, *The Making of the President (1960)* hit the *New York Times* best-seller list. It went on to sell more than four million copies and won the 1962 Pulitzer Prize for general nonfiction.

> *"To go against the dominant thinking of your friends, of most of the people you see every day, is perhaps the most difficult act of heroism you can perform."* — T. H. W.

Inspiration from Within

"Each disaster became a stepping-stone for growth."
— Erin Brockovich

Christina Aguilera

Star Search Reject

Pop singer Christina Aguilera (1980–) has released three albums, which have sold more than 30 million copies worldwide and earned her five Grammy Awards and sixteen Grammy nominations.

With a head full of dark blonde curls and an awe-inspiring voice, eight-year-old Christina Aguilera hoped to wow the judges of *Star Search* by performing "The Greatest Love of All." Her performance did not impress the judges enough for her to best the reigning champion. Two years later, she auditioned for the cast of the TV show *The New Mickey Mouse Club*. The producers rejected her because they thought she was too young. Nevertheless, her audition left a lasting impression. Two years after her initial audition, the producers called Aguilera and asked her to join the cast. Her two years on the show provided her with invaluable experience in dancing, acting, and singing. Unfortunately, Aguilera's celebrity negatively affected her school life. When she tried to return to her old school, she was targeted by jealous classmates. After several incidents, she transferred schools, only to face the same problems at her new school. Finally, she dropped out and finished high school with the help of a tutor.

After *The New Mickey Mouse Club* was canceled, Aguilera and her agent struggled for four years to launch her solo career. Finally, through her old Disney ties, she landed a contract to sing the pop version of "Reflections" from Disney's *Mulan*, which eventually led to a recording contract with RCA records. In 1999, Aguilera's debut album was released; and the first single, "Genie in a Bottle," quickly topped the charts and sold more than eight million copies. Aguilera also won a Grammy for Best New Artist in 1999, beating out her former *Mickey Mouse* costar, Britney Spears.

> *"What is it in us that makes us feel the need to keep pretending? . . . We gotta let ourselves be." — C. A.*

Muhammad Ali

No One Thought He Would Win

Born Cassius Marcellus Clay Jr., Muhammad Ali (1942–) is a boxer who won an Olympic light-heavyweight gold medal and became world heavyweight champion three times.

After a neighborhood punk knocked him down and stole his bicycle, Cassius Clay decided he was not going to let anyone push him around again; so he learned how to box. Less than six years later, the eighteen-year-old earned an Olympic gold medal in boxing in the light-heavyweight category. After bulking up and switching weight divisions, he made boxing his career. In his first four years of fighting, Clay amassed a 19-0 record, which included fifteen knockouts. He had crushed boxing greats Tony Esperti, Doug Jones, Henry Cooper, and Lamar Clark — who had delivered more than forty knockouts in his previous bouts. Clay also trounced Archie Moore, a boxing legend who had previously been one of the young boxer's trainers. Clay's record was good enough to make him the top contender for the world heavyweight boxing championship title, but no one thought he would win — especially the current titleholder, Sonny Liston. Even legendary sports commentator and Las Vegas oddsmaker Jimmy "The Greek" Snyder, renowned for his ability to pick the winners, thought Liston would be the inevitable winner and gave him the odds on favorite at 7 to 1.

Yet, on February 25, 1964, Clay proved the skeptics wrong with his defeat of Liston after the titleholder refused to leave his corner for the seventh round. Clay's problems should have been over, but new ones were just about to begin. The day following the match, Clay announced that he had become a Muslim and wished to be called by a new name: Muhammad Ali. In April 1967, Ali refused to be drafted by the Army to fight in Vietnam because war was against his religion. He fought this battle for his beliefs without using his fists. Ali was stripped of his heavyweight title — after having successfully defended it nine times — and his boxing license was suspended. He was also sentenced to five years in prison for draft evasion, but the courts agreed to release him pending an appeal.

Ali never lost hope, saying, "If I pass this test, I'll come out stronger." His boxing license was restored in 1970, but not his title. The title would not be restored to him until he defeated champion Joe Frazier, which is exactly what Ali did. He also won another, more important fight when the U.S. Supreme Court reversed his conviction for evading the draft. By the time Ali retired from boxing in 1980, he was the only heavyweight champion to win the title three times. He held a professional boxing record of 56-5-0, with thirty-seven knockouts in sixty-one fights and nineteen successful title defenses. In 1999, Ali was named "Sportsman of the Century" by *Sports Illustrated*. Six years later, he received the Presidential Medal of Freedom and the prestigious "Otto Hahn Peace Medal in Gold" from the United Nations Association of Germany for his work with the U.S. civil rights movement and the United Nations.

> *"I never thought of losing, but now that it's happened, the only thing is to do it right. That's my obligation to all the people who believe in me. We all have to take defeats in life." — M. A.*

Woody Allen

Recommended to Seek Psychiatric Counseling

Actor, director, comedian, and writer Woody Allen (1935–) has been nominated twenty-one times for his work. He has won three Academy Awards.

In 1952, Allen S. Konigsberg first submitted his writing to newspapers, but he was too shy to use his real name. Using part of his name, he submitted his work under the name Woody Allen. By the time he was seventeen, his jokes were being used by *New York Post* columnist Earl Wilson and by the legendary comedian Bob Hope.

After high school graduation, he enrolled at New York University, focusing on motion picture production. One of his professors told Allen that if he ever wanted to work, he would need to get psychiatric counseling first. Allen received a D at the end of his first semester and was eventually expelled for his failing grades. He had similar lack of success at City College.

By that point, Allen knew he had the ability to become a comedy writer and decided he did not need college.

He had already sold more than 20,000 of his jokes. Allen began performing in Greenwich Village cafes and then at local nightclubs and on a couple of talk shows. He also had several short stories published in magazines, including *The New Yorker.* He got a job as a writer and actor on the original *Candid Camera,* but television did not hold his attention for long, and he eventually gave motion pictures another look. Since 1965, Allen has starred in forty-seven movies, most of which he wrote, directed, or produced. During his career, Allen has amassed numerous awards for his writing, acting, and directing, including several Academy Awards, Golden Globes, and lifetime achievement awards.

"If you're not failing every now and again, it's a sure sign that you're not doing anything very innovative." — W. A.

Jane Austen

Bad First Impressions

Jane Austen (1775–1817) is an English writer famous for her novels *Sense and Sensibility, Pride and Prejudice, Mansfield Park, Emma, Northanger Abbey, Persuasion,* and other titles.

Most writers are nervous about exposing themselves to criticism, but Jane Austen was extremely shy. To prevent people from noticing what she was doing, Austen wrote on scraps of paper that she tucked away under her desk blotter when anyone entered her room. At some point, she collected the scraps and compiled them into a complete book titled *First Impressions.* In 1797, she gathered up the courage to show the novel to her father. He liked it so much that he queried a publisher to see if the firm would be interested in it. The publisher rejected it by return of post. Discouraged, Austen shelved *First Impressions* and focused her attention on a second novel, *Susan*. Six years later, in 1803, Austen managed to get a publisher interested enough to buy the book, but the firm never published it.

After these two major setbacks, Austen went to work on a new novel. It took her eight years before she dared to send it to a publisher. This time, a publisher purchased it and issued the book under the title *Sense and Sensibility*. It was a huge success, and the first edition sold out within a year. The success of the novel encouraged Austen to revise her original novel, *First Impressions*. It was published two years later under a new title: *Pride and Prejudice*. Today, *Pride and Prejudice* is Austen's most famous work and placed second in a 2003 BBC poll as the best-loved book in the United Kingdom. It has been adapted for television, stage, and motion pictures and has inspired numerous other works, including the best-selling novel by Helen Fielding, *Bridget Jones's Diary*.

> *"There will be little rubs and disappointments everywhere, and we are all apt to expect too much; but then, if one scheme of happiness fails, human nature turns to another; if the first calculation is wrong, we make a second better." — J. A.*

Lucille Ball

Hopelessly Inept

Lucille Ball (1911–1989) was a comedic actor and star of the hit television series *I Love Lucy*.

As a child, Lucille Ball treasured Saturday nights. That was when she and her grandfather hopped into the family's car and headed into the city to see a vaudeville show in Jamestown, New York. Sitting in the dark, the shy brunette watched wide-eyed, wondering if she would ever get past her own shyness to make people laugh. Ball was elated when her mother finally agreed to send her to the John Murray Anderson School for the Performing Arts. Her shyness and awkwardness made her seem hopelessly inept next to the grace and style of her fellow classmate, Bette Davis. Ball barely lasted six weeks before the instructors advised her mother not to waste any more money on a second term. Even worse, the head of the school, John Murray Anderson, told the teenager to "try another profession — any other."

Discouraged but determined, she decided to try her luck on Broadway. Time after time, directors and casting agents rejected her. A production assistant told her to "go home" because she "wasn't meant for show business." She managed to land a few parts in a show chorus, but was fired before the show opened. At twenty-two, Ball gave up on New York and decided to start over in Hollywood. She won a few small walk-on parts that eventually led to a few substantial roles in a string of B movies. Her movie career never really blossomed, but she did gain two major things from Hollywood: a head full of bright red hair and a Cuban husband, Desi Arnez.

By this point, she was nearly forty, which was considered over the hill by Hollywood standards. Not ready to give up on performing, Ball turned her attention to a relatively new medium called television. At the time, she had been doing a radio show, *My Favorite Husband*, which CBS was transforming into a television series. She thought it was a good idea but wanted Arnez to play the part of her husband. The network insisted that the public would not accept him as her husband. Exasperated, she reminded them of the truth, "We *are* married!" The couple had been married for more than ten years by then.

Realizing that the network executives were not going to change their minds, she came up with a plan to prove to them that America would accept her marriage to Arnez. Performing at vaudeville theaters, Ball and Arnez made audiences laugh with a skit that would eventually become the pilot for their television show. Their success on the vaudeville circuit was enough to convince CBS, and Ball returned to Hollywood. On October 15, 1951, *I Love Lucy* aired. Within four months, it was the most popular show in the country. During her lifetime, Ball earned four Emmy Awards for her television performances. Today, she is considered one of the greatest comedic actors of all time.

> *"I don't know anything about luck. I've never banked on it, and I'm afraid of people who do. Luck to me is something else: hard work and realizing what is opportunity and what isn't."* — *L. B.*

Wernher von Braun

From Failure in Math and Physics to Rocket Scientist

Wernher von Braun (1912–1977) was the director of NASA's Marshall Space Flight Center and the chief architect of the Saturn V launch vehicle, the super booster rocket that propelled the United States to the Moon.

Wernher von Braun did not do well in middle school. He failed his mathematics class and nearly failed a physics class. His father decided that academics was not his son's strong point and sent him to a boarding school to learn a trade. That might have been the end of this story had it had not been for a copy of *Die Rakete zu den Planetenräumen* (*By Rocket to Interplanetary Space*). Wernher von Braun had sent for the book and was immediately intrigued by the mathematical equations found throughout its first half. Wanting to understand them, he delved into calculus and trigonometry and graduated a year ahead of his class.

After graduation, von Braun was introduced to Professor Hermann Oberth, author of the *Die Rakete zu den Planetenräumen*. He eventually worked alongside the professor while studying at the Institute of Technology of Berlin. Once his studies were finished, von Braun took a job working for the German army to develop ballistic missiles. Soon he became leader of the "rocket team," which developed ballistic missiles for the Nazis during World War II. Von Braun, who had designed his rockets for space exploration and not as weapons, was dismayed at the Nazis' intended use of the missiles. When he casually complained about this turn of events to a young female dentist, who turned out to be a Gestapo spy, he was arrested and accused of trying to sabotage Germany's rocket program. He spent two weeks in jail before his release was arranged.

His release allowed von Braun to engineer the surrender of five hundred of Germany's top rocket scientists, along with plans and test vehicles, to the Americans in 1945. After the war, von Braun immigrated to the United States where he was finally able undertake the work he had wanted to do. Von Braun helped design America's first space probes and supervised the development of the Saturn V rockets used in the Apollo space programs. He became one of the most important rocket developers and a prominent spokesperson for space exploration in the United States.

"I have learned to use the word impossible with the greatest caution." — W. v. B.

Sister Frances Xavier Cabrini

Dismissed by the Convent

Sister Frances Xavier Cabrini (1850–1917), founder of the Missionary Sisters of the Sacred Heart of Jesus, was legendary for her work with the poor in New York during the late 1800s.

Born two months premature, Francesca Cabrini never fully recovered from the early setback and was constantly sick. When she was six, she began dreaming of leaving her small Italian village to become a missionary in China. Nothing could dissuade her — not the local townspeople who mocked her for her dream and not her sister, Rosa, who told her, "a missionary order would never accept a girl who is ill most of the time."

When Cabrini turned eighteen, she applied to the Daughters of the Sacred Heart Convent, but was rejected her because of her health. Undaunted, she returned home, determined to build up her health and apply again. It took six years before the order finally accepted her, and Francesca Cabrini became Sister Frances Xavier. Instead of being assigned overseas, however, she was assigned to teach at a local school. She applied to numerous organizations working in Asia, but they all rejected her.

Finally, one of her superiors suggested that she consider starting her own missionary order. The idea sparked new hope and, with the help of girls from an orphanage, she founded the Missionary Sisters of the Sacred Heart in 1880. For the next eight years, she developed the order with the goal of working in Asia. She at last gained the attention of Pope Leo XIII, who decided to send her overseas — not going to the East but west to the United States. He wanted her to help run an orphanage, school, and convent in New York City.

Cabrini dutifully followed the pope's orders, but when she arrived in New York City she discovered that the archbishop in charge had changed his mind because funding for the projects had fallen through. He advised her to return to Italy. Instead, she started a school, convinced the archbishop that an orphanage was indeed necessary, and took charge of the tiny hospital. Although Cabrini never fulfilled her dream of doing missionary work in China, she filled a much bigger purpose. By the time she died, she had founded more than seventy hospitals, schools, and orphanages throughout the United States, Europe, and South America. In addition, more than two thousand members had joined the Missionary Sisters of the Sacred Heart, the religious order she founded. In 1946, she was canonized by Pope Pius XII, making her the first American citizen to attain sainthood. Her body is enshrined inside a high school chapel in New York — the Mother Cabrini High School.

> *"Difficulties? What are they, Daughters? They are the mere playthings of children enlarged by our imagination, not yet accustomed to focus itself on the Omnipotent."* — *F. X. C.*

Jim Carrey

Booed Off Stage

Comedian and actor Jim Carrey (1962–) is most famous for his performances in the movies *Ace Ventura: Pet Detective, The Mask, Dumb and Dumber, The Cable Guy, Liar, Liar,* and *Bruce Almighty.*

STANDING IN FRONT OF THE audience at Yuk-Yuks in Toronto, determined to amaze the crowd with his ventriloquism act, fifteen-year-old Jim Carrey was instead booed off the stage. Perhaps the audience did not like Carrey's ventriloquism act or the polyester suit his mom had insisted he wear. The negative reaction didn't dissuade Carrey from his chosen path, however. He had already learned he could make people feel better with his impressions and physical comedy. In a 2004 *60 Minutes* interview with Steve Kroft, Carrey observed, "I had a sick mom, man. I wanted to make her feel better. Basically, I think she [lay] in bed and took a lot of pain pills. And I wanted to make her feel better. And I used to go in there and do impressions of praying mantises, and weird things, and whatever. I'd bounce off the walls and throw myself down the stairs to make her feel better."

After his father lost his job when Carrey was only sixteen, he had to drop out of school and get a full-time job to help support the family. For a while, the Carreys were homeless and lived in a yellow Volkswagen van. The poverty made young Carrey more determined than ever to follow his dreams.

Two years after his first performance, Carrey returned to Yuk-Yuks and finally received the reaction he had been hoping for — laughter. The success prompted him to move to Los Angeles. By age twenty-one, Carrey's comedy act was a hit, especially after he appeared on *The Tonight Show*. Yet, the act did not satisfy him. At the time, Carrey's performance consisted primarily of impressions. Carrey compared it to "saying to the world that those people are more interesting than me. And that's just not true."

The comedian decided to follow his instincts and go against everyone else's advice — he threw out his old act and focused on his own humor. At first, fans made it clear they preferred the old act. "People would be screaming at me to do my old act, and getting actually violent and angry at me. . . . It was a crazy experiment. But it was so good because it made me comfortable with the creative process — with being on a limb, you know? And I've been there ever since."

When he wasn't performing in comedy clubs, Carrey

turned to acting. He landed a couple of bit parts in the movies and one on a quickly canceled television show before finally landing a role on *In Living Color.* The show's popularity helped Carrey land the title role in *Ace Ventura: Pet Detective*, which launched Carrey's career in comedy films. As of 2007, Carrey had won two Golden Globes and two People's Choice Awards. He has also received an astounding twenty-one MTV Movie Award nominations and received nine MTV Movie Awards.

> *"If you are not in the moment, you are either looking forward to uncertainty, or back to pain and regret."* — J. C.

Stephen Crane

Deemed Too Outrageous

Stephen Crane (1871–1900) was an American novelist who wrote *The Red Badge of Courage.*

Stephen Crane learned quickly that one of the biggest problems writers face is finding a publisher. After several publishers turned him down because they thought his novella would be too outrageous for their readers, Crane decided to publish the work himself. He borrowed $700 from his brother and published *Maggie: A Girl of the Streets* himself under a pseudonym. Only two copies sold; the rest remained piled up along the walls of his room. He had already begun work on his second novel, *The Red Badge of Courage*, which was serialized in the *Philadelphia Press* before being published as a novel in October 1895. Many Civil War veterans hailed the second novel as an amazingly realistic account of life during the Civil War, a remarkable accomplishment considering Crane had no first-hand knowledge of the war. *The Red Badge of Courage* became extremely successful and led publishers to reissue Crane's first novel, *Maggie: A Girl of the Streets*. This time the novella received wider recognition. The book's success also led the *New York Journal* to hire Crane as a correspondent covering the Greco-Turkish War.

Crane published several additional novels as well as two books of poetry and a sequel to *The Red Badge of Courage*, which remained his most famous novel. The book was made into a movie twice, once in 1954 and again in 1974.

"You cannot choose your battlefield, God does that for you; but you can plant a standard where a standard never flew." — S. C.

Pat Croce

Rejected from School and Team

Pat Croce (1954–) is an author, entrepreneur, and TV personality who went from being a physical therapist to founding the Sports Physical Therapists chain, which sold for approximately $40 million in 1993. He has written four self-help books, including three that topped the *New York Times* best-seller list.

Pat Croce's dream was to play professional football for his hometown team, the Philadelphia Eagles, but all his ambition and positive thinking could not make up for a body that was too small. Rather than be slaughtered on the field, he decided that the next best thing to playing for the Eagles was working for the Eagles, and he set out to become their the team's conditioning coach. Croce's new goal was to attend college and become a physical therapist, but every school rejected his application. Finally, he was admitted to the University of Pittsburgh. After graduation, he tried several times to obtain a position with the Eagles, but each attempt was met with failure. During his job hunt, Croce noticed that sports medicine centers operated only at universities.

He decided that this needed to be changed and, in 1979, he opened the first sports medicine center situated in a U.S. hospital. After establishing the center, Croce accepted the coveted position of conditioning coach with a Philadelphia sports team — the Philadelphia Flyers hockey team, and not the Eagles. Eventually, he expanded from being a conditioning coach and opened his own privately owned sports medicine center called Sports Physical Therapists. Over the next nine years, he expanded the business into a chain of forty centers in eleven states. Sports Physical Therapists quickly became popular with professional sports teams across the country, including the Eagles.

"If something you try doesn't work and the door slams shut, that's okay. Just never stop trying." — P. C.

Emily Dickinson

An Eccentric, Dreamy, Half-educated Recluse

Unheralded during her lifetime, Emily Dickinson (1830–1886) is considered today one of the most widely known poets of the nineteenth century.

THOMAS WENTWORTH HIGGINSON, LITERARY EDITOR of the *Atlantic Monthly*, believed he was able to recognize a good poem. At least that is what he wrote to Emily Dickinson when he rejected her poetry. Yet Dickinson continued to send him her poetry. During their correspondence, she sent Higginson more than one hundred poems. Higginson never published any of them and simply urged her to study her craft further.

Samuel Bowles, editor of the *Springfield Republican*, also failed to recognize the innovation in Dickinson's poetry. He published only one of the more than fifty poems she sent to him. The consensus at the time was that poetry should contain strong rhyme, regular meter, and simple illusions — all things that her poetry lacked. Of the more than 1,800 plus poems Dickinson wrote, only a few were published, all anonymously, before her death. Her unpublished poems were found by Dickinson's sister and, ironically, with Higginson's help, she managed to get them published. The publisher had little faith in the book and, fearing that it would not sell, the firm required the family to underwrite the costs of publication. Titled simply *Poems*, the book had to be reprinted twice within the first two months of publication.

Still, Dickinson could not escape criticism from the *Atlantic Monthly*, even after her death. In 1892, Thomas Bailey Aldrich, editor of the *Atlantic Monthly*, warned that "an eccentric, dreamy, half-educated recluse in an out-of-the-way New England village — or anywhere else — cannot with impunity set at defiance the laws of gravitation and grammar" and predicted that "oblivion lingers in the immediate neighborhood." Today, Dickinson is regarded as a major figure in nineteenth century American literature; her name has become linked forever to the study of poetry.

> *"We'd never know how high we are till we are called to rise, and then, if we are true to plan, our statures touch the sky."* — E. D.

Phil Donahue

No One Would Hire Him

Media personality Phil Donahue (1935–) created and starred in the first tabloid talk show, *The Phil Donahue Show*, for twenty-seven years from 1970 until 1996.

EVEN THOUGH PHIL DONAHUE, A Notre Dame graduate with experience working at his school's radio station, came armed with audition tapes and letters of reference, he still had no luck landing a position as a radio broadcaster. Discouraged, Donahue worked at a bank until he could secure a permanent job in radio. Finally, in the fall of 1958, Donahue landed a job with a small radio station in Adrian, Michigan. The professional on-air experience gave him material to use to audition at larger stations. Eventually, he obtained a position with WHIO-AM in Dayton, Ohio. While there, he conducted interviews with Jimmy Hoffa and Billy Sol Estes, which were broadcast nationally. However, he was still unable to land a position at a larger station. After nine years of rejections, he gave up and took a job selling vacation plans.

Donahue hated that job and quickly returned to broadcasting, but not to radio. This time, he accepted a position at WLWD-TV, also in Dayton, as host of a television show. On November 6, 1967, *The Phil Donahue Show* premiered.

Although the show was based on Donahue's old radio show, it went against the conventional talk-show format popular in the late 1960s by featuring controversial subjects, a single guest or topic, and audience participation. The show soon became a hit and, after being acquired by Multimedia Productions, was broadcast nationwide. The show, renamed *Donahue*, enjoyed a twenty-seven-year run on national television.

"In reality, the most important things happen when you don't look for them." — P. D.

Dwight D. Eisenhower

Denied Promotion Three Times

Dwight David Eisenhower (1890–1969), a five-star general in the U.S. Army, became the thirty-fourth president of the United States.

DWIGHT D. EISENHOWER'S APPLICATION TO the U.S. Naval Academy at Annapolis, Maryland, was rejected because, at twenty-one, he was considered too old. West Point was his second choice, and, luckily, he was accepted there. While at the school, Eisenhower was demoted from the rank of sergeant to private for "wild dancing." Despite that lapse, he graduated in 1915. In 1939, Eisenhower was a mere colonel with an unremarkable military career; he had been rejected three times for promotion and was considering retiring. He might have done just that if World War II had not erupted. The war gave Eisenhower the opportunity to demonstrate his keen intellect and abilities as a military strategist. By 1942, he was head of the U.S. forces in Europe. Promoted through the ranks at a rapid-fire pace, within a year Eisenhower had reached the highest rank in the army: four-star general.

After World War II ended, Eisenhower served as chief of staff of the U.S. Army until 1948, when he decided to resign. Instead, he accepted he position of supreme commander of the North Atlantic Treaty Organization (NATO). He held that position until 1951, when he found himself drafted — not into the military but into politics.

Eisenhower had ignored people's pleas urging him to run for president in 1948; he intended to ignore them a second time in 1951. In a letter to then-President Harry Truman, he wrote, "I do not feel I have any duty to seek political nomination." At first, Eisenhower believed that the press exaggerated accounts of the movement to draft him and that it was not as widespread as reported. He changed his mind after seeing the results of the New Hampshire primary. Eisenhower won the contest for the Republican presidential nominee with 50 percent of the votes. He decided to run for president the next day. Interestingly, General Douglas MacArthur, another prominent general of World War II, predicted that Eisenhower would "back down before the final showdown." MacArthur was wrong. Not only did Eisenhower not back down, he won by a landslide. Eisenhower served two terms as the thirty-fourth president. During his term, he ended the Korean War, helped launch the space race, expanded Social Security, and began the interstate highway system.

"No one can defeat us unless we first defeat ourselves." — D. D. E.

F. Scott Fitzgerald

Rejected in Love and Work

Francis Scott Fitzgerald (1896–1940), author of *The Great Gatsby*, is considered by many as one of the greatest writers of the twentieth century.

Being placed on academic probation at Princeton was enough to make F. Scott Fitzgerald drop out of school and join the Army. He hoped to see the world, but he got no further than the military base in Montgomery, Alabama. However, his misfortune turned around when he met and fell in love with a young woman named Zelda Sayre. Fitzgerald knew that if he was ever going to convince her to marry him he would need to prove that he could support her. Fitzgerald did not intend to stay in the Army; he wanted to be a writer and had already submitted his first novel to a publisher, Charles Scribner's Sons. Scribner's had rejected it but encouraged Fitzgerald to resubmit the novel after he revised it. Wanting to demonstrate his worth to his love, Fitzgerald revised the work and submitted it again, only to find himself rejected twice: first by the publisher and then by Sayre, who broke off their engagement.

In 1919, Fitzgerald was slated to go overseas. However, the war ended before he could be shipped out, and he was discharged from the Army instead. Still wanting to prove himself to Sayre, he headed to New York, and then to St. Paul, Minnesota, where he focused all his energy on revising his novel and getting it published. He continued to submit his work to publishers and magazines and continued to receive rejections. Fitzgerald did not let this stop him; he hung the rejection letters on his walls to motivate himself. His walls were covered before his first novel, *This Side of Paradise*, was published. Fitzgerald married Sayre the following week. The book became a smash hit and was the most popular novel of the year. Fitzgerald continued to write, publishing four more novels, including his most famous work, *The Great Gatsby*, and numerous short stories.

"Never confuse a single defeat with a final defeat." — F. S. F.

Harrison Ford

Least Likely to Succeed

Actor Harrison Ford (1942–) starred as Han Solo in the *Star Wars* film series, as Dr. "Indiana" Jones in *Raiders of the Lost Ark* and its two sequels, and in numerous other hit movies.

In high school, Harrison Ford might have been labeled a "nerd" except for his C grade point average. That did not stop him from becoming a target for bullies, especially since he never played sports and was a member of the school's radio club. Unpopular, he was ignored by girls and graduated without ever going on a date. His classmates voted him "least likely to succeed."

Once in college, Ford got his first taste of acting after enrolling in a drama class. He was not particularly interested in acting but was looking for an easy A to raise his grade point average. Just weeks before graduation, he was expelled after he failed a philosophy class. Bitten by the performing bug, he moved to Hollywood and looked for work as an actor. Initially, he had more success finding carpentry work than acting jobs beyond small parts on a variety of television series. Still, he landed a minor role in the movie *American Graffiti*. When Ford asked George Lucas about a part in his upcoming science fiction movie, *Star Wars*, the film director rejected him because he wanted "new faces."

Unable to find another acting job, Ford agreed to read the part of Han Solo during the screen tests to earn some money. His reading landed him the role. *Star Wars* became an instant hit, and Ford became an overnight sensation. The movie was so successful that critics predicted that everyone cast in the film would be forever typecast in their *Star Wars* roles. Ford was passed up for the lead role in a subsequent movie directed by Lucas *Raiders of the Lost Ark*. However, after Lucas's first choice, Tom Selleck, became unavailable, Ford stepped in and earned critical praise for his portrayal of Indiana Jones.

Today, Ford is considered one of the most successful actors alive. He was listed in the *2001 Guinness Book of World Records* as the richest male actor in the world. In 2001, the American Film Institute gave him its Lifetime Achievement Award. Amazingly, he has been nominated only once for an Oscar (Best Actor for *Witness*), an award he did not win.

> *"All I would tell people is to hold on to what was individual about themselves, not to allow their ambition for success to cause them to try to imitate the success of others. You've got to find it on your own terms."* — H. F.

Henry Ford

Inventor of a Useless Novelty

Henry Ford (1863–1947) was the founder of the Ford Motor Company and is considered the father of modern assembly lines used in mass production.

IN 1893, HENRY FORD RECEIVED a promotion to chief engineer at Edison Illuminating Company. He was elated, but not at the rise in status. He knew the new job would give him more time and money to devote to his experiments. For the next three years, Ford spent his free time clanking and thumping in his tiny workshop. When he finally finished his creation, a gas-powered vehicle that he called a quadricycle, Ford discovered that it was too big to fit through the doors. No problem; he simply knocked down the wall. The quadricycle turned quite a few heads as its creator — with his thick mustache, bow tie, and bowler hat — drove it around town, sitting atop the contraption's velvet bench. Although Ford was not the first person to create a gasoline-powered vehicle, he was among the few who succeeded in making it run.

The Edison Company offered Ford the general superintendency of the company, but only if he agreed to give up working on the gas engine and devote himself to something more "useful." He refused and left the company to start his own business constructing gasoline-powered vehicles. After he spent more than $85,000 without results, his investors backed out and the company folded. He tried again, this time selling shares in his company to raise more money, but this attempt also failed.

In 1903, Ford tried again. He set about recruiting twenty people willing to invest in his company. One of the people Ford approached was his attorney, Horace Rackham. Rackham, knowing the inventor's history, was reluctant and sought the advice of the president of Michigan Savings Bank. The banker advised against the investment, saying, "The horse is here to stay, but the automobile is only a novelty, a fad, a passing fancy." Rackham ignored his banker's advice and invested his money. It turned out to be a very good decision. Ford achieved the results he had hoped for, and the profits of the Ford Motor Company reached more than $1 million by 1907.

"Think you can, think you can't; you will always be right." — H. F.

M. C. Hammer

Ill-prepared for Fortune

Rap artist M. C. Hammer (1962–) has released more than ten albums, including the hit singles "U Can't Touch This" and "Too Legit to Quit."

Stanley Kirk Burrell convinced not one but two record companies to produce his first album. However, after he and his partner went separate ways before the record was completed, he discovered that no one would take a chance on him by himself. With the help of two of his friends, Burrell hawked his first single out of the back of his car before teaming up with Felton Pilate, a music producer and member of the group Con Funk Shun. Together, the two men produced Burrell's debut album in Pilate's basement studio.

Despite having no money for marketing, Burrell sold more than sixty thousand copies of the album before attracting the attention of an executive at Capitol Records. Capitol gave him a multi-album contract and a $750,000 advance. Burrell, who had changed his name to M. C. Hammer, re-released his first album under then new title *Let's Get It Started.* The album quickly climbed the charts, selling more than 1.5 million records. His second album, *Please Hammer Don't Hurt 'Em*, was also a huge hit and became the first hip-hop album to go Diamond. He eventually sold more than twenty-five million albums worldwide, earned three Grammys, seven American Music Awards, and two MTV Awards.

Although the records made him a millionaire, Hammer was ill-prepared to handle the fortune. His overly extravagant lifestyle eventually forced him to declare bankruptcy in 1996. That same year, he also broke his leg; his wife was diagnosed with cancer; and his friend, Tupac Shakur, was murdered. The string of tragedies helped Hammer refocus his life. He reaffirmed his Christian beliefs in 1997 and became an evangelist with his own show on the Trinity Broadcasting Network. He continues to perform music and release records.

> *"In life, it is the moments that we are cut back that we should look forward to new growth in our lives. Bigger, better, stronger and multiplying ourselves by sharing what we have learned with others."* — M. C. H.

Stephen Hawking

Lacked Drive and Inspiration

Stephen Hawking (1942–) is a British theoretical physicist and writer of the best-selling novel *A Brief History of Time*, which stayed on the London *Sunday Times*'s best-seller list for 237 weeks.

Genius is not enough to guarantee success. A person must also have drive, which was the one attribute twenty-one-year-old Stephen Hawking appeared to be lacking. Hawking had already earned a degree from Oxford and was working on his Ph.D. at Cambridge, but his research was not going well. He was bored with life. As it would turn out, far worse problems lay ahead. Hawking began having bouts of clumsiness and had even fallen a few times for no apparent reason. Yet, it was not until his father noticed the change in his son's movements that he consulted a doctor. Numerous tests and consultations led to only one possible diagnosis. Hawking had amyotrophic lateral sclerosis (ALS), also known as Lou Gehrig's disease. ALS is a progressive, incurable, and fatal disease. Hawking's doctors told him that he had only a few years to live.

At first, Hawking gave up. Continuing his research seemed pointless since it was unlikely he would be able to finish it. Then, he was confronted with a thought that scared him even more than dying — the idea that he might die before achieving anything good with his life. This new thought reinvigorated him. He became engaged and then married his girlfriend, got a job, and — most importantly — he continued his studies.

More than forty years have passed since the doctors

made their pessimistic prediction, and Hawking continues to do his life's work. In a 2005 interview he stated, "It is a waste of time to be angry about my disability. One has to get on with life and I haven't done badly. People won't have time for you if you are always angry or complaining." Living by that credo, Hawking has published six books and several hundred papers, and is considered one of the world's leading theoretical physicists. His most popular book, *A Brief History of Time*, was on the best-sellers list for 237 weeks.

> *"I have noticed even people who claim everything is predestined, and that we can do nothing to change it, look before they cross the road."* — S. H.

Billy Idol

No One Believed in Him

Born William Broad (1955–), Billy Idol is the English rock musician behind the hit songs "Rebel Yell" and "Dancing with Myself."

NO ONE BELIEVED WILLIAM BROAD could do it. When Broad told his father that he was quitting college to pursue a music career, his father told him that he would never be able get a real job after his musical career failed. When Broad decided to pursue it anyway, his father refused to talk to him for more than two years. Broad would not stop, even when his first band quit after two months. Instead, he formed a new band, Generation X. Within a year, Generation X released a self-titled debut album. It was moderately successful, and the band released two more albums before folding because of management hassles. For six months, Broad's career stalled.

Broad later recalled that time, saying, "I've discovered that everything in my life that seemed to crash was a part of what pushed me forward." Just when he was ready to give up on music, his enthusiasm rejuvenated after he watched people's reaction to a song he had released with his old band. He changed his name to Idol and become a solo act. He initially went by the stage name Idle from a high school report card on which a teacher had written, "Billy is idle." Eventually he decided that the name Billy Idle no longer fit — he wanted to be an idol and calling himself one would be a great start. In 1981, Idol released a mini-LP "Dancing with Myself" and "Mony, Mony," which remained on the charts for almost a year. Idol followed these hits with others such as "White Wedding," "Rebel Yell," and "Cradle of Love."

"If your world doesn't allow you to dream, move to one where you can. If you don't believe in something, find something to believe in." — B. I.

Michael Jordan

Fueled by Disappointment

Michael Jordan (1963–) is considered one of the greatest basketball players of all time. During his career in the NBA, he won five NBA MVP awards, ten All-NBA First Team designations, nine All-Defensive First Team honors, three All-Star MVPs, ten scoring titles, and six NBA Finals MVP awards.

Jordan was only a freshman when he first tried out for his high school's varsity basketball team. Despite his six-foot-tall physique, he did not make the team. Undaunted, Jordan tried out again as a sophomore. He was cut for a second time. Devastated, he struggled through the rest of the school day. When he got home, he promptly shut himself in his room and dissolved into tears. Looking back, he admits, "It's probably good that it happened. It made me know what disappointment felt like. And I knew that I didn't want that feeling ever again."

Fueled by this resolve, Jordan continued to practice. Mother Nature gave him an added edge by giving him a four-inch growth spurt, and he finally made the basketball team his junior year. Nevertheless, when the list of the top three hundred U.S. college basketball prospects was published right before his senior year, his name was not on it. However, Jordan was good enough to land a full basketball scholarship at the University of North Carolina (UNC). UNC appreciated Jordan, and he was a starter for the team from the beginning. By the end of his freshman year, he was a national celebrity after sinking a fifteen-foot jump shot in the final seconds of the 1982 NCAA championship game. Jordan was the third overall pick when he was drafted by the Chicago Bulls in 1984. During his professional basketball career, Jordan was NBA Rookie of the Year and set NBA records for the most points scored. He has won multiple MVP awards, several NBA championships, and two Olympic gold medals; however, Jordan has always kept things in perspective. In his own words: "I have missed more than 9,000 shots in my career. I have lost almost 300 games. On 26 occasions, I have been entrusted to take the game-winning shot and missed. And I have failed over and over and over again in my life. And that is why I succeed."

"You have to expect things of yourself before you can do them." — M. J.

John F. Kennedy

Graduated at the Bottom of His Class

John F. Kennedy (1917–1963) was the thirty-fifth president of the United States.

While at Choate Rosemary Hall, a Connecticut prep school, John F. Kennedy's headmaster reported that he was "casual and disorderly" and that he "studies at the last minute, keeps appointments late, has little sense of material values, and can seldom locate his positions." As the result of these behaviors, Kennedy graduated near the bottom of his class. Because of his family's influence, he was able to get into Harvard University, where he ran and lost his election for class president when he was a freshman. He also failed to win a post on the student council as a sophomore.

During World War II, Kennedy volunteered for the U.S. Army, but he was rejected because of physical weaknesses. The U.S. Navy accepted him. During his military service, Kennedy was awarded for his heroism after rescuing three men when their boat was rammed by a Japanese destroyer. He even towed one of the men three miles until they reached shore.

After being discharged in 1945, Kennedy served in the U.S. Senate until 1959, when he decided to run for president. He was not expected to win. His own father predicted, "He won't have a chance. I hate to see him and Bobby work themselves to death and lose." Franklin D. Roosevelt Jr., son of the former president and a U.S. representative, also questioned Kennedy's chances, saying that Kennedy was too "politically immature" to become president. Kennedy ran anyway and became the youngest man ever elected president of the United States.

"Those who dare to fail miserably can achieve greatly." — J. F. K.

Bruce Lee

Told to Forget About Kung Fu

Bruce Lee's (1940–1973) skill on screen as both an actor and martial artist has made him one of the most influential martial artists of the twentieth century.

Bruce Lee spent his entire life studying martial arts. After coming to the United States from Hong Kong, Lee landed the role in the television series *The Green Hornet*. He was convinced that the role would make him a star, but it was canceled after one season. Lee then focused his energies on a movie project titled *The Silent Flute*, but the deal fell through. Then, to add injury to insult, literally, he severely injured his back after failing to warm up properly during a workout session. The doctors told him to rest and forget about kung fu because he would never be able to kick again.

For the next three months, Lee lay flat on his back. He decided that if he could not work his body, he would work his mind. He wrote down his thoughts on martial arts and the methods he used. By the end of his six months of forced rest, Lee had written eight volumes of notes, each two inches thick. During this time, he also wrote his own personal affirmation:

I, Bruce Lee, will be the highest paid Oriental superstar in the United States. In return, I will give *the most exciting performances and render the best quality in the capacity of an actor. Starting in 1970, I will achieve world fame and from then onward till the end of 1989 I will have in my possession $10,000,000. Then I will live the way I please and achieve inner harmony and happiness.*

Finally able to work again, Lee was recruited by Warner Brothers to help develop a television series called *Kung Fu.* Lee presented numerous ideas; but in the end, despite Lee's heavy involvement, the starring role in the series went to David Carradine. Warner Brothers later admitted that Lee had never even been considered for the role.

Warner Brothers' rejection led Lee to accept an offer by a Hong Kong film producer, Raymond Chow, to make a movie. After their introduction, Lee told Chow "You just wait; I'm going to be the biggest Chinese star in the world." Lee returned to Hong Kong and began filming. From 1971 to 1972, Lee starred in three movies: *The Big Boss*, *Fist of Fury*, and *Way of the Dragon*. Lee rose to stardom throughout Asia. For his next film, he focused on his determination to reach stardom in the United States. *Enter the Dragon*, the first movie to be produced jointly by a Chinese and American studio, was a huge success during its original theatrical release, grossing approximately $25 million in North America and $90 million worldwide. Tragically, Lee died two weeks before the movie was released. However, he is still regarded as the most influential and famous martial artist of the twentieth century.

"Dedication, absolute dedication, is what keeps one ahead — a sort of indomitable obsessive dedication and the realization that there is no end or limit to this because life is simply an ever-growing process, an ever-renewing process." — B. L.

Marilyn Monroe

Lacked Star Quality

Born Norma Jeane Mortenson, Marilyn Monroe (1926–1962) was one of the most popular movie stars of the 1950s and appeared in such classics as *Gentlemen Prefer Blondes, Some Like it Hot*, and *Monkey Business*.

After being admitted to the Blue Book Modeling Agency, Marilyn Monroe was told by director Emmeline Snively that she had "better learn secretarial work or else get married" because she would not make it as a model. Monroe refused to quit, and within two years she had become one of the agency's most successful models and had appeared on several magazine covers.

However, she did not intend to spend her career modeling, and she enrolled in several drama courses to pursue her lifelong dream of becoming an actress. In 1946, she signed a one-year contract with Twentieth Century-Fox, but she appeared in only one movie for the company before being released from her contract. The decision was reportedly made because production chief Darryl Zanuck did not like her appearance. She managed to obtain a contract with Columbia, but that company let Monroe's contract lapse in 1949 because producer Harry Cohn did not believe that Monroe had "star quality." It was only after her uncredited role in *The Asphalt Jungle* received a strong response from audiences that the studios took notice of her. After signing with Twentieth Century-Fox a second time, Monroe earned more than $200 million for the studio. Her legend continues to live on long after her premature death.

In 1999, Monroe was named the "Number One Sex Star of the Twentieth Century" by *Playboy* magazine and the "Sexiest Woman of the Century" by *People Magazine.*

"If I'd observed all the rules, I'd never have got anywhere." — M. M.

Joe Namath

Out of Harmony with His Coach

During his thirteen-year career as a professional football player, Joe Namath (1943–) threw 173 touchdowns and 220 interceptions, played on three division champion teams, and earned a league championship win and a Super Bowl win.

As an athletic high school student, Joe Namath played a variety of sports and received offers from six professional baseball teams upon graduation. Yet, Namath did not want to play baseball; he wanted to play football. Instead of accepting the offers, he applied to Penn State and the University of Maryland. Unfortunately, his SAT scores were below the minimum necessary for entrance. He tried retaking the test but still missed the mark by three points. Instead, he went to the University of Alabama.

Initially, he did not like the university, but as far as Namath was concerned Alabama had one thing going for it — legendary head football coach, Paul "Bear" Bryant. Namath was placed under Bryant's guidance. The coach and the student hit it off, but that did not stop Namath from being suspended from the final two games (which included the Sugar Bowl) after he broke the team's rules. Bryant would later call Namath "the greatest athlete I have ever coached."

After graduation, Namath signed up with the New York Jets. He was soon at odds with the team's coach, Weeb Ewbank. Although Namath was the American Football League Rookie of the Year and an AFL All-Star in 1965 and 1967, experts predicted that the conflict between the young football player and Ewbank would be the Jets' downfall. William N. Wallace, football analyst for the *New York Times*, observed in August of 1968, "The New York Jets would do well to trade Joe Namath right now. . . . It is unlikely that the Jets can ever win with Namath and Ewbank out of harmony." The Jets kept Namath and that same year the team won the 1968 American Football League championship and became the first AFL team to win the Super Bowl. During his career, Namath became the first quarterback to pass more than 4,000 yards in one season. He also completed 1,886 passes for 27,663 yards and 173 touchdowns.

"If you aren't going to go all the way, why go at all?" — J. N.

Ignace Paderewski

Instructed to Give Up Piano Pursuits

Ignace Paderewski (1860–1941) was a pianist and composer who eventually became the third prime minister of Poland.

Polish pianist Ignace Paderewski was told that he would never become a great pianist because his middle fingers were too short. One of his piano teachers even suggested that he study another instrument. Paderewski tried the flute, the clarinet, the bassoon, the horn, and even the trombone. None of them held the appeal that the piano did for him. Each time, he went back to the instrument that he loved, piano. After graduating from high school, he worked as a teacher for a few years. Like his other pursuits, he soon gave it up and went to Germany to continue his music studies. Again, his instructors advised him that he did not have enough talent to make a career as a pianist. Again, Paderewski did not listen; he went to Vienna to study with Theodor Leschetizky, the most famous piano teacher at that time. Leschetizky told Paderewski that he was too old to develop a dependable technique, but still Paderewski would not quit. Paderewski practiced constantly. Finally, in 1887, he made his first public appearance in Vienna. He was an overnight sensation and quickly became popular nationally. His popularity spread after landing performances in Paris, London, and the United States. His name has become synonymous with the highest level of piano virtuosity, and he is still considered one of the greatest pianists of his time.

"Before I was a genius, I was a drudge." — I. P.

Phil Rizzuto

Too Short for Baseball

Hall of Fame shortstop Philip Rizzuto (1917–2007) played for the New York Yankees from 1941 to 1956.

In 1936, Phil Rizzuto tried out for the Brooklyn Dodgers. The team's manager, Casey Stengel, turned him down and told him, "Kid, you're too small. You ought to go out and shine shoes." Rizzuto refused to listen and instead tried out for the New York Yankees. The Yankees also thought he was short — Rizzuto was only five feet, six inches tall — but team executives liked him enough to send him to a farm team for experience and training.

In 1941, Rizzuto played his first major league game. He played for the Yankees for the rest of his career, which was interrupted for three years when he joined the Navy during World War II. He was voted the American League's Most Valuable Player in 1950. Ironically, the Yankees had just hired Stengel — the same man who had rejected Rizzuto for the Dodgers. Many believe that Rizzuto's best years occurred under Stengel, who guided Rizzuto and the New York Yankees to World Series wins in 1949, 1950, 1951, 1952, 1953, and 1956. Both men have since been inducted into Baseball's Hall of Fame

"I like radio better than television because if you make a mistake on radio, they don't know. You can make up anything on the radio." — P. R.

Auguste Rodin

An Uneducable Idiot

Auguste Rodin (1840–1917) was a French artist who sculpted *The Age of Bronze* and *The Thinker.*

Auguste Rodin was rejected three times by the École des Beaux-Arts, a French art school. Instead, he studied at a trade school for decorative sculpture. Rodin suffered from severe visual difficulties that he developed as a child. The condition caused him numerous difficulties in school and is probably the reason his father called him an idiot and his uncle labeled him "uneducable."

Although the condition took away most of his eyesight, it gave him a heightened sense of touch, giving him the ability to infuse his sculptures with emotion, which had an enormous effect on late-nineteenth century art. Success would not come easily for him, though. At one point, Rodin's lack of success combined with the death of his sister led him to give up on becoming an artist, and he entered a Christian order. However, a priest encouraged Rodin to continue sculpting, and he eventually left the order. Shortly thereafter, in 1864, Rodin submitted one of his sculptures, *The Man with the Broken Nose*, to the Paris Salon, the official art exhibition of the Académie des Beaux-Arts, which was considered the greatest art event in the world at the time. The salon rejected Rodin's work.

In 1877, the Paris Salon finally admitted Rodin's *The Age of Bronze* — although just barely. The sculpture was immediately attacked by critics for its lack of theme. It proved to be so realistic that skeptics accused Rodin of using plaster molds from live models to cast the sculpture rather than sculpting it himself. Rodin vigorously denied the charges and defended himself by showing photographs to prove that the model and the sculpture differed. To further prove the accusations wrong, Rodin made his next sculpture larger than life. He also accepted a commission to design the doorway for the planned Museum of Decorative Arts in Paris, which involved creating figures that were smaller than life. Many of Rodin's best-known works began as figures for the doorway, such as *The Three Shades*, *The Kiss*, and *The Thinker*, which is the most highly renowned and recognizable of his sculptures and has been used in everything from cartoons to advertising.

"Nothing is a waste of time if you use the experience wisely." — A. R.

J. K. Rowling

Rejected by Twelve Publishers

Joanne Rowling (1965–), better known as J. K. Rowling, is the author of the seven novels that comprise the *Harry Potter* fantasy series.

JOANNE ROWLING HAD ALWAYS DREAMED of being a writer, yet she failed to complete any of the adult novels that she had started. One day, during a delayed train trip, she got another idea; she would write a children's book. It took her three years to finish writing the book. At the time, she did not own a computer — or even a typewriter — and did all the writing longhand. When she had completed the book, she typed it on a second-hand manual typewriter and contracted an agent.

Her agent immediately sent the manuscript out to twelve publishers, but each rejected the work. He tried other publishers, and finally, Bloomsbury agreed to publish the book, *Harry Potter and the Philosopher's Stone.* Rowling received an advance of just $3,000. The head of the company's children's fiction division warned her that there was no financial reward in children's books.

With money she received from a grant from the Scottish Arts Council, Rowling purchased a word processor and steadied her turbulent finances while she finished a second book in the series, *Harry Potter and the Chamber of Secrets.* Even before *Harry Potter and the Philosopher's*

Stone had been published, it garnered the attention of Arthur Levine, the editorial director of Scholastic Books. After a bidding war, Scholastic secured the American rights for *Philosopher's Stone* for $100,000. In June 1997, Bloomsbury published *Harry Potter and the Philosopher's Stone* with an initial print run of only one thousand copies, half of which were distributed to libraries. More than a year later, the book hit American shelves under a slightly different title, *Harry Potter and the Sorcerer's Stone*, to highlight the book's magical theme.

Sales of the book greatly exceeded expectations. Almost half a billion of Rowling's books about the young wizard Harry Potter have been published in more than six hundred languages. In 2004, *Forbes* magazine estimated that she had earned more than $1 billion from her books, making her the first person ever to become a billionaire as a writer. In 2006, *Forbes* placed her as the second richest woman entertainer in the world, right behind Oprah Winfrey.

> *"It is important to remember that we all have magic inside us."*
> *— J. K. R.*

Madame Schumann-Heink

Saved by a Diva's Tantrum

Ernestine Schumann-Heink (1861–1936) was a well-known operatic contralto.

Marie Wilt, a soprano with the Vienna Opera, was so impressed by Ernestine Schumann-Heink's singing abilities, she arranged for the fifteen-year-old to audition with the director of the Imperial Opera in Vienna. The director was not impressed and advised the young singer to go home, buy a sewing machine, and become a dressmaker. Thankfully, another singer, Amalie Matern, arranged for Schumann-Heink to audition at an opera house in Dresden. The director there recognized her talent and hired Schumann-Heink. She debuted in Dresden in 1878, but she was fired a couple of years later when she married without the management's consent.

After several months of struggling, she landed a job with the Hamburg Opera and performed bit parts there for the next seven years. One fateful night Marie Goetze, principal contralto of the opera, threw a tantrum at the last minute and refused to go on. Schumann-Heink was selected as an emergency replacement, and although she had had no opportunity to rehearse, the audience loved her performance. A miffed Goetze canceled her next appearance. Again, the role was handed to Schumann-Heink. It marked the start of a wonderful career. In her prime, Schumann-Heink's voice had a range, a quality, and a power that surpassed most other singers, allowing her to sing in both soprano and contralto ranges.

"Know what you want to do — then do it. Make straight for your goal and go undefeated in spirit to the end." — E. S.

Cybill Shepherd

Cancelled After One Season

Cybill Shepherd (1950–) is a Golden Globe Award-winning actor and singer who has appeared in *The Last Picture Show*, *Moonlighting*, *Cybill*, *Taxi Driver*, and *The L Word*.

In 1982, Cybill Shepherd was trying to break *back* into Hollywood after taking a hiatus to start a family. Earlier, she had appeared in several successful movies such as *The Last Picture Show*, *The Heartbreak Kid*, and *Taxi Driver*. Despite these achievements, Shepherd discovered that Hollywood did not always welcome former stars. She set out to hone her craft by working on stage and taking acting classes from a renowned drama coach. When this failed to revive her movie career, she turned her attention to television. She landed a role on an episode of *Fantasy Island* before being cast in a new nighttime drama, *The Yellow Rose*. With a cast that included Sam Elliott, Jane Russell, and Edward Albert, the show seemed destined to be a hit, but it was cancelled after its first season.

The role turned out to be a lucky break for Shepherd because it brought her to the attention of writer Glenn Gordon Carson. Carson was working on a new series for ABC about a former top model who, after losing her fortune, took over as the manager of a detective agency. *Moonlighting*, starring Shepherd as the former model, premiered on March 3, 1985, as a full-length movie followed by five episodes. The show soon developed a devoted fan base and ran for five seasons. Today, *Moonlighting* is considered one of the greatest spoofs of television detective shows and one of the first television series to mix comedy and drama successfully. It also helped revive Shepherd's career and launched a then-unknown actor, Bruce Willis, into movie stardom. Shepherd won two Golden Globes for Best Actress in a Television Comedy or Musical for her role on *Moonlighting* and was nominated for an Emmy Award for Outstanding Lead Actress in a Drama Series.

> *"We have to keep trying things we're not sure we can pull off. If we just do the things we know we can do, [we] don't grow as much. You gotta take those chances on making those big mistakes." — C. S.*

Steven Spielberg

Rejected from UCLA Film School

Steven Spielberg (1946–), a three-time Academy Award winner, is an American film director and producer. Among the many the films he has directed are *Jaws*, *E.T.*, and *Jurassic Park*.

Steven Spielberg was rejected three times from UCLA film school and the University of Southern California's School of Cinema-Television because of his poor grades. Spielberg then decided to accept a position at Universal Studios as an unpaid intern to gain experience and knowledge of the film industry. His first studio film, *The Sugarland Express*, was a box-office disappointment. His next film, *Jaws*, about a killer shark, started out with an unfinished script and impossible deadlines. It took three times longer to film than scheduled because of the problematic title character.

Spielberg survived these setbacks and used the problems plaguing the filming of *Jaws* to develop the script. He also used creative film techniques and relied on the audience's imagination to overcome problems with the mechanical shark. The resulting film earned more than $100 million in the United States. Spielberg turned down the chance to direct a sequel to *Jaws* in order to direct another movie he had written, *Close Encounters of the Third Kind.* The movie gave Spielberg his second hit, became an influential classic for generations, and earned eight Academy Award nominations, including Spielberg's first for best director. Although he did not win that year, he eventually won the award for his direction of *Schindler's List* and later, *Saving Private Ryan.* He has been nominated for the award an additional four times. Spielberg has also directed and produced other movie greats such as *Raiders of the Lost Ark, E.T.: The Extra-Terrestrial, The Color Purple,* and *Jurassic Park. Premiere* magazine listed him as the most "powerful and influential" figure in the motion picture industry; *Time* included him on its list of the "100 Greatest People of the Century"; and *Life* magazine called him "the most influential person of his generation."

"Failure is inevitable. Success is elusive." — S. S.

Sylvester Stallone

Voted Most Likely to End up in the Electric Chair

Actor, director, producer, and screenwriter Sylvester Stallone (1946–) is best known for his role as Rocky Balboa in the six *Rocky* films and his role as Rambo in the films of the same name.

When Sylvester Stallone was in high school, fellow students voted him "most likely to end up in the electric chair." Instead of turning to a life of crime after graduation as his classmates predicted, he attended college and studied drama. However, his University of Miami professors discouraged him from going into acting. He ignored their advice and unsuccessfully tried out for several roles, including parts in *Dog Day Afternoon*, *Serpico*, and *The Godfather*.

His mother had predicted that he would get into show business but told him it would be as a writer rather than an actor, despite the fact that Stallone had received a number of failing marks in English class. At first, Stallone ignored the prediction, but her words stayed with him. Finally, when no one would cast him in a substantial role, he decided to cast himself. He wrote his own screenplay, an epic movie about a fighter named Rocky, and set out to play the lead.

Studio after studio rejected his screenplay. Stallone finally found a studio willing to produce it, but only if a more established actor played the lead. Studio executives offered the struggling actor huge amounts of money to allow an actor such as James Caan, Ryan O'Neal, or Warren Beatty to star as Rocky in the film of the same name. Stallone held firm and refused to give up the role. *Rocky*, starring Stallone, was nominated for ten Academy Awards, including two for Stallone for Best Screenplay and Best Actor; it won three awards including the Academy Award for Best Picture.

"If you're gonna be a failure, at least be one at something you enjoy." — S. S.

Barbra Streisand

Debut Opened and Closed in One Night

Barbra Streisand (1942–) has won multiple Oscars, Emmys, Grammys, and Golden Globes as a singer, actor, composer, and director.

Barbra Streisand debuted at age nineteen in the off-Broadway revue, *Another Evening with Harry*. It opened and closed in a single night. Ignoring her mother's advice to take typing classes to ensure she could get a job, Streisand put her energies into becoming a star. She also refused to change her "too Jewish-sounding" last name. Instead, she accepted parts in a number of off-off-Broadway shows before landing a role in the musical *I Can Get It for You Wholesale*. Although she had only a small part, it led to a recording contract with Columbia Records.

Her first album, *The Barbra Streisand Album*, won two Grammy Awards, including Album of the Year. She was the youngest artist at that time to win the album award. During her forty-year (and still counting) career, Streisand has won eight more Grammys, two Oscars, six Emmy Awards, eleven Golden Globe Awards, a Tony Award, two Cable Ace Awards, the American Film Institute's Lifetime Achievement Award, and the Grammy Lifetime Achievement Award. Today, Streisand is one of the top-selling female artists in the United States and has sold more than seventy-one million albums in the United States alone.

"I go by instinct . . . I don't worry about experience." — B. S.

Fran Tarkenton

Three Super Bowl Losses and 2,781 Incomplete Passes

Francis "Fran" Tarkenton (1940–) is a former American football player and TV personality.

DESPITE HAVING MADE 2,781 INCOMPLETE passes during his football career and never having won any of the three Super Bowls he played in during his eighteen-year career with the National Football League (NFL), Fran Tarkenton still is referred to as the "greatest quarterback ever to play the game." By the time Tarkenton left professional football, he had completed 3,686 passes and held NFL records for most passing yards (47,003) and most touchdown passes (342).

Tarkenton's career always touched on victory and defeat, often at the same time. In 1975, the same year that Tarkenton suffered what many consider the worst loss of his career — the National Football Conference Divisional Playoffs — Tarkenton was named the NFL Most Valuable Player and the NFL Offensive Player of the Year. In 1999, Tarkenton placed fifty-ninth on the *Sporting News* list of the "100 Greatest Football Players" — proving that it is the art of playing the game, and not winning, that makes a player great. Tarkenton was inducted into the Georgia Sports Hall of Fame in 1977, the Pro Football Hall of Fame in 1986, and the College Football Hall of Fame in 1987.

"The failure to be perfect does not mean you are not a success; it is giving your best that helps you to understand the joy of receiving." — F. T.

Henry David Thoreau

Not an Influential Writer

Henry David Thoreau (1817–1862) was an American author, naturalist, transcendentalist, and philosopher best known for his novel *Walden* and his essay *Civil Disobedience*.

Henry David Thoreau never intended to be a writer. After attending Harvard, he was working as a teacher when he met Ralph Waldo Emerson, an encounter that would change his life and alter his career. Emerson encouraged Thoreau to start a journal. After much pestering on Emerson's part, Thoreau finally began recording his thoughts in a daily journal from which his books would eventually come. Emerson also encouraged Margaret Fuller, editor of a quarterly periodical called *The Dial*, to be the first to publish Thoreau's work. When Thoreau completed his first book, Emerson pressured Thoreau to submit it for publication. Every publisher Thoreau contacted rejected the manuscript. Emerson intervened, convincing his own publisher, James Munroe and Company, to publish the book on the condition that Thoreau would reimburse the company for any losses.

The book, *A Week on the Concord and Merrimack Rivers*, was released in 1849. Of the one thousand copies that were printed, only two hundred were sold; an additional seventy-five were given away, and the rest were shipped to Thoreau in 1853. Thoreau recorded the event in his journal, "I have now a library of nearly nine hundred volumes, over seven hundred of which I wrote myself." The experience put Thoreau deep in debt and fractured his friendship with Emerson. In 1854, Thoreau risked publishing a second book, *Walden*, which sold only slightly better than its predecessor. Thoreau spent the next ten years revising his unpublished manuscripts and trying to convince publishers to reissue revised editions of his earlier novels. However, *A Week* and *Walden* would be the only books published before Thoreau's death in 1862.

After Thoreau died, his sister took up the cause to get his the rest of his works published. In 1866, *A Yankee in Canada, with Anti-Slavery and Reform Papers* was published. The book reprinted an essay that Thoreau had written years earlier entitled *Resistance to Civil Government*, better known as *Civil Disobedience*. Although Thoreau may have wielded little influence as a writer when he was alive, his works have had a major impact on the world since his death.

Some of the greatest people in history have cited Thoreau's writings, especially *Civil Disobedience*. Mahatma Gandhi said, "Thoreau was a great writer, philosopher, poet, and withal a most practical man, that is, he taught nothing he was not prepared to practice in himself. He was one of the greatest and most moral men America has produced." Martin Luther King Jr., also influenced by Thoreau, said, "No other person has been more eloquent and passionate in getting this idea across than Henry David Thoreau. As a result of his writings and personal witness, we are the heirs of a legacy of creative protest." Others who have credited Thoreau's effect on their lives include John F. Kennedy, Martin Buber, Leo Tolstoy, Willa Cather, Ernest Hemingway, Sinclair Lewis, E. B. White,

William Butler Yeats, Frank Lloyd Wright, John Burroughs, John Muir, David Brower, and Emma Goldman.

> *"I wish to suggest that a man may be very industrious, and yet not spend his time well. There is no more fatal blunderer than he who consumes the greater part of his life getting his living. All great enterprises are self-supporting." — H. D. T.*

The Who

Quickly Rejected

The Who is considered by many to be one of the greatest and most influential rock bands of all time. In addition to its many hit songs, the band wrote and performed the classic rock opera *Tommy*.

The Who's first demo record was rejected by EMI because the group had not written any of their own songs. The band's guitarist Pete Townsend quickly sat down and wrote "I Can't Explain." Shel Talmy, a producer at EMI, was so spellbound by a demo of the new song that he immediately signed the band to a contract and scheduled a recording session. "I Can't Explain" was released eight weeks later by Decca and sold more than 100,000 copies. Since then, the Who has sold more than 150 million records and has landed in the Top 10 on VH1's "100 Greatest Artists of Hard Rock" and "100 Greatest Artists of Rock 'n' Roll." The band, one of the first rock groups to integrate synthesizers into their music, had a considerable influence on punk music and rock opera. Townsend is also said to have been the first guitarist to destroy a guitar on stage, ushering in a new tradition in both pop and rock music.

> *"I refuse to have my best efforts — already heavily filtered in advance and subjected to the constraints of finance and time — rejected by any criteria whatsoever."* — Pete Townsend

Robin Williams

Funny, But Not Likely to Succeed

Robin Williams (1951–) is an Academy Award-winning American actor and comedian who starred in the television show *Mork and Mindy* as well as in popular movies such as *Good Morning, Vietnam*; *Dead Poets Society*; *Mrs. Doubtfire*; and *Good Will Hunting*.

ROBIN WILLIAMS WAS VOTED "MOST humorous" in high school, but his classmates did not think his comedy would carry him far. They had also voted him "least likely to succeed." He was playing in local comedy clubs when he landed a small role on the television show *Happy Days*. His performance, most of it improvised, was extremely successful, and the role was spun off as the hit series *Mork and Mindy*. Overnight, Robin Williams became the featured celebrity on posters, coloring books, lunchboxes, and other merchandise promoting the show.

While filming the series, Williams moved into motion pictures as well. Unfortunately, his first two films, *Popeye* and *The World According to Garp*, flopped at the box office. After *Mork and Mindy* ended in 1982, he made several more films, but they, too, were all box-office disappointments. Then, in 1987, Williams landed the role of Adrian Cronauer in the movie *Good Morning, Vietnam*. The movie helped make his career and earned him a nomination for an Academy Award for Best Actor. He was nominated a second time in 1989 for his performance in *Dead Poets Society*. It was not until 1997 that he finally won an Oscar, for Best Supporting Actor, for his role in

Good Will Hunting. As of 2007, Williams has appeared in almost sixty movies.

"You're only given a little spark of madness. You mustn't lose it." — R. W.

Turn Lemons into Lemonade

"Difficulties are meant to rouse, not to discourage."
— William Ellery Channing

Rick Allen

A Determined Drummer

Rick Allen (1963–) is drummer for the rock band Def Leppard, which has released several multiplatinum and two diamond albums between 1980 and 2007.

After five years of practice on his mother's kitchen utensils, ten-year-old Rick Allen decided it was time to get a real drum set. His parents agreed to pay for half of the set if he agreed to take lessons. For the next five years, Allen climbed the narrow stairway to a dingy room above the town's tiny music store, where he learned the basics of playing drums. The first time he touched real drumsticks, he knew in his heart that he was destined to become a drummer.

His parents must have recognized that too, because they approved of Allen's decision to leave school when he was fifteen to tour as a professional drummer with the band Def Leppard. Within two years, Def Leppard's first album had topped the charts. A luminous life, a new record, and a new year stretched out before him as Allen drove to a New Year's Eve party in 1984 in his glossy new Corvette with his gorgeous girlfriend beside him. Although he was familiar with the road, he took a tight curve too fast. His car spun off the pavement and flipped repeatedly. Allen awoke in the hospital to discover his left arm had been severed at the shoulder and his right arm was seriously damaged.

Lying in the hospital bed, his right arm immobilized, a bored Allen started tapping on his hospital bed with his feet. He realized that losing his arm did not mean, he had lost his rhythm. He could still play the drums using his right arm, while playing kick and snare with his right foot. All he had to do was figure out a way to use his left foot to replace his arm. A friend who was good with electronics helped him design a new drum kit to suit his needs. "[A]n amazing thing happens at a certain point," Allen said later, "the information is in your brain and, very quickly, your brain is able to rewire itself and send that information to different places. I think it's called necessity. . . . It's something that if you're really determined enough, it just kinda of happens."

A few months later, Allen returned to his gig performing with Def Leppard. His fellow band members had remained on hiatus until Allen was able to return. Excited to have him back on the drums, they re-recorded parts of their new album to match their drummer's new style. The band's next album went multiplatinum. Allen's dreams expanded beyond music. He helped found the Raven Drum Foundation with the mission "to empower individuals in crisis through the healing power of the drum." He continues to work with and inspire others who are physically challenged.

"If you're thrown in the deep end you swim, and that's basically what I did. I had to do it and with the rest of the band behind me and the encouragement I got from people from all over the world, I knew that I was going to play." — R. A.

Julie Andrews

Not Famous Enough

Julie Andrews (1935–) is an award-winning actor and singer best known for her roles in *Mary Poppins* and *The Sound of Music.*

Her costar, among others, objected to casting Julie Andrews in the part of Eliza Doolittle in *My Fair Lady*. Before she was hired for the Broadway version, costar Rex Harrison told the director he had reservations about her ability to portray the character. However, the director insisted Andrews was the precise person for the role. Andrews went on to win critical acclaim and a Tony nomination for her performance in the musical, which was successful in New York and London. Still, producer Jack Warner did not believe that Andrews could successfully portray the role on the big screen. When it came time to cast the movie, Warner decided he wanted someone famous and gave the part to Audrey Hepburn.

Around the same time, Walt Disney purchased the film rights for P.L. Travers's book, *Mary Poppins*. For more than twenty years, Travers had refused to sell the rights because she did not believe a film version would capture the book's magic. Looking for a job after being rejected for the film version of *My Fair Lady*, Andrews auditioned for and won the lead in *Mary Poppins*, one of Disney's first live-action movies.

When Oscar time came around in 1964, *My Fair Lady* won the Best Picture Award, but the Academy Award for Best Actress went to Andrews. Hepburn was not even nominated. Harrison, however, won the Best Actor Award for his on-screen performance in *My Fair Lady*. In his acceptance speech, Harrison dedicated his award to both Andrews and Hepburn, referring to them as "his two fair ladies." Andrews also won the Golden Globe for Best Actress for her portrayal of Mary Poppins in the movie, which many consider one of the best musicals of all time.

"Perseverance is failing nineteen times and succeeding the twentieth." — J. A.

Douglas Bader

Crushed Dreams

Douglas Bader (1910–1982) was a fighter pilot for the Royal Air Force during World War II.

NO MATTER HOW GREAT THE pilot, planes crash, a sad fact that Douglas Bader learned too well. In December 1931, the young cadet was on the verge of completing his dream of becoming a pilot for the Royal Air Force (RAF) when his plane crashed. Because of his injuries, the doctors had to amputate both of his legs. Even with the loss of his legs, however, Bader vowed to pursue his dream. For seven long months, he struggled to learn to walk using prosthetic legs. Once that was accomplished, he learned to fly his plane. However, the medical board could not accept that a legless pilot was as good as one with legs, and they discharged Bader from the military.

Seven years went by before opportunity finally came knocking. World War II broke out in Europe, and England was desperate for competent pilots to help in the effort to defeat Adolf Hitler. Because of the need for pilots, Bader was allowed to rejoin the RAF. He racked up twenty-three victories before being shot down over enemy territory on August 9, 1941. When he attempted to bail out of his damaged aircraft, he discovered his prosthetic legs had become tangled. Luckily, the strap attaching his legs broke, and Bader managed to parachute to the ground. Without his legs, he was quickly captured by German forces.

Bader was taken to an enemy hospital to recover from injuries he had sustained in the incident. While he was there, he convinced his captors to help him acquire a new set of prosthetic legs. Once he received them, Bader immediately tried to escape. The attempt failed, but Bader was not one to accept failure. During his four-year internment with the Germans, Bader made countless attempts, even after he was transferred to the "escape proof" Colditz Castle. Finally, the guards confiscated his legs each night, a policy that kept Bader imprisoned until his release in 1944.

> *"Don't listen to anyone who tells you that you can't do this or that. That's nonsense. Make up your mind you'll never use crutches or a stick, then have a go at everything. Go to school; join in all the games you can. Go anywhere you want to. But never, never let them persuade you that things are too difficult or impossible." — D. B.*

Bill Belichick

A Coach in the Wrong Direction

Bill Belichick (1952–) guided the New England Patriots to three Super Bowl wins as the team's head coach.

As the son of an assistant football coach, Bill Belichick knew by the time he was ten that he wanted to follow in his father's footsteps. He obtained a degree in economics at Wesleyan University in Connecticut. When plans to pursue a master's degree fell though, he took an unpaid position as a special assistant with the Baltimore Colts. Slowly, Belichick worked his way up until he was the defense coordinator for the New York Giants under Coach Bill Parcells in 1985.

Six years and two Super Bowl wins later, Belichick accepted the position as head coach for the Cleveland Browns. Only thirty-seven, he was the youngest head coach in the league. Belichick coached the Browns for five years before he was fired because the team's owner thought the team "needed to go in another direction."

Belichick went in a familiar direction — he rejoined Parcells, who was coaching the New England Patriots. Belichick once again became the assistant head coach and defense coordinator under Parcells. The job lasted only a year before Parcells, with Belichick at his side, moved to the New York Jets.

When Parcells announced his retirement in 2000, it was assumed that Belichick would be hired to replace him as head coach of the Jets. However, only moments before the press conference to announce his hiring, Belichick scooped up a sheet of loose leaf paper and hastily scrawled out these seven words: "I resign as HC of the NYJ." Instead, Belichick took a position as head coach of the New England Patriots. It was a risky move. The Patriots' performance had been declining since Parcells had resigned as its head coach several years earlier, while the Jets were flourishing.

Under Belichick's guidance, the Patriots won their first Super Bowl in 2001. When the team returned to win the Super Bowl again in 2002, Belichick shouted, "They said we couldn't do it!" In 2004, the Patriots became the second team in NFL history to win three Super Bowls in four years.

> *"You're going to be criticized whatever you do. I just think that's the job. You have to make decisions that aren't popular. If it's fourth and 1, half the people in the stands want you to go for it, the other half don't want you to go for it. Whichever way you decide, you're going to make people angry. At that point, I get paid to make the decisions. I'll make them." — B. B.*

Ken Blanchard

Not Academic Enough

Kenneth H. Blanchard (1939–) is a management consultant and coauthor of the best-selling novel *The One Minute Manager.*

Ken Blanchard decided to pursue a career in sales after several vocational preference tests revealed that would be the best career for him. He quickly learned that the results of a vocational test and people's perceptions were two different things after he applied for a summer sales internship. Although he made it through several intensive interviews, he did not get the job. Blanchard ignored the vocational tests and obtained his doctoral degree in educational administration and leadership from Cornell University. When he tried for a position as a dean of students, however, he again met with failure because of lack of experience. His attempt to become a professor also failed after several academics told him that his writing was not "academic enough" for a university professor. He eventually realized that his writing style had been targeted not because it was weak, but because it was understandable.

He used this knowledge to help him when he began writing his first book on management techniques with his partner, Spencer Johnson. "Rather than writing as an art for our own satisfaction or the satisfaction of a few colleagues, we wrote for the satisfaction of the reader — managers all over the country," Blanchard said. Together Blanchard and Johnson wrote four drafts, which they presented to about 250 to 300 people to read and provide feedback.

When publishers rejected the finished work, a small book of only 112 pages, Blanchard and Johnson decided to publish it themselves in 1981. They sold more than twenty thousand copies of *The One Minute Manager* before selling the reprint rights to William Morrow. Since then, the best-selling book has sold more than seventeen million copies around the world, has been printed in twenty-seven languages, and has spawned a series of additional *One Minute* books.

"Learning is defined as a change in behavior. You haven't learned a thing until you can take action and use it." — Ken Blanchard and Don Shula

Milton Bradley

A Checkered Life

Milton Bradley (1836–1911) founded the Milton Bradley Company and is credited for launching America's obsession with board games.

As a lithographer, Milton Bradley completed his first big project for the Republican National Convention by producing images of the party's candidate. Unfortunately, Abraham Lincoln later grew a beard and inadvertently rendered the beardless lithographs worthless. Soon after, the Civil War erupted and further jeopardized Bradley's business. About to go broke, the young entrepreneur came up with an idea for a board game in which players moved game pieces over colored squares while attempting to make it to the end without ruining themselves financially. He called it the "Checkered Game of Life," although the name was eventually shortened to the "Game of Life." By 1861, Bradley had sold more than 45,000 copies of his game. Three years later, he created Milton Bradley and Company, which continues to manufacture games — including Bradley's first one — more than 140 years later.

"No one ever won a chess game by betting on each move. Sometimes you have to move backward to get a step forward." — Amar Gopal Bose

David Brown

Barred from Work

Movie producer David Brown (1916–) is responsible for producing *The Sugarland Express, Jaws, Cocoon,* and *Driving Miss Daisy.*

When he began school, David Brown wanted to be a physicist, but he had difficulties with both math and science. As a result, he changed his focus to journalism. After graduating from Stanford University and Columbia University School of Journalism, Brown headed to New York and started his journalism career. In 1951, Daryl F. Zanuck offered him the position of head of the story department at Twentieth Century Fox. Brown, who had never been interested in film, accepted the job.

His film career went smoothly at first. Brown worked his

way up to the number two position at Fox. While there, he helped launch Elvis Presley's and Marilyn Monroe's movie careers. He lost his job when, in 1963, he recommended a film that turned out to be a flop. Brown did not remain unemployed for long. He landed a position as editorial vice president at the New American Library. After about a year, he was fired because of a clash with a coworker. Brown was rehired by Twentieth Century Fox, only to be fired again — along with studio head Richard D. Zanuck — six years later in a studio upheaval.

Brown described this time as one of the lowest points in his life. "Our names were taken off the parking places right in front of us. Our offices were padlocked," Brown said. "That was terribly painful." For the next year, he worked at Warner Brothers Pictures as executive vice president in charge of creative operations and as a member of board of directors. He left the studio to form his own company with Zanuck, Zanuck-Brown Productions, which releases through Universal Pictures.

Pursuing his own ideas has created enormous success for Brown. Zanuck-Brown Productions is responsible for giving director Steven Spielberg his start in films; the studio produced both *The Sugarland Express* and *Jaws*. The team also produced *The Sting*, *Cocoon*, and *The Verdict* before splitting amicably in 1988. On his own, Brown has produced such films as *The Player*, *The Saint*, *Angela's Ashes*, *A Few Good Men*, and *Chocolat*. His Broadway musicals include *Dirty Rotten Scoundrels* and *Sweet Smell of Success*.

"Achieving success in any field requires a positive attitude. It also requires an ability to surmount disappointments and setbacks — by trying again and again to reach your goals." — D. B.

Jacques Cousteau

From Therapy to Destiny

Jacques Cousteau (1910–1997) was an explorer, ecologist, filmmaker, photographer, scientist, and researcher most famous for his pioneer work in marine conservation.

Jacques Cousteau was close to graduating from the French naval aviation school when his car spun out of control and crashed on a deserted mountain road. He survived, but his right arm was severely damaged, and doctors advised amputating it. He refused, and his arm was saved, but it took several years of therapy before he could regain full use of it. While stationed at Toulon, a fellow officer casually suggested to Cousteau that swimming might help rehabilitate his arm. The water therapy dramatically changed Cousteau's life. He quickly discovered that he loved being underwater, especially diving. Before long, he was spending all his time at the beach.

Cousteau became frustrated with the limited technology available — he wanted to dive deeper than the standard helmet and heavy suit apparatus allowed and he wanted more mobility. His frustration led him to invent the Aqualung, which consisted of a canister of compressed air, a regulator that supplied a constant flow of oxygen, and a mouthpiece that enabled the diver to breathe. Cousteau spent the rest of his life exploring the waterways of the world, all the while inventing and testing new equipment. He also won three Oscars for his filmmaking, hosted a popular television show, and authored several books.

"Sometimes we are lucky enough to know that our lives have been changed, to discard the old, embrace the new, and run headlong down an immutable course. It happened to me that summer's day, when my eyes were opened to the sea." — J. C.

George Cukor

Fired After Only Ten Days of Filming

George Cukor (1899–1983) directed numerous films including *David Copperfield, Camille,* and *My Fair Lady,* for which he won the Academy Award.

IN 1938, *GONE WITH THE Wind* was the most anticipated movie in production. Producer David Selznick selected every aspect carefully — especially the director. After weighing his options, he decided upon George Cukor. For a year, Cukor worked on the preproduction until he was finally ready to do the filming. Unfortunately, Cukor did not last two weeks before he was fired. Clark Gable, fearing that his own role would be overshadowed by the director's attentiveness to his female costars, announced that he could not go on and walked off the set. Gable refused to be directed by "a fairy" and gave Selznick an ultimatum: either Cukor or him. Afraid to lose Gable's star power, Selznick fired Cukor and brought in Victor Fleming to finish directing.

Cukor took everything in stride without harboring any resentment. After he was fired, he continued in secret to coach two of the film's major stars, Vivien Leigh and Olivia de Havilland, on weekends, which no doubt contributed to the actors' stellar performances and helped make the movie a success. He also went to work on the film version of the hit play *The Women*, then directed *The Philadelphia Story*. Both films are considered comedy classics, and the latter revived Katharine Hepburn's career. In 1964, Cukor won his first Academy Award for Best Director for his work on *My Fair Lady*. It was his fifth nomination for the award.

"You can't have any successes unless you can accept failure." — G. C.

Fannie Farmer

Advised to Abandon Her Education

Fannie Farmer (1857–1915) was a culinary expert and the editor of the *Boston Cooking School Cookbook*, better known today as the "Fannie Farmer Cookbook."

In 1873, Fannie Farmer's college plans stalled after she suffered a paralytic stroke during her senior year of high school. Although she was only sixteen, the doctors told her to abandon any ideas of furthering her education because she probably would never walk again. Although it took several years, Farmer eventually recuperated enough to work as a mother's helper, although she continued to walk with a significant limp. She had given up all thoughts of continuing her education until her employer urged her to enroll at the Boston Cooking School. Farmer decided to try it. After graduation, she was immediately hired as the school's assistant principal and, within two years, she had become the school's principal.

In 1896, she wrote and edited a cookbook. It was a follow-up edition to a cookbook published twelve years earlier by Mary J. Lincoln. Despite her position at the school and the book's previous success, Farmer could not find a publisher for the new version. One publisher reluctantly printed it but only after Farmer agreed to pay the costs herself. The *Boston Cooking School Cookbook*, also called the "Fannie Farmer Cookbook," was extremely popular and made Fannie Farmer a household name. During Farmer's lifetime, twenty-one editions of the cookbook were published. It has been translated into French, Spanish, and Japanese and has sold nearly four million copies. Farmer went on to teach doctors and nurses about diets and nutrition for people convalescing from illnesses. Her book on the subject, based on her own experiences, was published under the title, *Food and Cookery for the Sick and Convalescent.* Farmer was even invited to lecture on the topic at Harvard Medical School.

"The dictionary is the only place that success comes before work. Hard work is the price we must pay for success. I think you can accomplish anything if you're willing to pay the price." — Vince Lombardi

Wayne Gretzky

Too Small and Too Slow for Hockey

Known to fans as "The Great One," Wayne Gretzky (1961–) set forty regular-season records, fifteen play-off records, and six All-Star records during his hockey career. He also won four Stanley Cups, nine MVP awards, and ten scoring titles.

EARLY ON, WAYNE GRETZKY GOT used to being smaller than the other hockey players. By the time he was six, he was competing against ten-year-old players. When he was sixteen, he became the youngest player to compete in the World Junior Championships. Not only did he complete with eighteen- to twenty-year-old players, he bested them by finishing as the top scorer. He was voted to the tournament's All-Star team and was honored as the best forward. However, when National Hockey League (NHL) scouts looked at him, all they could see was Gretzky's size. The conventional wisdom dictated that hockey players needed to be big — at least six feet tall and two hundred pounds. Gretzky was only five feet eleven inches tall and weighed barely 165 pounds. One scout wrote that he "won't survive the rough play," and another deemed him "too small, too slow" to play for the NHL.

Rejected by the NHL, the seventeen-year-old Gretzky signed up to play for the World Hockey Association (WHA). In 1978, he became WHA Rookie of the Year. It would be his only year with the WHA, which folded the next year. Gretkzy's team was incorporated into the NHL, and again critics predicted that Gretzky would crumble in the face of the steep competition.

To compensate for being smaller and slower than his competitors, Gretzky developed his own style by using his eyes, his brain, and his father's advice to "skate where the puck is going, not to where it has been." In his first NHL season, Gretzky was awarded the Hart Memorial Trophy, given to the league's most valuable player; tied for the scoring lead with 137 points, a record for the most points scored by a first-year player; and was awarded the Lady Byng Trophy for being the league's most sportsman-like player. He won the Hart Memorial Trophy the next seven years. He also won the Art Ross trophy, an annual award given to the player who leads the league in scoring points at the end of the regular season, a record ten times. Gretzky is the only player to score more than two hundred points in a season, a feat he accomplished four times during his career. By the time he retired, he held sixty-one

NHL records that included 894 career goals, 1,963 career assists, 2,857 points, and 50 hat tricks.

"You'll miss 100 percent of the shots you don't take." — W. G.

Robert Jarvik

No Medical School Would Accept Him

Robert K. Jarvik (1946–) is the American scientist and physician famous for his work on the Jarvik-7 artificial heart.

After his father developed heart disease and required surgery, Robert Jarvik, an architecture and mechanical drawing student at the time, was so impressed by the doctors treating his father that he switched his major to premedicine. After graduating from Syracuse University, Jarvik discovered his mediocre grades made it almost impossible for him to get into medical school. After applying to and being rejected by approximately twenty-five U.S. medical schools, he attended the University of Bologna in Italy. After two years abroad, he transferred to New York University and graduated with a master of arts in occupational biomechanics in 1971. Jarvik took a job working at a surgical supply house, then applied for a lab assistant position with the artificial organs program at the University of Utah. The job as lab assistant helped pave the way for his acceptance to the university's medical school.

Jarvik was thirty when he earned his medical degree in 1976 — the same year his father died of an aneurysm. At the time, he had already begun working with William J. Kolff on an artificial heart, but it would be years before the device would be ready for use in a patient. Finally, on December 2, 1982, the first patient received the Jarvik-7 artificial heart. The patient survived 112 days. The second patient survived much longer — 620 days. Since then, approximately ninety other patients have used the Jarvik-7 while waiting for a heart transplant with a donor heart. Jarvik's most recent work has been with miniaturized heart-assist devices for people whose hearts need a boost or who are waiting for heart transplants.

"Leaders are visionaries with a poorly developed sense of fear and no concept of the odds against them." — R. J.

Stephen King

Trashed His Own Work

Stephen King (1947–) is the author of more than two hundred stories, fifty of which are best-selling horror and fantasy novels. Best known for his works such as *Carrie*, *The Shining*, *Misery*, *Christine*, and *Pet Sematary*, King also writes short stories, nonfiction, and other genres.

Stephen King had written only four pages of his new novel when he decided the work was dreadful and tossed it. Fortunately, his wife, Tabatha, spotted the crumpled pages and plucked them from the trash. After reading the rejected work, she placed the pages on King's desk with a note, "Please keep going — it's good." King considered her his harshest critic and wisely chose to follow her suggestion. When the book was finished, he submitted the manuscript, entitled *Carrie*, to publishers. All King's previous manuscripts had already been rejected. When the first responses came in, it appeared that *Carrie* would suffer the same fate. One editor told King, "We are not interested in science fiction which deals with negative utopias. They do not sell." King's own opinion of *Carrie* was not much better. He later said that after finishing *Carrie*, his "considered opinion was that I had written the world's all-time loser."

Nevertheless, King continued to submit the novel to publishers, including Doubleday, which had rejected his earlier novels. King received the surprising news that Doubleday planned to publish the novel via a telegram, because at the time he could not afford a phone service. Although readers bought fewer than half of the thirty thousand hardcover copies printed, the paperback version sold more than one million copies in its first year. *Carrie* became a successful movie and launched King's writing career. Today, he is one of the world's most successful writers, with more than seventy books published.

King later released his earlier novels under the pseudonym Richard Bachman, because he wanted to see if he could replicate his own success under a different name. The ruse did not fool his fans for long. A press release issued in 1985 observed that Bachman had died from "cancer of the pseudonym, a rare form of schizonomia." More than ten years later, a fifth Bachman book, *The Regulators*, was released. The publishers claimed that Bachman's widow had found the manuscript, but inside the back cover was an early picture of King. If that wasn't enough to erase the doubts, the "also by this author" list included works written by King, and the cover was designed so that when it was placed next to King's new novel, *Desperation*, the two books formed one picture. Although the original editions of the Bachman novels sold only moderately well, they are now among the most sought-after paperback novels.

"When you find something at which you have talent, you do that thing until your fingers bleed or your eyes pop out of your head." — S. K.

David Letterman

Fired for Unpredictable Behavior

David Letterman (1947–) is an American comedian and host of CBS's *Late Show with David Letterman*; he also hosted the show's predecessor, *Late Night with David Letterman*, on NBC.

David Letterman was once fired as a television weatherman in Indianapolis for his unpredictable behavior. His bizarre behavior included such antics as sarcastically predicting "hailstones the size of canned hams," congratulating a tropical storm for being upgraded to a hurricane, and erasing state boundary lines. After being fired, Letterman moved to Los Angeles where he landed regular roles on two series in the 1970s, *The Starland Vocal Band Show* and *Mary*. However, both were canceled by CBS after only a few episodes. Letterman eventually moved to NBC, where he created a series titled *Leave it to Dave*, but it never aired. He then had a morning talk show, *The David Letterman Show*, which earned two Emmy Awards for Letterman — one for hosting and one for writing — but the show was canceled after four months. By that time, Letterman had gained a loyal audience, and within a year, NBC offered him another show. Airing immediately after *The Tonight Show*, *Late Night with David Letterman* gave full rein to the wacky host. *Late Night* earned five Emmy Awards and thirty-five

Emmy nominations before Letterman moved to CBS to host *The Late Show*, which has earned nine Emmy Awards and more than fifty Emmy nominations.

"Nothing, believe me, nothing is more satisfying to me personally than getting a great idea and then beatin' it to death." — D. L.

Ronald Reagan

Doesn't Have the Presidential Look

After giving up an acting career, Ronald Reagan (1911–2004) became the thirty-third governor of California and the fortieth president of the United States.

IN THE 1940S, RONALD REAGAN was a major box-office draw in Hollywood and had already appeared in more than two dozen movies, including *Knute Rockne - All American*, the role that gave Reagan his lifelong nickname "The Gipper." During the late 1950s and early 1960s, he became even more famous when he hosted the number one rated show on television, *General Electric Theater.* He also served as the president of the Screen Actors Guild for seven years. By 1964, Reagan was looking for a new challenge and tried out for the starring role in an upcoming movie titled *The Best Man*. He was not selected for the role because, according to an executive at United Artists, "Reagan doesn't have that presidential look." The role went instead to Henry Fonda.

Reagan decided that if he could not play the part of a president, he would assume the role of governor. About a year after his rejection for the part, Reagan announced his candidacy for governor of California. Unlike the studio executives, the majority of Californians believed that

Reagan not only looked like a governor, but also had the qualifications for the job. Reagan served two terms as governor before trying again for the role of president. This time, though, the role he sought was not in a film but in real life. In 1976, Reagan made his first attempt to win the Republican Party nomination for president of the United States. He narrowly lost to incumbent President Gerald Ford, who went on to lose the general election to the Democrats' nominee, Jimmy Carter.

When Reagan tried again in 1980, he easily won the Republican nomination and beat incumbent Carter by a landslide. On January 20, 1981, Reagan was sworn in as the fortieth president of the United States. During the next eight years, he achieved record-setting economic expansion and job creation and a reduction in inflation. His performance in office has led many historians and academics to rank Reagan as one of the top American presidents.

"Every new day begins with possibilities. It is up to us to fill it with the things that move us toward progress and peace." — R. R.

Jerry Rice

Assigned Football as Punishment

Jerry Rice (1962–) is a former football wide receiver in the NFL. During his career, he was selected to the Pro Bowl thirteen times, was named All-Pro ten times, and has won three Super Bowl rings as a member of the San Francisco 49ers.

Jerry Rice's football career began after he was caught trying to play hooky from school; part of his punishment was being required to attend football practice. He became an All-State end and defensive back in high school, but he was not considered good enough by any of the bigger colleges to warrant a scholarship offer. Only one college recruited him, Mississippi Valley State in Itta Bena, but the school was not big enough to be in Division I.

Nevertheless, Rice seized the opportunity to attend college on a scholarship. It was a good move for both Rice and the Mississippi Valley State Delta Devils. As a key member of the team, Rice caught more than one hundred passes his junior and senior year and had twenty-eight touchdown receptions his senior year. The Delta Devils finished the season with a 24-6-1 record. The performance brought Rice to the attention of 49ers coach Bill Walsh, who picked the Mississippi player in the first round. Walsh's decision was immediately criticized because Rice was virtually unknown and had never played in a high-stakes arena.

During his first year as a professional with the 49ers, Rice dropped a record fifteen passes, but he also set a team record with 241 receiving yards in one game and made it onto the 1985-86 all-rookie team. In 1992, Rice earned the record for most touchdown receptions in a professional career; and in 2000, he was placed on the NFL All-Time team by the Pro Football Hall of Fame.

"To me, it was never about what I accomplished on the football field. It was about the way I played the game. I played the game with a lot of determination, a lot of poise, a lot of pride and I think what you saw out there . . . was an individual who really just loved the game." — J. R.

Molly Ringwald

Failure at Age Twelve

Molly Ringwald (1968–) rose to stardom in 1980s after she starred in several John Hughes movies including *Sixteen Candles*, *The Breakfast Club*, and *Pretty in Pink*.

Molly Ringwald began acting when she was five, and by the time she was eleven she had a part on a series, *The Facts of Life*. Unfortunately, her character was written out of the show after the first season. "I felt like I had failed," she said about the experience. Her mother told her it was for the best, but the words offered little comfort. Ringwald decided to take a year off from working. When she returned, she was cast in the 3-D film *Spacehunter: Adventures in Forbidden Zone*. Her performance was described by one reviewer as "atrocious." Despite the bad review, director Paul Mazursky cast her in his movie *The Tempest*, which earned her a Golden Globe nomination and brought her to the attention of another director, John Hughes, who quickly cast Ringwald in his next movie, *Sixteen Candles*. The movie transformed Ringwald into an idol to thousands of girls, and her face was soon plastered onto the covers of teen magazines. Ringwald also appeared in the movies *The Breakfast Club* and *Pretty in Pink* in the early 1980s.

"I don't really believe in regret. I think you can always learn from the past, but I wouldn't want a different life." — M. R.

Ray Romano

Fired After Two Rehearsals

Raymond Romano (1957–) is an American actor and comedian best known for his Emmy Award-winning role on the sitcom *Everybody Loves Raymond.*

In 1995, Ray Romano had been working as a stand-up comedian for several years and was looking for a new challenge. He tried out and landed a role on an upcoming series, *NewsRadio*. But after two rehearsals, the producers decided that his style of comedy was not right for the role, and he was fired. With his schedule free, Romano returned to the comedy clubs and appeared on *Late Night with David Letterman*. Impressed by Romano's performance, Letterman called Romano the following week and offered him a job. Letterman's production company, Worldwide Pants Incorporated, was looking for people to develop shows for, and he felt that Romano's style was exactly what they needed. The resulting collaboration led to the show *Everybody Loves Raymond*.

By 1999, when *NewsRadio* was ending its run, *Everybody Loves Raymond* had begun its third season. The show averaged more than thirteen million viewers and was the eleventh most-watched show on television, according to Nielsen Media Research. It continued for nine seasons and ranked in the top ten the last five years it was on the air. In 2001, Romano was named one of E!'s top twenty entertainers of the year. By 2004, he had become the highest paid television actor in history with a salary of $50 million, while his show had the highest revenue of any show on television, almost $4 billion. Romano was nominated six times for an Emmy Award for Outstanding Lead Actor in a Comedy Series, winning once in 2002, and received two nominations for a Golden Globe award for Best Performance by an Actor in a TV Series-Comedy.

"I have the show because I'm insecure. It's my insecurity that makes me want to be a comic, that makes me need the audience." — R. R.

Charles Schultz

Repeatedly Rejected

Charles Schultz (1922–2000) was an American cartoonist known worldwide for creating and drawing the *Peanuts* comic strip.

Charles Schultz was used to rejection. In high school, a teacher once asked him to do school drawings for the yearbook. When the yearbook came out, Schultz discovered that none of his drawings had made it in. When he asked his first love, a redheaded coworker, to marry him, she turned him down after her mother convinced her that a cartoonist would never amount to anything. He was rejected once again when he applied for a job as a cartoonist at Walt Disney Studios.

In 1947, Schultz began drawing a regular cartoon titled *Li'l Folks* for the *St. Paul Pioneer Press*. He attempted to syndicate the column with the Newspaper Enterprise Association, but the deal fell through. When he approached the United Feature Syndicate with his best strips, the syndicate insisted on changing the name because *Li'l Folks* was too similar to the name of another strip the firm was running. Schultz's strip became *Peanuts*, a name that upset the cartoonist. The first year, only seven newspapers bought *Peanuts*, but that number steadily grew.

By the mid-1960s, Schultz had won national awards for his cartoons and an Emmy for *A Charlie Brown Christmas*, and *Peanuts* had graced the cover of *Time* magazine. In 1999, when Schultz announced his retirement, *Peanuts* was featured in more than 2,600 newspapers, in twenty-one languages and seventy-five countries. Sadly, Schultz died in his sleep on the same day the last Sunday *Peanuts* comic went to press.

"Sometimes I lie awake at night and I ask, 'Why me?' And the voice says, 'Nothing personal, your name just happened to come up.'" — C. S.

Howard Schultz

218 Rejections for His Idea

Howard Schultz (1953–) is the chairman and chief global strategist of Starbucks, a leading coffeehouse in the United States.

His Il Giornale coffee shops were doing well, but Howard Schultz wanted to expand and grabbed the opportunity to purchase his own roasting facility as well as another line of coffeehouses. When he pitched his idea to 242 potential investors, however, he received 218 rejections. Still, he managed to get enough money from the twenty-four willing investors to go ahead with his plan.

Schultz soon learned that one of the investors was trying to buy out the coffeehouses secretly and make Schultz a mere manager instead of a shareholder. When he confronted the investor, the investor issued Schultz a take-it-or-leave-it ultimatum. Refusing to be backed into a corner, Schultz replied, "It's my idea. . . . You're not taking it away." It was only after the investor left that Schultz allowed himself to break down in tears.

His tears did not last long, and Schultz pushed forward to implement his own plan. His drive and determination convinced the other investors to rally behind him. They provided enough money to purchase the other coffeehouses, and adopted the old chain's name — Starbucks — as the name of the new company. Within ten years, Starbucks had expanded outside its Seattle home base. Today, it is the world's largest chain of coffee shops. As of November 2007, Starbucks had more than 8,500 stores worldwide with plans to expand to at least 40,000 stores.

"You are judged by the company you keep." — H. S.

Martin Scorsese

Second Choice . . . Film School

Martin Scorsese (1942–) is an American Academy Award-winning film director, writer, and producer.

Martin Scorsese owed his movie career to a failed entrance exam. He had intended to become a priest since he was fourteen, but he failed the entrance examination to Fordham University's divinity school and enrolled at New York University instead. While at NYU, he focused on filmmaking and received honors for several of his works. After earning his degree, he worked on a variety of British and American television shows and at NYU as a film instructor. The premier of *Mean Streets* in 1972 marked his breakthrough as a director. The film was not the first movie

Scorsese had directed and was not even a box-office success, but the critics praised it. Scorsese went on to direct other successful movies such as *Taxi Driver, Casino, Raging Bull,* and *Goodfellas.*

In 1980, Scorsese received his first Oscar nomination for Best Director for the movie *Raging Bull.* Other Oscar nominations followed: in 1988 for *The Last Temptation of Christ,* in 1990 for *Goodfellas,* in 2002 for *Gangs of New York,* and in 2004 for *The Aviator.* Each time, he failed to win the Oscar for Best Director.

In 2007, Scorsese's name again appeared on the ballot for an Academy Award for Best Director for his work on *The Departed.* This time he did not go home empty-handed. In his acceptance speech, Scorsese observed: "So many people over the years have been wishing this for me. Strangers. I go into doctor's offices, elevators, people saying 'you should win one, you should win one.' I go to get an x-ray and people are saying 'you should win one.' Friends would say, 'you should win one.' . . . This is for you."

> *"Defeat should never be a source of discouragement, but rather a fresh stimulus."* — Bishop Robert South

Erich Segal

From Unsuccessful Screenplay to Best-selling Novel to Award-Winning Movie

Erich Segal (1937–) is the author of the best-selling novel *Love Story* and the screenplay for the popular 1970 movie by the same name.

In the late 1960s, Erich Segal was a successful scholar who had published a study of the work of the ancient Roman playwright Titus Maccius Plautus as well as a writer who had collaborated on several screenplays, including the hit film *Yellow Submarine*. A Harvard graduate, he was a popular professor at Yale University. Despite such credentials, Segal could not get anyone interested in his first solo screenplay, and his agent suggested that he turn it into a novel.

The publisher who printed the novel, *Love Story*, did not have a lot of faith in it, and the first run was a mere 7,500 copies. The book became an overnight success and went through twenty-one hardcover printings in its first year, was on the *New York Times Book Review* best-sellers list for a year, was translated into more than twenty languages worldwide, and eventually sold eleven million copies in the United States.

With the book's success, Segal finally sold the screenplay to Paramount. The film version of *Love Story* placed in the top ten on American Film Institute's most romantic movies. The film won the Golden Globe Award for Best Motion Picture and was nominated for an Academy Award for Best Picture. It also won Segal a Golden Globe Award for Best Screenplay and nominations for an Academy Award (as a writerof the story and screenplay) and a Writers Guild of America Award for Best Drama Written Directly for the Screen.

"Love means never having to say you're sorry." — E. S.

Warren Spahn

Too Scrawny for Baseball

As a major league baseball pitcher, Warren Spahn (1921–2003) played twenty-one seasons and won more games than any other left-handed pitcher.

ORIGINALLY, WARREN SPAHN WANTED TO play first base on his high school baseball team, but that position had already been filled. Wanting to be on the team, Spahn hesitatingly mentioned to the coach that he had pitched on occasion. To the coach's amazement, the one-hundred-pound, fourteen-year-old had amazing control of his pitches. Spahn was not even out of high school before he was being considered for the major leagues. The New York Yankees scout decided Spahn was too "scrawny." The Boston Braves, however, offered him an immediate contract, but Spahn's father insisted that his son finish high school.

Unfortunately, a month after Spahn began playing for the Braves' minor league team, he tore several tendons in his left arm while trying out a new pitch. He went home to rest, but returned to the team two weeks later convinced that the injury was healed. He was wrong, and his powerful pitches injured the tendons even more severely. Spahn was sent home until the following spring. When he returned as scheduled, he was hit in the face by a wild throw. The blow broke his nose and, once again, Spahn was forced to sit on the sidelines. He finally was allowed to pitch in 1942, but his career was interrupted when he was drafted into the Army during World War II.

When he returned in 1946, Spahn was twenty-five years old and had not even thrown a ball in more than three years. It did not take him long to get back into the game. Spahn earned a spot on the National League All-Star team the following year, a position he would return to twelve more times. Spahn won more games during his career than any other left-handed pitcher. He was listed twenty-first on the *Sporting News* list of the "100 Greatest Baseball Players" and was inducted into the National Baseball Hall of Fame in 1973, the first year he was eligible.

"Hitting is timing. Pitching is upsetting timing." — W. S.

Thomas J. Watson

A Long Road to Success

Thomas J. Watson Sr. (1874–1956) was the president of International Business Machines, better known as IBM, from the 1920s to the 1950s.

Thomas J. Watson's father wanted him to study law, but Watson did not want to be a lawyer. Instead, he accepted a position as a teacher, but he quit that job after only one day. He worked as a bookkeeper in Clarence Risley's Market, then became a clerk for a store that sold pianos, organs, and sewing machines. Eventually, Watson obtained a job as a salesperson at the National Cash Register (NCR) Company. Amazingly, the man who one day would be called the "World's Greatest Salesman" failed to sell anything the first two weeks. He worked for fifteen years before being promoted to sales manager. While at NCR, Watson, along with the owner of NCR and twenty-eight others, was accused of illegal anticompetitive sales practices and convicted in federal court. Although the conviction was later overturned on appeal, the president of NCR fired him.

Watson's dismissal from NCR turned out to be a blessing. Soon after, he was hired by a struggling company, the Computing-Tabulating-Recording Company. In the early 1920s, Watson worked his way up the corporate ladder to become president of the firm; and in 1924, he renamed the company to the International Business Machine Corporation (IBM). Watson remained president of IBM for more than thirty years before handing the reigns over to his son. When Watson took over the company, IBM had barely more than four hundred employees and was close to bankruptcy. Today, IBM employs almost 330,000 employees worldwide with annual revenues close to $100 billion.

"If you want to increase your success rate, double your failure rate." — T. J. W.

Kanye West

Image Problems

Kanye West (1977–) is a record producer and rapper who has won numerous awards for his first two albums, including six Grammys.

Kanye West spent a year in Los Angeles trying to get a record contract, but the young rapper had no luck. He returned to his hometown of Chicago and began producing songs for local rappers. Eventually, he was able to get a job working as a producer for Jay-Z's Roc-A-Fella record label. West met with success as a producer of hit singles for artists such as Alicia Keys, Jay-Z, Foxy Brown, Janet Jackson, Brandy, Eminem, and Ludacris. Still, what he wanted most was to produce his own rap album. The executives at Rock-A-Fella records initially resisted because they thought West lacked the tough background and image of a rapper. As Damon Dash, then CEO of Rock-A-Fella, recalled, "Kanye wore a pink shirt with the collar sticking up and Gucci loafers."

In 2001, West began working on his own album, continually frustrated that people would not take him seriously as a rapper. In October 2002, West was in a near-fatal car accident after he fell asleep at the wheel. Inspired by the tragedy to try something new, he called Dash and asked him for a drum machine. Three weeks later, West was recording the vocals for a new song he had created, "Through the Wire." Although the vocals were mumbled because West's jaw was still wired shut, the song became his calling card and helped land him a record contract. "Death is the best thing that can ever happen to a rapper," West later said during a *Time* magazine interview. "Almost dying isn't bad either." A year and a half later, his first album was finally released. The first single from the album, "Through the Wire," peaked at fifteen on the Billboard Hot 100. The album was nominated for a Grammy Award for Album of the Year and won Best Rap Album and Best Rap Song for "Jesus Walks."

> *"It seems we living the American dream but people highest up got the lowest self esteem / The prettiest people do the ugliest things for the road to riches and diamond rings."* — From "All Falls Down," K. W.

Mae West

Arrested for Violating the Penal Code for Obscenity

Mae West (1893–1980) was an American actress, playwright, and screenwriter most famous for her bawdy double entendres.

MAE WEST BECAME THE TARGET of the Society for the Suppression of Vice after her first play, titled *Sex*, opened on Broadway in 1926. The police arrested the cast, but they waited for forty-one weeks — after the 375th performance of the play. West spent eight days in jail and received a $500 fine. The experience, she later confided, gave her enough material for a dozen plays.

Two years later, West opened two more plays. The first was a play titled *Pleasure Man*, which closed after its first performance when police arrested the entire cast for violating the penal code for obscenity. Although the charges were dropped after a mistrial, the play never reopened. West quickly opened *Diamond Lil*, which soon became one of her most successful plays. As the female lead in the play, West delivered her famous line, "Why don't you come up sometime and see me?" The play eventually was adapted into the Academy Award-nominated movie, *She Done Him Wrong*, the second of twelve motion pictures starring West.

"Everything's in the mind. That's where it all starts. Knowing what you want is the first step toward getting it." — M. W.

Everyone's a Critic

"There is no failure. Only feedback."
— Robert Allen

Louisa May Alcott

Dissuaded from Pursuing a Writing Career

Louisa May Alcott (1832–1888) was an American novelist best known for the novel *Little Women*.

After reading Louisa May Alcott's work, Editor James T. Field told her, "Stick to your teaching, Miss Alcott. You can't write." He offered to lend her forty dollars to start a kindergarten. Alcott listened to him . . . almost. She did open the kindergarten, but she did not stop writing. When the kindergarten failed to provide her with a decent income, she abandoned it and went back to working as a writer. During the Civil War, she worked as a nurse in a military hospital. Her experiences there led to one of her first published novels, *Hospital Sketches*. For the next five years, she published almost a book a year.

Still, it was not until *Little Women* was published that she clearly defined herself as a successful writer. The money she earned from that book enabled her to repay her debt to Field, a fact she mentioned in her note to him. Field laughed and graciously admitted that he had misjudged Alcott's abilities. Alcott went on to publish more than thirty books and collections of stories, all of which are still in print today more than a hundred years later. Alcott was also a strong advocate for women's rights and was the first woman to register to vote in her town of Concord, Massachusetts.

"I am not afraid of storms, for I am learning how to sail my ship."
— L. M. A.

Fred Astaire

A Wretched Performer

During his lengthy career, Fred Astaire (1899–1987) danced, sang, and choreographed his way through numerous films. He is considered one of the most influential dancers of all time.

LEGEND HAS IT THAT AN MGM studio employee described Fred Astaire's first screen test in a succinct nine-word report, "Can't act. Can't sing. Balding. Can dance a little." In a 1933 memo David O. Selznick, who had signed Astaire and commissioned the test, characterized the dancer's performance that day as "wretched."

Fortunately, Astaire already had a contract with RKO. After being loaned out to MGM to star in the movie *Dancing Lady*, Astaire was cast in his first RKO film, *Flying Down to Rio*. The RKO film paired him with another up-and-comer, Ginger Rogers. Although they did not received top billing on the film, the pair entranced Americans and the film soon launched them into the spotlight.

Astaire danced, sang, and acted on the stage and screen for more than seventy-six years. His career comprised more than forty motion pictures, including thirty-one musicals (ten of which also featured Ginger Rogers). In the 1930s, twenty-six of his recordings placed among the Top 10 songs; eight of them reached the number one spot. He received a National Artist Award from the American National Theatre, an honorary Oscar, several lifetime achievement awards, and was inducted into the Entertainment Hall of Fame. He also ranked fifth on the American Film Institute's list of the "50 Greatest American Screen Legends." Another famous dancer, Mikhail Baryshnikov, said about Astaire, "No dancer can watch Fred Astaire and not know that we all should have been in another business."

"Chance is the fool's name for fate." — F. A.

The Beatles

Dismissed as Out of Style

The Beatles, a four-person musical group from England, began releasing hits in the 1960s and went on to become are the best-selling musical group of all time according to the Recording Industry Association of America.

For five years, John Lennon, Paul McCartney, and George Harrison played their music around England and Germany, changing the name of the group almost as often as they changed gigs. The Quarrymen, the Silver Beetles, and Johnny and the Moondogs are among the many names they tried, but none of the names seemed to help their success. Lennon's aunt told him he would never make a living playing guitar; the group's failure to land a record contract reinforced that view. The band fired their first manager, Alan Williams, who retorted, "You'll never work again!" He advised his prospective replacement, Brian Epstein, "not to touch [the band] with a barge pole." Epstein ignored this advice, accepted the position as manager, and immediately set out to land the group a record contract. When he approached Decca Records, an executive there said, "We don't like their sound" and added, "Guitar groups are on the way out."

Several other British labels also turned them away. At the request of an EMI market executive who liked their sound, EMI record producer George Martin agreed to give them a chance on the condition that the group replace their drummer. The band, now calling themselves the Beatles, agreed and quickly hired drummer Ringo Starr. At their second recording session, the band produced "Love Me Do," which hit the top twenty charts in the United Kingdom. The band quickly followed this hit with another single, which led to the release of their first record in 1963. Their album *Please Please Me* soared to number one, where it remained for thirty weeks.

Having conquered the British airwaves, the Beatles began looking west toward the American market. Unfortunately, EMI's American counterpart, Capitol Records, refused to issue the records because British acts had never been commercially successful in America. Another American record label released the Beatles' singles, but they received little airtime. Dick Clark's popular TV show *American Bandstand* played the Beatles song "She Loves Me," but the teenage audience gave it just mediocre ratings. According to some reports, the teens erupted into fits of laughter at the group's appearance and odd haircuts when they were shown a photo of the Beatles.

Nevertheless, the Beatles' "British invasion" of the United States was unstoppable. Both the *CBS Evening News* with Water Cronkite and the *The Jack Parr Program* ran clips of Beatles performing. Anticipation began to build, and when the Beatles finally arrived in New York in 1964, they were a sensation. The first stop for the Beatles was an appearance on *The Ed Sullivan Show*. The rest, as they say, is history.

> *"You don't need anybody to tell you who you are or what you are. You are what you are!"* — John Lennon

Beethoven

A Hopeless Composer

Ludwig van Beethoven (1770–1827) was a German composer whose classical music compositions are considered by many to be the most influential ever written.

As a child, Ludwig van Beethoven impressed his teacher, Mozart, with his musical talent. After his mother died, however, Beethoven abandoned his studies and returned home. A few years later, another great composer, Joseph Haydn, invited Beethoven to study with him. Haydn soon regretted the invitation. His new student constantly broke music's most important rules. Furthermore, he seemed slow, plodding, and lacking in talent. The two parted ways. Haydn later advised an inquirer to avoid Beethoven because he "had never learned anything and would never do anything in a decent style." Another of Beethoven's music teachers said, "As a composer, he is hopeless." Beethoven continued to try other music teachers, but they also gave up on him. Finally, he gave up looking for music teachers and sought out patrons until he was able to support himself as his work became more popular. By age twenty-eight, the composer and pianist was making a good living in Vienna performing piano concerts and selling his compositions to publishers.

Despite Beethoven's popular success, critics viciously

attacked his work. During his lifetime, his symphonies were called "harsh and bizarre," "an orgy of vulgar noise," "laborious without effect," and "a crude monstrosity." Beethoven ignored his critics, in part because a far greater problem plagued him. Beginning in his late twenties, he experienced hearing problems and periods of deafness. He tried countless cures and treatments, but by the time he was fifty-five, he had gone completely deaf.

Just as he did not let critics stop him, Beethoven refused to let deafness end his career. Although he contemplated suicide, he abandoned the idea, writing that "it seemed impossible to leave the world until I had produced all that I felt called upon me to produce." Near the end of his life, he went into isolation, sharing little of what he wrote with the public. Whether it was this isolation, his deafness, or the fact that he no longer felt he had to please his contemporaries, these final works possessed a complexity that would not be appreciated until long after Beethoven's death.

"One must not hold one's self so divine as to be unwilling occasionally to make improvements in one's creations." — L. v. B.

Alexander Graham Bell

Inventor of a Valueless Toy

Alexander Graham Bell (1847–1922) was an inventor and scientist, most famous for perfecting the telephone and inventing the first metal detector.

Alexander Graham Bell was not the first to think of transmitting a person's voice over electrical wires. Most scientists, though, considered the idea fanciful and impossible. In fact, it was considered so improbable that in 1865 Joshua Coopersmith was arrested and charged with fraud after he attempted to raise funds for such a device. Bell took a more cautious approach and did not look for financial backers until he had patented the device. His search for investors, however, was fruitless. No one was willing to take a risk on what was viewed as "only a toy."

William Orton, president of Western Union, the largest communications company in America, scoffed at the idea. Bell offered Western Union exclusive rights to his invention for the bargain price of $100,000. Orton turned him down, noting in an internal memo that Bell's device had "too many shortcomings to be seriously considered as a means of communication. The device is inherently of no value to us." When Bell presented his invention at the White House, President Rutherford B. Hayes observed, "That's an amazing invention, but who would ever want to use one?"

A year later Bell answered the president's question by installing his "amazing invention" — which he called a telephone — in the White House. Today, there are well over one billion telephones in use around the world.

"When one door closes another opens. But we often look so long and so regretfully upon the closed door that we fail to see the one that has opened for us." — A. G. B.

Jon Bon Jovi

A No Ability, No-Talent Performer

Jon Bon Jovi (1962–) is the lead singer of the rock band Bon Jovi, which has produced Top 40 hits like such as "You Give Love a Bad Name," "Livin' On a Prayer," and "It's My Life."

JON BONGIOVI'S CRITICS DID NOT expect him to get far — in his life or his musical career. They told him, "You don't have the ability. You don't have the talent. You don't have what it takes." He ignored the negative comments and chose to listen to his parents instead. They encouraged him to be the best that he could be, even if what he wanted to be was a rock star. Bongiovi began by organizing a band in high school. One of its first performances was at a local talent show. The band placed last.

After graduation, the band broke up, but Bongiovi did not give up his dream. In 1980, he recorded several demo tapes at his cousin's record studio, where he had been working as a janitor. Record companies rejected his demos, but a local radio station agreed to include one of his songs on a compilation tape. The song, "Runaway," began getting frequent airplay, leaping from one radio station to another until it was being played across the country. Suddenly, the same companies that had rejected Bongiovi's work earlier now participated in a bidding war to get him to sign with them.

Realizing he needed a band, Jon Bongiovi recruited his former band mate David Bryan, who in turn found Alec John Such, Tico Torres, and Richie Samborra. By 1983, the newly formed group had a record contract with Polygram.

The group derived its name from the anglicized version of Bongiovi's last name: Bon Jovi. The group's self-titled debut came out on January 21, 1984, and went gold, as did the follow-up album, "7800 Fahrenheit," released in April 1985. The band opened for legendary bands such as the Scorpions, KISS, and Judas Priest, but the members wanted more. They wanted to be superstars.

For their next album, the group hired professional songwriters. The strategy helped push Bon Jovi's third album, *Slippery When Wet* to gold and then platinum within six weeks of its release. That was just the beginning. To date, Bon Jovi has released more than twelve albums, including two "best of" albums, and has sold more than 35 million albums in the United States and more than 120 million albums worldwide. In 2007, the band won its first Grammy for Best Country Collaboration for the song "Who Says You Can't Go Home."

"The harder I worked, the luckier I got." — J. B. J.

Enrico Caruso

Deemed Without Talent as a Singer

Enrico Caruso (1873–1921), an Italian opera singer, was a pioneer in recorded music and one of the world's most famous tenors.

Enrico Caruso's mother had big dreams for her third child. She told him "My boy, I am going to make every sacrifice to pay for your voice lessons." Sadly, she died long before she could help those dreams come true. At eleven, the motherless boy dropped out of school to help provide for his family. Several years went by before Eduardo Missiano, an aspiring baritone, heard Caruso singing at a local swimming pool. Missiano believed that Caruso had talent and introduced him to his teacher, Guglielmo Vergine. Vergine, however, concluded that Caruso could not sing and would never amount to much. The teacher compared Caruso's voice to the sound of "wind whistling through the shutters." Still, he reluctantly agreed to teach the boy. The two worked together for three years before parting ways.

In his twenties, Caruso made his debut in *L'Amico Francesco* at the Teatro Nuovo in Naples. Caruso could sing, but he had never learned how to act; and his performance was often met with boos and hisses. For five years, he lived on the edge of obscurity and poverty as he struggled to make a name for himself. Slowly, his reputation grew, and he began playing more and more opera houses throughout Italy. However, it was not until his widely reported stellar performance in *Fedora* that he was considered an international sensation.

For more than twenty years, Caruso was a dominant force in the opera world. In 1903, he crossed the Atlantic and performed for the first time at the New York Metropolitan Opera. The "King of Tenors" continued to perform there, in more than thirty-five operas, every winter until his death. A generous man, Caruso shared the fortune his success brought him. During World War I, he gave $5 million to the Italian Red Cross and used his concerts to raise an additional $21 million for the Allied armies.

What makes a good singer? *"A big chest, a big mouth, ninety percent memory, ten percent intelligence, lots of hard work, and something in the heart." — E. C.*

Mary Higgins Clark

Light, Slight, and Trite Writing

Mary Higgins Clark (1927–) is the author of twenty-four best-selling suspense novels, including *Where Are the Children?*, *A Stranger Is Watching*, and *Where Are You Now?*

For six years, Mary Higgins Clark submitted the same short story to publisher after publisher. She received more than forty rejection letters before the story was finally published. One letter referred to her writing as "light, slight, and trite." Undeterred, Clark wrote her first book, a fictionalized account of the relationship between George Washington and his wife. The book took three years to write but failed to sell once it was published. Disheartened, she started her own business writing and marketing radio scripts. This kept her going until her agent convinced her to try writing another book. This time, she wrote a suspense novel.

Writing the novel proved to be a challenge. Clark described the process: "The first four months of writing the book, my mental image is scratching with my hands through granite. My other image is pushing a train up the mountain, and it's icy, and I'm in bare feet." Simon and Schuster agreed to publish the book *Where Are the Children?* for a $3,000 advance.

Less than three months later, Clark received another check, this one for $45,000, after the publisher sold the paperback rights. The book became a best seller and was adapted into a movie in 1986. Clark has written almost thirty suspense novels, all of which have become best-sellers. Many of her novels have been adapted into television movies. All of her novels are currently in print, with *Where Are the Children?* in its seventy-fifth printing. In 2001, the Mystery Writers of America established the Mary Higgins Clark Award in her honor. The award recognizes outstanding authors of suspense fiction.

"If you want to be happy for life, love what you do." — M. H. C.

Katie Couric

Too Young to Be Taken Seriously

Katie Couric (1957–) is the weeknight news anchor and managing editor of the *CBS Evening News*. Before becoming the first woman to serve as solo news anchor on network TV, Couric was cohost of NBC's *The Today Show* for fifteen years.

Being an assignment editor in CNN's Washington bureau helped Katie Couric learn the practical details of broadcasting while giving her a chance to do on-the-air reporting. The on-air stints ended when the president of CNN said he did not like her voice and never wanted her on the air again. She took the criticism in stride and started working with a voice coach. Slowly, she found her way back on television, but her efforts were constantly hampered by directors who thought she appeared too young to be taken seriously.

Couric moved to Washington, DC, to work as a late-night news reporter for the NBC affiliate. While there, she won a local Emmy and an Associated Press award for one of her stories. With those successes, she began eyeing a bigger prize: the anchor's chair. When she approached her news director with the idea, he advised her to look for a "really small market somewhere." She ignored this advice and accepted a position working for NBC as a deputy Pentagon correspondent, which put her in position to work as anchor substitute and substitute host for the NBC morning show, *Today*. She joined *Today* as a national correspondent in 1990 and then became a substitute cohost for Deborah Norville. The position turned permanent when Norville left the show. In 2006, Couric became managing editor and anchor for the *CBS Evening News*. Couric is the first woman to serve as the solo anchor for the weekday evening news on a major television network.

"You can't please everyone, and you can't make everyone like you." — K. C.

Edward Estlin Cummings

Dedicated to Rejection

Edward Estlin Cummings (1894–1962) is best known for the unconventional use of typography and punctuation in his more than nine hundred poems.

Although Edward Estlin Cummings, better known as e. e. cummings, had already published twelve books by 1934, the poet had trouble finding a publisher for his new book of poems. Cummings tried fourteen publishers but was rejected by every one of them. Even worse, he was in his late thirties and still relying on his mother for financial support. Still, he got a loan from his mother and decided to publish the book himself. He also changed the title of the book to *No Thanks* and dedicated it to the publishers who had rejected the book. In order to ensure that the meaning was not lost, Cummings carefully constructed the dedication so the publishers' names resembled a funeral urn.

One of the most prominent and influential poets of the twentieth century, Cummings is best known for his more than nine hundred poems. In his poems he transformed capitalization, punctuation, syntax, and typography to serve his own purposes. He is famous for interrupting sentences or words, changing word order, and ignoring grammatical conventions to make the poem a visual image. One of his better-known poems, "r-p-o-p-h-e-s-s-a-g-r," was designed to look like a leaping grasshopper with the syllables and letters of the word "grasshopper" scattered throughout the poem and parentheses, punctuation, capital letters, and other devices used to reflect the poem's meaning. During his lifetime, Cummings also published two novels, several plays, and various essays, as well as numerous drawings, sketches, and paintings.

To be nobody-but-yourself — in a world which is doing its best, night and day, to make you everybody else — means to fight the hardest battle which any human being can fight; and never stop fighting. — E. E. C.

Clint Eastwood

B-Movie Reject

Clint Eastwood (1930–) is an American actor, director, producer, and composer with numerous films to his credit including *Dirty Harry*, *Unforgiven*, and *Million Dollar Baby*.

Clint Eastwood's first roles for Universal Studios were minuscule parts in B-movies. His career at Universal was cut short when a studio executive fired him and told him, "You have a chip on your tooth, your Adam's apple sticks out too far, and you talk too slow." Ironically, fellow actor Burt Reynolds was fired at that same meeting.

Eastwood reportedly worked as a mechanic and a garbage collector to make ends meet before he landed a role on the TV show *Rawhide*. During a break in shooting, Eastwood starred in a low-budget Western filmed in Italy. The movie, *A Fistful of Dollars*, referred to as a "spaghetti western," became a huge hit in Italy and prompted the director to hire Eastwood to appear in two sequels, *For a Few Dollars More* and *The Good, the Bad, and the Ugly*.

The three movies were eventually released worldwide and turned Eastwood into an international star. He has starred in almost sixty movies, about half of which he directed. Eastwood has been nominated for an Academy Award for Best Actor twice and lost both times. However, four of his movies have earned him eight nominations for directing and producing. *Unforgiven* and *Million Dollar Baby* won Eastwood Academy Awards for Best Director and Best Picture.

"I don't believe in pessimism. If something doesn't come up the way you want, forge ahead. If you think it's going to rain, it will." — C. E.

Peter Falk

Rejected for Not Being Perfect

Actor Peter Falk (1927–) has won five Emmy Awards for his portrayal of the title role in the television series *Columbo*.

When Peter Falk was three, a tumor developed in his right eye. The entire eye had to be removed and replaced with a glass eye. When he was old enough to consider what he wanted to do with his life, he initially rejected the idea of being an actor because he did not feel he could do the job. Eventually, he decided to give it a try, but discovered that he would have to be willing to battle Hollywood's promotion of physical perfection. Although Falk was rejected for many roles because of his glass eye, he got his first big chance when he landed a role in the 1958 movie *Wind Across the Everglades*. After that, Columbia Pictures considered offering him a contract, but the studio eventually decided against it because of Falk's physical imperfections. He succeeded anyway, and got a number of parts in movies and on television during the 1960s. Falk was twice nominated for an Academy Award for Best Supporting Actor; and in 1961, he became the first actor nominated for both an Oscar and an Emmy in the same year.

However, it was the role he began playing in 1968 — the rumpled, far-from-perfect detective Colombo — that made him famous. Falk won five Emmys and a Golden Globe for his performance as the TV detective. He portrayed the character for thirty-five years in more than seventy television movies. He also published his memoirs, *Just One More Thing*, which took its title from Colombo's signature parting remark to each suspected murderer.

"Why did it take [12 years] to decide to be an actor? Obviously fear — fear of failure, but fear by itself is too simple. It was fear coupled with my highly romantic, ridiculously unrealistic notion of what constituted an actor." — P. F.

William Faulkner

Couldn't Hold a Steady Job

Nobel Prize winner William Faulkner (1897–1962) was an American novelist and poet. His works include *The Sound and the Fury* and *As I Lay Dying* and the short stories "A Rose for Emily," and "Barn Burning."

William Faulkner's neighbors called him "Count, No 'Count" because he rarely held a steady job. He was once fired from his job as postmaster because he read the magazines before delivering them and often became so immersed in his writing that he ignored the customers. After Faulkner's first two works were published, at least twenty publishers rejected his third novel, *Sartoris* (later republished as *Flags in the Dust*), before it was finally accepted for publication. One publisher told him that the company "didn't believe that [he] should offer it for publication" because it was "diffuse and non-integral with neither very much plot development nor character development."

Thoroughly disgusted by the publication process, Faulkner decided that he would write his next book about "the most horrific tale [he] could imagine" with the sole intention of making money. The result was *The Sound and the Fury*. Initially, the book fared little better than his other novels, although Faulkner did find a publisher for it. Alfred Harcourt, president of Harcourt, Brace, told Faulkner's editor that he was "the only damn fool in New York who would publish it."

Faulkner won the 1949 Nobel Prize in literature for

The Sound and the Fury, among other works. Still selling well today, the book is frequently listed on college syllabi as required reading. Faulkner donated the cash grant that came with the prize to establish a fund to encourage new fiction writers. The result is the PEN/Faulkner Award for Fiction. "Count No 'Count" also won the Pulitzer Prize for Fiction twice, in 1955 and in 1963.

"Always dream and shoot higher than you know you can do. Don't bother just to be better than your contemporaries or predecessors. Try to be better than yourself." — W. F.

Debbi Fields

Entrepreneur Without Business Backing

Debbi Fields (1956–) is the founder and former chairperson of Mrs. Fields Cookies, a cookie manufacturer that today is a $450 million company.

THE BUSINESS WORLD PUTS ITS faith in market reports and consumer surveys, not compliments. Research showed that people liked crispy cookies, and not the soft, chewy cookies that Debbi Fields baked. In addition, Fields had almost no business experience and had not completed community college. However, she did have conviction, a terrific cookie recipe, plus a library card that she used to check out every book on business she could find.

Although most believed that a store could not survive just selling cookies, Fields managed to convince both her husband and a bank to finance her operation. On August 13, 1977, she opened her first store in Palo Alto, California. That first day, Fields waited all morning, but no customers entered the store. She had bet her husband that she could make fifty dollars the first day, so she set out to find customers. Fields hit the streets, giving away cookies to anyone willing to try them. Her plan worked. She won the bet with her husband and started her career and a successful business. Within ten years, Fields had opened more than four hundred Mrs. Fields Cookies stores with annual sales reaching $87 million. By 2001, Fields had more than 650 U.S. and 65 international stores in eleven different countries.

> *"The important thing is not being afraid to take a chance. Remember, the greatest failure is to not try. Once you find something you love to do, be the best at doing it." — D. F.*

Ian Fleming

Panned by the Critics

Ian Fleming (1908–1964) first created and then chronicled the adventures of James Bond in a series of novels and short stories.

When Ian Fleming's first book, *Casino Royale*, was published in 1954, the critics panned it for having an unrealistic plot, graphic sexual content, and violent brutality. Criticism did not bother Fleming. He readily admitted he wrote "trivial piffle" and had no literary ambitions. His first novel — a spy story featuring agent James Bond — sold seven thousand copies, which was enough to encourage Fleming to keep writing. He eventually wrote eleven more novels and nine short stories about the secret agent Bond. The books were only moderately successful until 1961 when President John F. Kennedy listed one of Fleming's books, *From Russia with Love*, as one of his top ten favorite books. This sparked an interest in the books that intensified after the release of the first James Bond movie, *Dr. No*, the following year.

Like the books, the first Bond movie was not expected to be much of a success and was given a budget of only $1 million. Its success ensured that a sequel, *From Russia with Love*, soon followed, which tragically was the last movie President Kennedy saw before his death. More than forty years later, the Bond books are still going strong and the more than twenty Bond movies have grossed more than $4 billion worldwide.

"You only live twice. Once when you are born and once when you look death in the face." — I. F.

Frederick Forsyth

No Reader Interest in His Work

Frederick Forsyth (1938–) is an English author known for his thrillers and crime novels such as *The Day of the Jackal*, *The Odessa File*, *The Dogs of War*, *The Fist of God*, and *The Afghan*.

After working for several years as a reporter and publishing a book on the Biafran War, Fredrick Forsyth decided to turn his attention to writing fiction. It took him only a month to complete his first manuscript, *The Day of the Jackal*, which several British publishers promptly rejected. One publisher told Forsyth that the book "had no reader interest."

Forsyth eventually found a publisher for *The Day of the Jackal*. After it was finally published, critics took Forsyth to task for his simplistic and "graceless prose" style, shallow characterization, and for using "every stereotype in the filing system." Forsyth said in an interview with the *Los Angeles Times*, "My books are 80 percent plot and structure. The remaining 20 percent is for characters and descriptions. I try to keep emotions out. Occasionally a personal opinion will appear in the mouth of one of my characters, but only occasionally. The plot's the thing. This is how it works best for me."

Despite the negative response from critics, *The Day of the Jackal* became an international best seller and, according to *Publishers Weekly*, was the fourth best-selling novel in the United States in 1971 and 1972. *Jackal* was also made into a major motion picture and earned Forsyth the Edgar Allan Poe Award for Best Novel from the Mystery Writers of America. Since then, Forsyth has written fifteen additional novels and is credited with helping define a new genre of thriller— the "documentary thriller" — that educates readers in addition to entertaining them.

"The talent of success is nothing more than doing what you can do well, and doing well whatever you do." — Henry Wadsworth Longfellow

Sigmund Freud

Harsh Predictions for His Future

Often referred to as "the father of psychoanalysis," Sigmund Freud (1856–1939) was an Austrian neurologist and psychiatrist known for his theories about the unconscious mind, dreams, and sexual desire.

When Sigmund Freud was eight, his father predicted that he would "come to nothing." His own father's harsh words did not stop him from entering medical school and becoming a neurologist. Becoming a doctor did not satisfy Freud, and he decided to write a book. It took two years of writing before his book was ready for publication. For a year and a half, the scientific community ignored *The Interpretations of Dreams* and only a couple of periodicals even mentioned it. Eventually, it received a few caustic reviews in psychological journals, but that did not increase the book's sales. The first printing of six hundred copies sold out more than eight years after the book was published. For all his work, Freud was paid $209.

Freud did not let his lack of success or the attitude of his contemporaries affect him or prevent him from publishing additional works, which received wider acceptance than his first book. Eventually, his reputation grew, as did the reputation of his first book, *The Interpretation of Dreams*. Today, the book is considered one of Freud's most original and important works. *The Interpretation of Dreams* was translated into at least a dozen languages and was printed seven more times during Freud's lifetime.

"From error to error, one discovers the entire truth." — S. F.

John Gardner

Rejected for Fifteen Years

John Gardner (1933–1982) was an American novelist and university professor. His books on the art of writing are considered classics by most writers and writing teachers.

John Gardner submitted his first novel, *The Resurrection*, to publishers for fifteen years before finally getting it published. Initially, it attracted very little attention; one reviewer called it "pretty muddled." His second novel, *The Wreckage of Agathon*, received the same treatment. It was not until his third novel, *Grendel*, was published that he was recognized as a major contemporary writer. During the long years before his work received any recognition, Gardner continued to write. After his success, Gardner commented on the sequence of his novels, noting that some of his recently acclaimed books had been written earlier and rejected by publishers. "When you're sitting writing for fifteen years, and [nobody's] liking you, you do build up a backlog. I've been publishing an early work, a late work, an early work."

Gardner's most influential works were published after his death. *On Becoming a Novelist*, *On Writers and Writing*, and *The Art of Fiction: Notes on Craft for Young Writers* were all published posthumously. Today, these books are used as textbooks in countless creative writing courses and are considered by many to be "must reads" for all aspiring writers. Probably the best advice Gardner offered for new writers was this: "Nearly every beginning writer sooner or later asks (or wishes he dared ask) his creative writing teacher, or someone else he thinks might know, whether or not he really has what it takes to be a writer. The honest answer almost always is 'God only knows.'"

Considering Gardner spent his life teaching fiction writing, it seems only fitting that his words continue to instruct long after his death.

"We pay a heavy price for our fear of failure. It is a powerful obstacle to growth. It assures the progressive narrowing of the personality and prevents exploration and experimentation. There is no learning without some difficulty and fumbling. If you want to keep on learning, you must keep on risking failure — all your life." — J. G.

George Frideric Handel

A Fickle Friend of Fame

George Frideric Handel (1685–1759) was a leading composer of concerti grossi, operas, and oratorios during the Baroque period, He is most famous for his oratorio *Messiah*.

BY THE AGE OF EIGHTEEN, George Frideric Handel was already considered a musical prodigy. He had been appointed to the post of church organist before becoming a violinist and harpsichordist at the Kaiser's opera house in Hamburg. Before long, he was composing his own works and became an overnight success. By the time he was forty, he was world-famous.

Fame, however, proved to be a fickle friend. Audiences were inconsistent, and competition with rival composers was fierce. At times, he found himself broke and on the verge of bankruptcy. He also faced health problems, and in 1737, when he was only fifty-two, he suffered a stroke that left his right arm limp, four fingers permanently paralyzed, and made focusing difficult. Handel was forced to stop performing altogether until he recovered. He improved physically, but the combination of the public's rejections, his health problems, and debt proved to be too much for his spirit. By 1741, Handel had announced his retirement and gave his farewell concert.

Handel was four months into his retirement when Charles Jennings visited him. Jennings had written the words for an extended musical composition, known as a libretto, and he wanted Handel to compose the music for it. The libretto inspired Handel to start writing music again.

For the next twenty-four days, he wrote almost nonstop. When he was finished, he had completed a 260-page manuscript that he titled *Messiah*.

Today, *Messiah* is Handel's most famous piece and is considered by many as his best work. It, along with Handel's other works, were major influences on many of the composers who came after him including Haydn, Mozart, and Beethoven. The latter once said, "Handel is the greatest composer who ever lived. I would bare my head and kneel at his grave."

"Ah, but a man's reach should exceed his grasp — or what's a heaven for?"
— Robert Browning

Rex Harrison

Muddled His Only Line

Rex Harrison (1908–1990) was an English actor who won both an Academy Award and a Tony Award for his portrayal of the role of Professor Henry Higgins in the movie and stage versions *My Fair Lady*.

Eighteen-year-old Rex Harrison discovered that being on stage for the first time could be nerve-wracking. The young British actor was supposed to walk across the stage to say his one line, "Fetch a doctor, baby!" Unfortunately, it proved too difficult for Harrison, who muddled the line and said instead, "Fetch a baby doctor!" People told him that he should give up the dream of being an actor because only those with "exceptional talent could succeed."

Harrison ignored the jibes and instead landed a few prominent roles in movies in the 1930s and 1940s, including that of the king in *Anna and the King of Siam* and that of the jealous conductor in *Unfaithfully Yours.* Still, his career did not take off, and after a scandalous extramarital affair with an actress, Harrison seemed headed for obscurity. The actor was not ready to call it quits, however. He returned to the stage, which many say helped refine his acting skills. Harrison won two Tony Awards for his performances in *Anne of the Thousand Days* and *My Fair Lady.* This helped revive his film career, and he was nominated for an Academy Award for Best Actor for his portrayal of Julius Caesar in the movie *Cleopatra* in 1963. In 1964, he won the Academy Award for Best Actor for the role for which he is best known, Professor Henry Higgins in *My Fair Lady.*

"Exhilaration is that feeling you get just after a great idea hits you, and just before you realize what's wrong with it." — R. H.

Joseph Heller

Lacked Craft and Sensibility

Joseph Heller (1923–1999) was an American novelist and playwright best known for his novel *Catch-22.*

JOSEPH HELLER'S BOOK INSPIRED THE popular phrase, catch-22. The term easily could have been catch-18, however, since that was the original title of the book. The publisher, Simon and Schuster, discovered that another book with a similar title — *Mila 18* by Leon Uris — was scheduled to be released at the same time as Heller's book. Heller scrambled for a new title and eventually settled on *Catch-22* as the new title. He chose 22 because Simon and Schuster was the twenty-second publisher to read the book and the only one willing to publish it. *The New Yorker* and the *Atlantic Monthly* gave *Catch-22* bad reviews. The *New York Times* wrote, "It gasps for want of craft and sensibility" and called the book "an emotional hodgepodge."

Although its title has come to mean "a no-win situation," *Catch-22* won over enough people to have sold more than ten million copies. Heller went on to publish another eight novels, two collections of short stories, and several other works. However, many believe that *Catch-22* remains his best work. Heller himself once observed, "When I read something saying I've not done anything as good as *Catch-22* I'm tempted to reply, 'Who has?'"

"We do have a zeal for laughter in most situations, give or take a dentist."— J. H.

Katharine Hepburn

Box Office Poison

For more than seventy years, Katharine Hepburn (1907–2003) appeared on stage, film, and television. She earned four Oscars for her performances in *Morning Glory, Guess Who's Coming to Dinner, The Lion in Winter,* and *On Golden Pond.*

Katharine Hepburn dreamed of being famous even as a child. Unfortunately, after a sequence of unsuccessful movies early in her career, she became labeled as "box office poison." The label originated from a 1938 poll of motion picture exhibitors. Hepburn, who had already won an Oscar for Best Actress, shared the list with many other film notables, including Fred Astaire, Joan Crawford, Mae West, Greta Garbo, Marlene Dietrich, and Edward Arnold.

Ignoring the list, Hepburn continued her work as an actress with her usual tenacity. She eventually landed a role in *The Philadelphia Story*, which turned out to be highly successful and is now considered a comedy classic. Ironically, the movie was directed by George Cukor, who had recently been fired from the movie *Gone with the Wind*. Hepburn, too, had originally planned to participate in the film, in the lead role of Scarlet O'Hara. She did not believe the role was right for her, however, and she was replaced by Vivien Leigh.

Hepburn's career continued for the next sixty years. She starred in more than fifty movies and won three more Oscars. She currently holds the record for the most best actress Oscar nominations (twelve) and the most best actress wins (four) and is one of only four actors to win back-to-back Oscars for leading roles. Hepburn has been nominated for an Emmy Award five times, winning the award in 1975 for her lead role in *Love Among the Ruins*. She was also nominated for two Tony Awards and has received numerous lifetime achievement awards. In 1999, the American Film Institute ranked Hepburn number one on its Greatest American Screen Legends list.

"We are taught you must blame your father, your sisters, your brothers, the school, the teachers — you can blame anyone but never blame yourself. It's never your fault. But it's always your fault, because if you wanted to change, you're the one who has got to change. It's as simple as that, isn't it?" — K. H.

Buddy Holly

Labeled a No-Talent

One of the pioneers of rock and roll, Buddy Holly (1936–1959) hit the charts in the 1950s with the songs "That'll Be the Day," "Peggy Sue," and "Oh, Boy!"

After only a few months singing professionally, Buddy Holly shared the bill with Elvis Presley and opened for Bill Haley and the Comets, a famous rock-and-roll band of the 1950s. But when he landed his first record contract with Decca Records, none of the songs that were released hit the charts. Paul Cohen, who oversaw scouting and artist development at Decca, called Holly the "biggest no-talent I ever worked with" and released him from his contract.

Holly continued to tour and recorded several new songs under the guidance of producer Norman Petty. However, when Holly and Petty tried to find a new record label to release the songs, Roulette, Columbia, RCA, and Atlantic Records all turned them down. Finally, Coral/Brunswick agreed to release the songs. Because Coral/Brunswick was a subsidiary of Decca, the record company was able to re-release some of Holly's earlier songs. When the new version of "That'll be the Day," came out, it slowly climbed the charts until finally reaching the top. Several other songs by Holly, such as "Peggy Sue" and "Oh Boy," became hits as well. Although a fatal plane crash cut short Holly's career, his work had a major impact on rock and roll. In 2004, *Rolling Stone* magazine ranked him as thirteenth on its list of "100 Greatest Artists of All Time."

"If anyone asks you what kind of music you play, tell him 'pop.' Don't tell him 'rock 'n' roll' or they won't even let you in the hotel." — B. H.

Jennifer Hudson

Not Quite the Next American Idol

Jennifer Hudson (1981–) was a finalist on the hit television show *American Idol* before starring in the 2006 movie *Dreamgirls.*

It took a giant leap of faith for Jennifer Hudson to leave a successful career performing on Disney's cruise line for a simple audition, especially since seventy thousand other singers were also trying out. Still, Hudson flew to Atlanta and auditioned for the television show *American Idol* and a chance to go to Hollywood. Her gamble paid off, and she landed a spot as one of the show's top twelve performers. Simon Cowell, a judge for the show, told Hudson that she was "out of her league." As if to prove his point, she twice landed among the bottom three, but then received enough votes to remain on the show. On the sixth episode, she sang "Circle of Life," impressing Cowell as well as the song's writer, Elton John. Revising his initial opinion, the judge proclaimed that Hudson had "finally proved why she was among the top twelve."

She was stunned and disappointed when voters cast her once again among the bottom three contestants, ending her role on the show. "I cried all the next day," she later admitted. "It definitely hurt."

About a year later, after Hudson had finished touring with other *American Idol* contestants, a New York casting agency asked her to try out for a role in an upcoming movie, *Dreamgirls*. After two auditions and two rejections, she was asked to try out once more. The third time was definitely the charm — she landed the role of Effie White in *Dreamgirls*. Hudson beat out almost eight hundred people — including Fantasia Barrino, who had appeared with Hudson on *American Idol* and had eventually won the title. After the movie proved to be a huge success, Cowell admitted on national television, "I'd like to be the first to admit a massive dose of humble pie. That was extraordinary, Jennifer, and I feel very proud of you."

To date, Hudson has won more than eighteen awards for best supporting actress or "best breakthrough performance" from organizations such as the New York Film Critics, the Los Angeles Film Critics Association, the Southeastern Film Critics Association, and the National Board of Review. She has also won an Academy Award for Best Performance by an Actress in a Supporting Role, a Screen Actors Guild Award for Best Supporting Actress, an NAACP Image Award for Best Supporting Actress in a Movie, and a British Academy Film Award for Best Actress in a Supporting Role.

"Simon [Cowell] said to me that you only get one shot at the big time. But you know what, Simon, I got shot number two." — J. H.

John Irving

Only Mildly Interesting

John Irving (1942–), best-selling American novelist and Academy Award-winning screenwriter, who wrote *The World According to Garp*, *Cider House Rules*, and *A Prayer of Owen Meany*.

Truth is often stranger — and harsher — than fiction. In John Irving's novel *The World According to Garp*, a prominent literary magazine harshly rejects a short story written by the main character. The rejection letter reads, "The story is only mildly interesting, and it does nothing new with language or with form. Thanks for showing it to us, though."

The book's editor thought the rejection was unrealistically harsh. Irving disagreed — not because he believed in his literary vision, but because the rejection was not the creation of his imagination. Irving had submitted the short story in the novel to several publications and had received that exact rejection letter from *The Paris Review.* In fact, the story had also been rejected by the *American Review* and by magazines such as *The New Yorker* and *Esquire.* After seeing the original rejection letter, the editor agreed to let the work stand as it was. The "mildly interesting" short story, titled "The Pension Grillparzer," was considered one of the strongest portions of the novel and won the Pushcart Prize for short fiction. *The World According to Garp* received similar laurels. It has sold several million copies, was nominated for a National Book Award in 1979, won an American Book Award in 1980, and became a popular movie starring Robin Williams and Glenn Close. Irving has also won a Rockefeller Foundation Grant, a National Endowment for the Arts fellowship, a Guggenheim Grant, and won the Academy Award for Best Adapted Screenplay, which was based on his best-selling book *Cider House Rules.*

"You've got to get obsessed and stay obsessed."— J. I.

Thomas Jefferson

Accused of Cowardice and Dereliction of Duty

Thomas Jefferson (1743–1826) was the third president of the United States and one of the primary authors of the Declaration of Independence.

In 1796, Thomas Jefferson, the principal author of the Declaration of Independence, lost his bid for the presidency to John Adams. When he ran again in 1800, his opponents called him an atheist and enemy of Christianity. They also accused Jefferson of cowardice and dereliction of duty for his actions nineteen years earlier when he was governor of Virginia. In 1781, two days after his term as governor had expired, the British marched toward his Monticello home in Virginia. Rather than staying and waiting two weeks for the legislature to choose a new governor, Jefferson moved his family to safety. Jefferson was cleared of any wrongdoing, but public disapproval over his actions remained so strong that he was never again elected to office in Virginia. By focusing attention on the past, his opponents hoped to defeat Jefferson in his bid for the presidency.

Despite the criticism leveled against him, Jefferson won the election and became the third president of the United States. During his two terms of office, he was responsible for the Louisiana Purchase, the Embargo Act of 1807, and the Lewis and Clark Expedition. Jefferson is still considered one of the most influential founding fathers of the United States. Numerous memorials honor him, such as the Jefferson Memorial in Washington, DC, which includes a nineteen-foot statute of him. His face is also featured on the Mount Rushmore Memorial, the two dollar bill, the nickel, and the one hundred dollar Series EE savings bond.

> *"In matters of style, swim with the current; in matters of principle, stand like a rock." — T. J.*

James Joyce

Destroyed His Own Prose in a Fit of Rage

James Joyce (1882–1941) was an Irish writer best known for his novels *Ulysses* and *A Portrait of the Artist as a Young Man.*

JAMES JOYCE'S COLLECTION OF SHORT stories, *Dubliners*, was rejected more than twenty times before it was published in 1914. When it was finally released, someone bought the entire first run and promptly burned every book. Joyce's next work, *A Portrait of the Artist as a Young Man*, a semiautobiographical novel, was actually a rewrite of an original manuscript that Joyce had partially destroyed in a fit of rage. It, too, was initially rejected by at least one publisher who told Joyce that the writing needed "time and trouble spent on it to make it a more finished piece of work." The second book, which did not sell well during Joyce's lifetime, has since been ranked by the Modern Library as the third greatest English language novel of the twentieth century.

When the first few sections of his next book, *Ulysses*, were published in the *Little Review* even before Joyce had finished the novel, it caused a sensation. The U.S. government immediately confiscated copies of the work and banned it for being "obscene." The magazine's editors were fined. The book remained banned for the next twenty years. Nevertheless, Joyce finished *Ulysses*. Because of its length (250,000 words) and vocabulary of 30,000 words, the *New York Times* predicted, "The average intelligent reader will glean little or nothing from it . . . save bewilderment and a sense of disgust." The prediction could not have been more wrong. *Ulysses* is considered to be the best English-language novel of the twentieth century, according to its ranking on the Modern Library list. The work has had an enormous impact on a wide variety of songs, films, and novels. Nobel Prize–winning authors William Faulkner, Samuel Beckett, and Toni Morrison are among the many authors who have been influenced by Joyce's work.

"A man of genius makes no mistakes. His errors are volitional and are the portals of discovery." — J. J.

John Keats

Prearranged for Positive Reviews

John Keats (1795–1821) was a principal poet during the English Romantic period.

John Keats's first volume of poems was published in 1817. It received positive reviews — because Keats's friends had arranged them — but it sold only a few copies, and the publishers later admitted they regretted publishing it. Reviewers attacked Keats's second volume of poetry, a trend that would plague him throughout his short life. One critic wrote, "[Keats's] friends, we understand, destined him to the career of medicine, and he was bound apprentice to a worthy apothecary in town. . . . It is a better and wiser thing to be a starved apothecary than a starved poet, so back to the shop, Mr. John."

Despite having written only fifty-four poems during his lifetime, Keats is regarded as a prominent poet from the English Romantic era. He died when he was only twenty-seven. At his request, his tombstone does not bear his name. Instead it reads, "This grave contains all that was Mortal, of a Young English Poet, who on his Death Bed, in the Bitterness of his heart, at the Malicious Power of his Enemies, Desired these words to be engraved on his Tomb Stone: Here lies One Whose Name was writ in Water."

"Failure is, in a sense, the highway to success, inasmuch as every discovery of what is false leads us to seek earnestly after what is true and every fresh experience points out some form of error which we shall afterward carefully avoid." — J. K.

Maya Lin

Hoped to Fade into Anonymity

Maya Lin (1959–) is an American artist and architect and designer of the Vietnam Veterans Memorial in Washington, D.C.

MAYA LIN HAD HOPED TO study both architecture and sculpture while attending Yale, but the school did not permit students to study both. She chose architecture, but she secretly sneaked across campus and took art classes as often as she could. This love of art inspired her to enter a nationwide competition to design the Vietnam Veterans Memorial. The judges eventually selected her design from among more than fifteen hundred submissions.

Winning the chance to design the memorial, however, led to numerous difficulties for Lin. Although government agencies had approved her design, many veterans favored a more traditional sculpture for the monument. Claiming that her design insulted the memory of those who had died in the war, disgruntled veterans attacked the twenty-year-old college senior with racial and sexual slurs. They questioned why an Asian woman (Lin was the American-born daughter of Chinese parents) had been selected to design a memorial for a war that had been fought in Asia.

The heated debated raged for more than a year before a compromise was finally reached. As a result, a more traditional bronze statue was constructed at the entrance to the monument that Lin had designed. After completing the project, Lin went to Harvard to finish studying architecture — disillusioned, slightly bitter, and hoping to fade into anonymity after all the controversy. As she later recalled, "When it was over, I wanted to pretend it never happened. I went back to school and tried to forget it. I refused to talk about the memorial or do another one."

Lin was not even named at the memorial's dedication ceremony in 1982. No one, not even Lin herself, could have imagined the effect the memorial would have on visitors. The V-shaped black marble wall with the 58,000 names inscribed on it soon became the most visited public monument in the country. It had a profound impact on veterans and other Americans, who sought it out as a place of remembrance for those they had lost during the war. By 1994, the memorial had to be restored to repair wear from the constant attention from visitors. Lin eventually designed other structures including the Civil Rights Memorial in Montgomery, Alabama, and the Wave Field at the University of Michigan. In 1994, she became the subject of an Academy Award–

winning documentary, *Maya Lin: A Strong Clear Vision*. Lin, who has a studio in New York City, served on the selection jury of the World Trade Center Site Memorial Competition.

"To fly, we have to have resistance." — M. L.

George Lucas

Unexceptional

George Lucas (1944–) is an American screenwriter, director, and producer famous for his creation of the epic *Star Wars* saga.

GEORGE LUCAS WROTE AND DIRECTED his first movie, *THX 1138*, in 1971. The film was not well received, and its lackluster performance at the box office scared away potential backers for his next movie, *American Graffiti*. Francis Ford Coppola stepped in as executive producer, which convinced Universal Studios to finance it.

American Graffiti was a success, earning five Academy Award nominations, including two for Lucas (one for director and one for co-screenwriter). Even so, Lucas continued to have difficulty finding financing for his third film, a science fiction movie like the ill-fated *THX 1138*.

In a last-ditch effort, Lucas convinced a reluctant Twentieth Century Fox to support the film, which he called *Star Wars*. Still, the studio doubted it would make any money. Throughout the filming, Lucas faced overwhelming obstacles — editing problems, glitches with special effects, and schedule setbacks. When the film was finally finished, only forty theaters ordered it for showings. To counter this, the studio stipulated that theaters reserving *The Other Side of Midnight*, a popular upcoming film, would also have to order *Star Wars*. Lucas, however, had taken his own steps to ensure the movie's popularity by releasing the story in novel and comic format. *Star Wars* grossed more than any other movie released at that time and remains one of the highest grossing movies ever made. It earned $215 million in the United States and $337 million overseas during its original theatrical release. Stanley Kauffman, a film critic for the *New Republic*, was one of many who missed the film's potential. He observed in his review, "The only way *Star Wars* could have been exciting was through its visual imagination and special effects. Both are unexceptional." *Star Wars* received ten Academy Award nominations, winning for Best Costume Design; Best Film Editing; Best Sound; Best Music, Original Score; Best Art Direction, Set Decoration; and Best Effects, Visual Effects.

Star Wars has been re-released several times, most recently under the title *Star Wars IV: A New Hope*. The movie and its characters continually appear on "top 100" lists compiled by such groups as the Writers Guild of America (which chose it as the sixty-eighth greatest screenplay of all time) and the American Film Institute (AFI) (which listed it as one of the top films of the twentieth century). The movie has also been cited by the AFI as one of the most thrilling and one of the most inspirational American films of all time. *Star Wars* characters Han Solo and Obi-Wan Kenobi have won their own citations as being among the greatest American film heroes of all time.

"Good luck has its storms." — G. L.

Ricky Martin

Too Small and Young-Looking

Ricky Martin (1971–) is a Grammy Award–winning pop singer with more than thirty hit singles including "She Bangs," "Nobody Wants to be Lonely," and "Livin' La Vida Loca."

RICKY MARTIN AUDITIONED FOR THE boy band Menudo three times before he was selected. The manager did not particularly like his voice and thought that Martin was too small and young-looking for the band. For the next five years, Martin toured with Menudo until he turned sixteen, the boy band's mandatory retirement age.

After finishing high school, Martin decided to launch his solo career. His first solo album sold more than five hundred thousand copies worldwide, a respectable number but far from the sales Menudo had posted. Martin persisted and, with each album he released, his popularity and sales increased. His second album, released two years later, did slightly better, selling more than a million copies worldwide. His third album sold more than seven million copies worldwide.

Yet, it was Martin's fifth album that really sold well. It sold more than 660,000 copies in its first week and debuted at number one. It eventually sold more than seventeen million copies and went platinum seven times. Martin has released several additional albums and sold more than fifty-five million albums worldwide, charting twenty-one Top 10 hits on the U.S. Latin charts — eight of which reached number one — and more than thirty hit singles. Martin has also won several Grammy Awards, MTV

Video and Music Awards, and Billboard Awards.

"Politicians create the boundaries; we in the music business get rid of them." — R. M.

Herman Melville

A Ridiculous Writer

Herman Melville (1819–1891) was a novelist, short story writer, and essayist. He is best known for having written the American epic *Moby Dick*.

Although Herman Melville published several novels, he could not support himself as a writer and worked as a New York City customs inspector for most of his life. He lived in such obscurity that when he died, the *New York Times* misspelled his name in his obituary. When his most famous work, *Moby Dick*, was published in 1851, it sold fewer than four thousand copies and earned Melville only $550. The critics tore it apart, one calling it "sad stuff, dull and dreary," while another said it was "ridiculous."

More than thirty years after his death, after another manuscript was found carefully stored in the family's breadbox; interest in Melville's work was revived. The manuscript — *Billy Budd, Sailor* — was published and helped make Melville a household name. His works have influenced other great writers including Thomas Mann, E. M. Forster, D. H. Lawrence, Albert Camus, Thomas Pynchon, and Cormac McCarthy. Today, his books and characters have become so deeply a part of American culture that they are mentioned in everything from science fiction to heavy metal music. Starbucks, the world's largest chain of coffee houses, got its name from a character in *Moby Dick.*

"He who has never failed somewhere, that man cannot be great." — H. M.

Arthur Miller

Too Depressing

American playwright Arthur Miller (1915–2005) is famous for his brief marriage to actress Marilyn Monroe as well as his numerous plays, including *The Crucible, A View from the Bridge, All My Sons*, and *Death of a Salesman.*

ARTHUR MILLER'S FIRST SUCCESS AS a playwright came at the University of Michigan. The school initially rejected his application to attend, but Miller eventually graduated from the university with a degree in English in 1938. That year, Miller headed for New York to make a name for himself. It took six years and twenty-two plays before he was able to get one of his works produced on Broadway. *The Man Who Had All the Luck* won the Theatre Guild's National Award, but critics panned the play, and it closed after only four performances.

After this failure, Miller turned to novels to earn enough money to support his family. Although his books were successful, Miller was drawn to the stage and he resumed writing plays. In 1947, he wrote the play *All My Sons*, which ran for 328 performances and won two Tony Awards, and the New York Drama Critics Circle Award.

Despite this, Miller had difficulty finding a producer for his next play, *Death of a Salesman.* Producer Cheryl Crawford stated her reasons for rejecting it with the comment, "Who would want to see a play about an unhappy traveling salesman? Too depressing." Miller eventually succeeded in finding a producer for the play, and *Death of a Salesman* premiered at the Morocco Theatre in 1949. The play was a critical success, winning a Tony Award for Best Play, a New York Drama Critics' Award, and a Pulitzer Prize. Also hugely successful with audiences, the play ran for 742 performances and earned Miller an estimated $2 million.

Miller went on to write additional plays. Today, he is considered by many to be one of the greatest dramatists of the twentieth century. Miller also earned an Emmy Award, the George Foster Peabody Award, the John F. Kennedy Award for Lifetime Achievement, the Tony Lifetime Achievement Award, and the Lifetime Achievement Award for his plays.

"Maybe all one can do is hope to end up with the right regrets." — A. M.

Conan O'Brien

An Unknown and Unworthy Successor

Conan O'Brien (1963–) is an Emmy-winning writer, comedian, and host of late-night variety show *Late Night with Conan O'Brien.*

After graduating magna cum laude from Harvard University with a B.A. in U.S. history, Conan O'Brien moved to Los Angeles to pursue a career as a writer. One of his first jobs was working on a short-lived comedy on Fox titled *The Wilton North Report. Newsweek* referred to the show as "a disastrous late-night comedy and talk show." After that fiasco, O'Brien began writing for comedy series such as *Not Necessarily the News*, *Saturday Night Live*, and *The Simpsons*. Except for occasional appearances in *Saturday Night Live* skits, he rarely appeared in front of the camera.

When David Letterman announced that he was moving to CBS, O'Brien was not even on the list of possible choices to replace him as host of NBC's late-night show. However, network executives could not agree on a replacement among the comedians on the list. Running out of options, producer Lorne Michaels suggested O'Brien. Michaels' recommendation, combined with an audition tape in which O'Brien hosted a fake show with the help of real celebrities Mimi Rogers and Jason Alexander, impressed NBC executives, and O'Brien got the job.

Audiences, however, reacted with much less enthusiasm. They looked at the unknown as an unworthy successor to Letterman. So few people turned out to see the show that the network arranged for interns to fill the empty seats. By the end of the first year, even the executives had lost their faith in O'Brien. TV critic Tom Shales suggested the host "return to Conan O'Blivion from whence he came."

The network almost canceled *Late Night with Conan O'Brien*, but executives reconsidered when they realized they had nothing to replace it. The show remained on life support, and O'Brien was offered a mere thirteen-week contract. During that short time, O'Brien polished his comedic skills and gained confidence on camera. Since then, *Late Night* has won the Writers Guild Award for Best Writing in a Comedy/Variety Series five times. The show has also been nominated for numerous Emmy Awards for its comedic writing. O'Brien is scheduled to take over as host of *The Tonight Show* in 2009.

"If you apply the must-succeed-every-time standard to a creative thing, you ruin it." — C. O.

Laurence Olivier

A Ranting, Writhing Romeo

Laurence Olivier (1907–1989) was an actor, director, and producer; recipient of Academy, Golden Globe, Emmy, and British Academy of Film and Television Arts Awards; and is generally regarded as the best actor of the twentieth century.

In his first professional role, Laurence Olivier, dressed in a police uniform, stepped elegantly onto the stage, only to trip over a doorsill and fall headfirst into the floodlights. The pratfall, in *The Ghost Train* at the Brighton Hippodrome, was not the most auspicious start for the actor, but it marked the beginning of a promising career. By 1933, Olivier had landed a role opposite Greta Garbo in the movie *Queen Christina*. The young actor's luck was short-lived, however. Within two weeks, Garbo exercised her star power and had Olivier fired. Although he got a few more parts, a big break eluded him. By 1935, after a play he was starring in closed after only a week, he told his friend Emlyn Williams, "I'm all washed up. I'll never make it."

Instead of quitting, Olivier took a part in a production of *Romeo and Juliet*. The reviewers tore his performance apart. One critic observed that Olivier's "blank verse was the blankest" he had ever heard, while another described Olivier as a "ranting, writhing Romeo." Audiences disagreed, however, and the scheduled six-week run was extended to six months. The production also introduced Olivier to his second wife, Vivien Leigh, who played the role of Ophelia to his Hamlet about a year later.

Leigh renewed Oliver's interest in movies. They starred opposite each other in the 1937 movie *Fire Over England*. It was the first of four movies in which the two starred together. Olivier returned to Hollywood in 1938 to star in *Wuthering Heights*, which became a box office hit. During his career, Olivier appeared in sixty movies, two dozen television programs, and countless stage performances. He won four of his fourteen Academy Award nominations and received the Academy's Honorary Award in 1979 for the full body of his work.

"Life is enthusiasm, zest." — L. O.

George Orwell

Writer with the Wrong Point of View

George Orwell (1903–1950) is the pseudonym of Eric Blair and the name he used to publish the popular novels *Animal Farm* and *Nineteen Eighty-Four*, among others.

In 1927, Eric Blair quit his job as a policeman to pursue a career as a freelance writer. He moved to Paris for a year, but was forced to return to England when he became ill and ran out of money. In 1930, he completed his first novel, *A Scullion's Diary*, and immediately submitted it to a publisher. While the publisher found it interesting, they also deemed it "too short and fragmented." Blair revised it, but the first publisher again rejected it, as did another publisher. Thoroughly dejected, Blair all but abandoned the manuscript and took a job teaching.

This might have been the end of the story had it not been for a Blair's friend, who brought the manuscript to the attention of Victor Gollancz who agreed to publish it. Blair had one request: He wanted the book published under a pseudonym. Rather than choose one himself, he offered Gollancz four possibilities and asked him to choose one. Gollancz picked George Orwell. On January 9, 1933, *Down and Out in Paris and London* by George Orwell was released. The first printing sold out immediately and was soon followed by second and third printings. Blair released a new novel each year for the next six years before taking a break from novel writing to work for the BBC. In 1943, shortly after his mother died, he left the BBC to become the literary editor of the *Tribune*. While there, he wrote another novel, a satire that he finished in early 1944.

Although he had proven himself as both a writer and a novelist, Blair — under the name of Orwell — again had difficulty finding a publisher. Over the next year, numerous publishers in England and the United States rejected his manuscript. Most rejected the novel on political grounds. T. S. Elliot, then an editor for Faber and Faber, commented that the book did not present "the right point of view from which to criticize the political situation at the present time." Another editor stated, "I think the choice of pigs as the ruling caste will no doubt give offence to many people, and particularly to anyone who is a bit touchy, as undoubtedly the Russians are." The Dial Press rejected the novel because editors there thought that "there [was] not much demand for animal stories in the U.S.A."

Finally, in August 1945, *Animal Farm* was released. Although it was not enormously successful until after

Orwell's death, the book has since become one of his most famous works. Orwell is also famous for *Nineteen Eighty-Four* — written shortly after *Animal Farm* — which introduced a number of new terms: "big brother," "thought police," doublethink," and even the abbreviation of love as "luv." The novel made Orwell a familiar name and led to the use of the term "Orwellian" to describe actions of a totalitarian society such as those depicted in his novels.

> *"No one I met at this time — doctors, nurses, practicantes, or fellow-patients — failed to assure me that a man who is hit through the neck and survives it is the luckiest creature alive. I could not help thinking that it would be even luckier not to be hit at all."* — G. O.

James Redfield

Attacked by Reviewers

Author James Redfield (1950–) wrote the best-selling novel *The Celestine Prophecy*, which has sold more than twenty million copies worldwide.

In 1989, James Redfield quit his job to become a writer. He embarked on his new career by taking a trip to the New Age sacred sites in Sedona, Arizona, a journey that would inspire his first book, *The Celestine Prophecy*. After he finished the book in 1991, Redfield began looking for publishers. After a fruitless search, Redfield decided that the only way to get his book published was to do it himself. He invested his life savings into his own publishing company, Satori, and printed three thousand copies of *The Celestine Prophecy*. When sales at bookstores skyrocketed, he printed more copies, and then more. Within a year, he had sold one hundred thousand copies of his book.

His self-made success soon garnered the attention of Warner Books, which bought the rights to the book and released it in hardcover. Once the book came to their attention, reviewers attacked it. One stated, "It sounds like the speech of those planet-saving alien robots in fifties science-fiction movies." Another said the book was "exactly the kind of work that thrives at a time when organized faith is in retreat, and when every variety of garbage — systematic garbage, with pretensions to establishing a homemade religion — floods to fill the gap." The book touched a more positive nerve with readers, however, and soon the book was number one on the *New York Times* fiction best-seller list, where it remained for three years. Since then, *The Celestine Prophecy* has sold more than twenty million copies worldwide, been translated into thirty-five languages, and served as the basis for a movie of the same title released in 2006.

"If we knock on the door until it opens, not taking no for an answer, our lives will be transformed as we step up into a higher awareness." — J. R.

The Rolling Stones

Endured Criticism and Censorship

The Rolling Stones, an English rock-and-roll band, has released more than fifty-five albums and had more than thirty top-ten singles in the United Kingdom and the United States as of 2007.

THE ROLLING STONES HAD BEEN playing gigs around England for a year before they hired Eric Easton to manage their group. Easton had doubts about the band's lead singer, Mick Jagger, and told his partner, Andrew Loog Oldham, "The singer will have to go." At the time, Jagger was studying business at the London School of Economics, and the rock-and-roll band was promoting a bad-boy image.

Jagger stayed as the lead singer for The Rolling Stones and, within a year, the group topped the charts. Unfortunately, many of the songs they sang were deemed "unsuitable" by the BBC. Through the years, the band's work would often be the target of criticism and censorship. For example, their song "Let's Spend the Night Together" topped the charts in England, but most U.S. radio stations avoided playing it, instead opting to broadcast the flip side of the record, "Ruby Tuesday." When the group performed the song on *The Ed Sullivan Show*, U.S. executives required them to change the lyrics to "Let's spend *some time* together" to make the song less suggestive.

The Rolling Stones have continued to perform together for more than forty years. During that time, they have released fifty-five albums and thirty-seven Top 10 singles. They were inducted into the Rock and Roll Hall of Fame in 1989. The group placed fourth on *Rolling Stone* magazine's list of "100 Greatest Artists of All Time."

"Failure doesn't mean you are a failure . . . it just means you haven't succeeded yet." — Robert Schuller

Arnold Schwarzenegger

Rigid and Unconvincing

Arnold Schwarzenegger (1947–) is a former bodybuilder and actor who became the thirty-eighth governor of California.

Arnold Schwarzenegger came to America from Austria to act in the movies. Everyone told him it could not be done. Not only did he have a name that was hard to spell and pronounce, he had a heavy accent. Although Schwarzenegger got a movie role, another actor dubbed his lines. His accent was not a problem in his next film, since he played a deaf-mute. Schwarzenegger never lost faith. He later observed, "I said 'that's what I want do' and eventually, it did happen and I became the highest paid entertainer and all because I never listened to 'it can't be done.'"

After his performance in his third movie, *Stay Hungry*, Schwarzenegger was awarded a Golden Globe for Best New Male Star. Although it was not his first movie, it was his first "speaking" role. Six years went by before he landed a part in *Conan the Barbarian*. Critics slammed his performance. They said the actor's heavy Austrian accent was difficult to understand and that his movements were rigid and unconvincing. Despite the criticism, *Conan the Barbarian* earned $100 million, and Schwarzenegger became a top star in the action film industry. He appeared in twenty-six more movies including such hits as *The Terminator*, *Predator*, *True Lies*, *Kindergarten Cop*, *Total Recall*, *Last Action Hero*, and *Commando*.

In 2003, Schwarzenegger left acting and went into politics. In his first run for office, he was elected governor of

California in a special recall election. In 2006, he was reelected to serve a full term in office.

> *"The mind is the limit. As long as the mind can envision the fact that you can do something, you can do it, as long as you really believe one hundred percent." — A. S.*

George Bernard Shaw

Possessed No Hint of Any Creative Power

Irish author George Bernard Shaw (1856–1950) wrote more than sixty plays including *Androcles and the Lion*, *Pygmalion*, and *Man and Superman*.

BETWEEN 1876 AND 1885, GEORGE Bernard Shaw wrote five novels. However, when he attempted to have them published, London publishers rejected his work. His first novel, *Immaturity*, remained unpublished for more than fifty years. The other four were finally released as "padding" for propagandist magazines edited by his friends. For the next few years, Shaw worked as a newspaper writer and music critic. In 1895, he became a drama critic for the *Saturday Review*. Although he had written plays before, they had never been produced or published. Being a playwright intrigued Shaw, however, and he wrote *Candida*, a poignant look at marriage and the relationships between men and women. The work was produced in 1898, his first play to receive attention.

Shaw's plays received mixed reviews. Arnold Bennett, a reviewer for *The Academy*, wrote in 1901, "One might still be hopeful for Mr. Shaw's future as a dramatist, despite his present incompetence, if there were any hint in his plays of creative power. But there is no such hint." Anthony

Comstock, secretary for the Society for the Suppression of Vice, called Shaw "an Irish smut-dealer." Shaw did not let these criticisms bother him. He continued writing plays, including a series of classic comedy-dramas such as *Androcles and the Lion* and *Pygmalion*, which would become the basis for the hit Broadway show and movie *My Fair Lady*. In 1925, Shaw was awarded the Nobel Prize in Literature. He also won an Academy Award for Best Writing (Screenplay) in 1938 for *Pygmalion* after it was adapted for film.

> *"When I was a young man, I observed that nine out of ten things I did were a failure. I didn't want to be a failure, so I did ten times more work." — G. B. S.*

Frederick W. Smith

Launched an Unfeasible Business

Frederick Smith (1944–) is the founder, chairman, president, and CEO of Federal Express, also known as FedEx, the first overnight express delivery company in the world.

Frederick W. Smith had a vision that others could not see. While attending Yale University, he described his concept — a company offering overnight delivery service — in a term paper. The professor said the idea was "interesting" and "well-formed," but that, "in order to earn better than a 'C,' the idea must be feasible."

Smith had planned to attend Harvard Law School, but this plan was sidetracked by the Vietnam War. He served two tours of duty in the Marines from 1966 to 1970. When he returned from Vietnam, Smith decided that instead of attending law school, he would raise enough money to launch his own business — a business that was based on the same "unfeasible" concept he had written about years earlier in his paper. He called his delivery company Federal Express. Smith encountered many roadblocks in his efforts to raise the initial startup funds for his business. He later recalled in a *New York Times* interview, "People thought we were bananas. We were too ignorant to know that we weren't supposed to be able to do certain things."

Smith succeeded in raising the money to start his business, but on Federal Express's first night of operation, the business shipped only 186 packages. In the first three months, Federal Express lost more than $30 million, and drivers often had to pay for gas out of their own pockets. Smith was in danger of losing his investors' money as well as the capital that his brothers and sisters had given him. On the verge of declaring bankruptcy, Smith renegotiated his bank loans and kept his fledgling business going. Finally, by 1976, the company had begun to show a profit; and two years later it was stable enough to offer shares on the New York Stock Exchange. By 1984, Federal Express revenues surpassed $1 billion. Twenty-five years later, Federal Express has grown into a network of companies worth more than $34 billion.

"Anybody who works themselves into exhaustion or incoherence doesn't have the discipline to do the job to begin with." — F. W. S.

John Steinbeck

An Immature Embarrassment

John Steinbeck (1902–1968) was an author and winner of both the Nobel Prize and the Pulitzer Prize. His books include *Of Mice and Men*, *The Pearl*, and *The Grapes of Wrath*.

After graduating from Stanford University, John Steinbeck moved to the publishing hub of America, New York City, with the hopes of becoming a successful writer. It would take him four years and countless rejections before he would get his first work published. Shortly after his first novel, *Cup of Gold: A Life of Henry Morgan, Buccaneer*, was published, one of the book's harshest critics called it an "immature experiment" and an "embarrassment." The critic turned out to be Steinbeck himself.

Steinbeck found fault with his other works as well, including the Pulitzer Prize-winning novel *The Grapes of Wrath* and *Of Mice and Men*. A *Time* magazine critic joined in attacking *Of Mice and Men*, calling it "an oxymoronic combination of the tough and tender, . . . [that] will appeal to sentimental cynics, cynical sentimentalists . . . Readers less easily thrown off their trolley will prefer Hans Andersen." The book was eventually made into three movies and is still in print more than seventy years later. In 1962, Steinbeck won the Nobel Prize for Literature for his "realistic and imaginative writing, combining as it does sympathetic humor and keen social perception." Today, Steinbeck is one of the most widely known and most read American writers. Many of his works continue to be included on required reading lists in American and

Canadian high schools.

> *"It is the nature of man to rise to greatness if greatness is expected of him." — J. S.*

Elizabeth Taylor

Lacked Talent and Necessary Look

Elizabeth Taylor (1932–) is a two-time Academy Award-winning actor. She has appeared in numerous films including *National Velvet*, *Cleopatra*, and *Father's Little Dividend*.

After two years of trying to convince Universal Studios to give her a chance, nine-year-old Elizabeth Taylor won a role in her first movie, *There's One Born Every Minute*. The movie bombed. Studio executives told Taylor she had no talent and did not have "the look" necessary for a child actor. After Universal dropped her contract, she appeared in the movie *Lassie Come Home* for MGM. Taylor earned very little for her work in the film — about $150 a week less than the four-legged star of the movie received.

The movie was successful and ignited Taylor's career. The following year she was cast in three movies, including *National Velvet*, which grossed more than $4 million and earned Taylor a long-term contract. During Taylor's more than sixty-year career, she has appeared in more than sixty-five movies, among them such classics as *Cat on a Hot Tin Roof*, *Doctor Faustus*, *Cleopatra*, and *Who's Afraid of Virginia Woolf?* Taylor has won two Academy Awards, a Golden Globe, the American Film Institute's Lifetime Achievement Award, and the Golden Globe's Cecil B. de Mille Award for Lifetime Achievement.

She has also received the Jean Hersholt Humanitarian Award and the Presidential Citizens Medal in recognition of her philanthropy.

"It's not the having, it's the getting." — E. T.

Jules Verne

Too Scientific

Jules Verne (1828–1905) was a French author, often referred to as the "father of science fiction." His most famous works include *Journey To The Center Of The Earth*, *Twenty Thousand Leagues Under The Sea*, and *Around the World in Eighty Days*.

At the tender age of sixteen, Jules Verne bravely read his first full-length play to a group of family and friends. He stopped after the first act when the audience burst into unsolicited laughter. This setback caused him to burn the script, but it did not stop him from writing. Still, it would be another nineteen years before any of Verne's stories would be read by the public. After graduation, Verne went to Paris, France, to study for the bar, but instead he began writing librettos for operettas. When Verne's father discovered his son's new occupation, he cut off financial support, and Verne was forced to work as a stockbroker to support himself.

After he married in 1857, his wife encouraged Verne to search for a publisher for his stories. For the next six years, publishers rejected Verne's work, saying the stories were "too scientific." They were finally published after Verne revised his manuscripts. Verne, then thirty-five, went on to publish fifty-four novels as well as numerous short stories, essays, plays, and poems. Many of them became best-sellers, including *20,000 Leagues under the Sea, Around the World in 80 Days*, and *Journey to the Center of the Earth.*

"Anything one man can imagine, other men can make real." — J. V.